THE SCOTTISH POLICE OFFICER

The structure of policing is undergoing change in Scotland at present and the profile of the police officer differs from that of the past. This book takes an informative approach and offers a unique account and insight into the Scottish police organisation, describing the 'Scottish police officer' from the point of recruitment through to training, development and specialist policing.

Written by an ex-senior police officer, this book examines how the qualified police officer goes about his/her daily work policing Scotland and how this has changed over time as a result of organised crime, terrorism and the changing priorities of the public and politicians. The contribution of non-police officers such as police civilian staff, auxiliaries and the private sector, plays a key role in the policing of Scotland in the twenty-first century and is considered at length. As police supervision and management are crucial to the organisation's success, the subjects of personnel development, promotion and management in the police are examined with comment on the suitability of the system in the twenty-first century.

The Scottish Police Officer concludes with commentary on the future profile of the Scottish police officer and makes some general comparison with their colleagues in the rest of the UK and the European Union. This will be an essential text for police officers in Scotland and elsewhere and students and academics in the areas of law, politics, management, police studies, criminology and criminal justice.

Daniel Donnelly is a retired senior police officer and Honorary Senior Research Fellow at the Centre for Criminal Justice and Police Studies, University of the West of Scotland. He has obtained the degrees of BA, MBA and PhD and has regularly taught at a number of Scottish universities. Daniel is the author of *Municipal Policing in Scotland* (Dundee University Press 2008); co-editor/author of *Policing Scotland* 1st and 2nd editions (Willan 2005 and 2010), and author of *Municipal Policing in the European Union: Comparative Perspectives* (Palgrave Macmillan 2013).

THE SCOTTISH POLICE OFFICER

Daniel Donnelly

Routledge
Taylor & Francis Group
LONDON AND NEW YORK

First published 2014
by Routledge
4 Park Square, Milton Park, Abingdon, Oxon, OX14 4RN

and by Routledge
605 Third Avenue, New York, NY 10017

Routledge is an imprint of the Taylor & Francis Group, an informa business

British Library Cataloguing in Publication Data
A catalogue record for this book is available from the British Library

Library of Congress Cataloging-in-Publication Data
Donnelly, Daniel
The Scottish police officer / Daniel Donnelly.
pages cm
1. Police—Scotland. 2. Police—Recruiting—Scotland. 3. Police—Scotland—Personnel management. I. Title.
HV8197.A3D66 2013
363.2'209411—dc23
2013013910

ISBN13: 978-0-415-67160-6 (hbk)
ISBN13: 978-0-415-67161-3 (pbk)
ISBN13: 978-0-203-08343-7 (ebk)

Typeset in Bembo
by RefineCatch Limited, Bungay, Suffolk

Dedicated to the police officers and police support staff of Police Scotland

CONTENTS

ILLUSTRATIONS

Figures

Tables

Boxes

PREFACE

The idea for this book came about in 2008 when no date had been set for an Independence Referendum for Scotland and the notion of a single police service in Scotland had not as yet appeared on any political agenda. We now know there will be an Independence Referendum in 2014 and as of 1 April 2013 the national Police Service of Scotland came into being.

Scottish policing is experiencing major organisational change in the first part of the twenty-first century and this transition is destined to produce a more distinct model of policing in Scotland. Only time will tell how this will impact on individual police officers but what is apparent at the present time are signs of an emerging uniqueness in Scottish law enforcement compared to the rest of the UK.

The present book gives the reader an overview of what is involved in being a police officer in Scotland, how the country is policed, who oversees the police and how non-police officers contribute to policing. Some explanation is given of the historic constitutional reform of policing introduced in 2013 and a final comment is made as to what lies ahead for the Scottish police officer.

ACKNOWLEDGEMENTS

A number of people from all corners of Scotland took time from their busy schedules to assist me in the writing of this book – far too many to mention. The book could not have been written without the dedicated assistance of the library staff who furnished books and journal articles on a regular basis over the years. As always, a special thanks to John Burke and the staff at the Hamilton Campus Library, University of the West of Scotland; Carole Jesmont at the Strathclyde Police Library, Jackton; the staff at the Mitchell Library, Glasgow; the staff at the National Library Scotland, Edinburgh; the staff of the Highland Library, Inverness; and the staff at the National Police Library, NPIA, Bramshill. As always, a big thank you to all the staff at the Scottish Police College for their continued support and help. A special mention, too, must go to Mary Munro and her team at the www.cjscotland.org.uk website for the invaluable record which they provide on all matters pertaining to Scottish criminal justice.

I also wish to acknowledge the work done by the Justice Analytical Services of the Scottish Government who continue to publish important statistical information on policing and the criminal justice system, some of which is included in the present text. The Scottish Police Performance Framework is an excellent example.

I am also indebted to the previous Strathclyde Police Force for furnishing profile information of police recruits for 2008–2010.

My grateful thanks to the Police Mutual Assurance Society for giving permission to include reference to their 2012 study Portrait of the Police.

A special mention is due to Brian Willan who encouraged me to take on this project before he retired from the publishing business. Last but not least my sincere thanks to Nicola Hartley of Routledge for her endless patience over a long period of time.

Every endeavour has been made to ensure that information in the book is accurate as at the end of December 2012. Any errors and shortcomings remain my responsibility.

ABBREVIATIONS

A&E	Accident and Emergency
ACC	Assistant Chief Constable
ACDP	Accelerated Careers Development Programme
ACPO	Association of Chief Police Officers
ACPOS	Association of Chief Police Officers in Scotland
ANPR	Automatic Number Plate Recognition
APA	Association of Police Authorities
ASB	Anti-Social Behaviour
ASPS	Association of Scottish Police Superintendents
BBV	blood-borne virus
BEM	Black and Ethnic Minority
BNP	British National Party
BSIA	British Security Industry Agency
CC	Chief Constable
CCTV	closed circuit television
CEOP	Child Exploitation and Online Protection Centre
CHIS	Covert Human Intelligence Sources
CID	Criminal Investigation Department
CIP	Community Improvement Partnership
COPFS	Crown Office and Procurator Fiscal Service
CPO	Community Police Officer
CPP	Community Planning Partnership
CRB	Criminal Records Bureau
CSM	Crime Scene Management
CSO	Community Support Officer
CSP	Community Safety Partnership
CT	counter-terrorism

DCC	Deputy Chief Constable
DNA	deoxyribonucleic acid
DPA	Data Protection Act
DPSLM	Diploma in Police Service Leadership and Management
EAW	European Arrest Warrant
EC3	European Cybercrime Centre
ECHR	European Convention on Human Rights
EEA	European Economic Area
EEI	Early and Effective Intervention
EEW	European Evidence Warrant
EHRC	Equality and Human Rights Commission
EPSU	Energy and Protective Security Unit
EU	European Union
FOI	Freedom of Information
FPN	Fixed Penalty Notice
FTE	full-time equivalent
G4S	international security company
GCSE	General Certificate of Secondary Education
GHA	Glasgow Housing Association
GPA	Gay Police Association
GSOC	Garda Siochana Ombudsman Commission (Ireland)
HIV	human immunodeficiency virus
HMICS	HM Inspector of Constabulary for Scotland
HMRC	Her Majesty's Revenue and Customs
HSE	Health and Safety Executive
ICO	Information Commissioner's Office
ICP	Independent Commission on Policing
ICT	Information and Communication Technology
IDMG	Inter-Departmental Ministerial Group
IPCC	Independent Police Complaints Commission (E&W)
IPSOS	Market Research Company (IPSOS MORI)
MAPPA	Multi-Agency Public Protection Arrangements
MEP	Member of the European Parliament
MP	Member of Parliament
MPS	Metropolitan Police Service
MSP	Member of Scottish Parliament
NCA	National Crime Agency
NGO	non-governmental organisation
NHTU	National Human Trafficking Unit
NIB	National Intelligence Bureau
NIM	National Intelligence Model
NIPB	Northern Ireland Policing Board
NPIA	National Police Improvement Agency
NRM	National Referral Mechanism

NSCU	National Sexual Crimes Unit
NSIR	National Standards for Incident Reporting
NSV	National Security Vetting
OECD	Organisation for Economic Cooperation and Development
OIM	offshore installation manager
ONS	Office for National Statistics
PAW	Partnership for Action Against Wildlife Crime
PCC	Police and Crime Commissioner
PCCS	Police Complaints Commission(er) for Scotland
PCSO	Police Community Support Officer
PCU	Priority Crime Unit
PDR	Personal Development Review
PF	Procurator Fiscal
PIDS	Passive Infrared Detection Systems
PIRA	Provincial Irish Republican Army
PIRC	Police Investigations and Review Commissioner
PMAS	Police Mutual Assurance Society
PNB	Police Negotiating Board
POCA	Proceeds of Crime Act 2002
PONI	Police Ombudsman for Northern Ireland
PSNI	Police Service for Northern Ireland
PSoS	Police Service of Scotland
RIPA	Regulation of Investigatory Powers Act 2000
RSAMD	Royal Scottish Academy of Music and Drama
RUSI	Royal United Services Institute
SACRO	Safeguarding Communities – Reducing Offending
SCC	Strategic Command Course
SCCCJ	Scottish Consortium on Crime and Criminal Justice
SCD	Specialist Crime Division
SCDEA	Scottish Crime and Drugs Enforcement Agency
SCDP	Senior Careers Development Programme
SCDS	Senior Careers Development Service
SCJS	Scottish Criminal Justice Survey
SCQF	Scottish Credit and Qualifications Framework
SEPA	Scottish Environment Protection Agency
SIA	Security Industry Authority
SID	Scottish Intelligence Database
SIO	Senior Investigating Officer
SNP	Scottish National Party
SOC	Scenes of Crime
SoFMH	School of Forensic Mental Health
SOPO	Sexual Offences Prevention Order
SOPs	Standard Operating Procedures
SPF	Scottish Police Federation

SPPF	Scottish Police Performance Framework
SPSA	Scottish Police Services Authority
SPWA	Strathclyde Police Women's Association
SQA	Scottish Qualifications Authority
UKBA	UK Border Agency
UKHTC	UK Human Trafficking Centre
UNODC	United Nations Office of Drugs and Crime
VRU	Violence Reduction Unit
WDF	Women's Development Forum
WHO	World Health Organisation

TABLE OF STATUTES

Acts of Parliament

Crime and Courts Act 2013
Crofters' Holding (Scotland) Act 1886
Equality Act 2010
Glasgow Police Act 1800
Metropolitan Police Act 1829
Police Act 1919
Police (Scotland) Act 1857
Proceeds of Crime Act 2002

Acts of the Scottish Parliament

Freedom of Information (Scotland) Act 2002
Offensive Behaviour at Football and Threatening Communications (Scotland) Act 2012
Police and Fire Reform (Scotland) Act 2012
Scotland Act 2012
Wildlife and Natural Environment (Scotland) Act 2012

Regulations

Police Service of Scotland Regulations 2013
Police Service of Scotland (Police Cadets) Regulations 2013

1

INTRODUCTION

The Scottish police officer

According to geneticists working on a national project aiming to discover the origins of Scots through using DNA, every Scot is an immigrant and there are no fewer than 100 different male and female lineages present in Scotland's modern population. Examination of DNA has revealed Scotland is an exceptionally diverse nation with lineages extending to all parts of the globe. Links can be traced back to ancient and medieval times, Saracens from the Near East, women from Sheba on the Red Sea, and connections exist as far distant as Siberia, the Arctic, the Adriatic, and most of Europe – 'it is a national mosaic of glittering, exotic complexity' (Moffat 2012). Such studies help uncover the people who made Scotland and help us understand who the Scots really are.

The population of Scotland may be relatively small at 5 million but for a nation of this size, millions of native Scots have left their country over the centuries to set down roots in all corners of the world. As a result, generations of Scots emigrants can be located in Canada, the USA, Australia, New Zealand, India, South Africa, Europe, Ireland and England. A wide variety of occupations have been taken on by these expatriates – French aristocrats, Polish resistance fighters, Texan ranchers, New Zealand shepherds, Australian gold miners and Confederate rebels (Hunter 2007). The Scots have been a migratory people since medieval times and from 1825 to 1938 over 2.3 million left Scotland to go to many overseas destinations (Devine 2011: 85). Many of Scotland's industrial workers also left home with a profound understanding of working-class politics and a belief in the trade union movement and with unparalleled experience and leadership qualities went on to form trade unions wherever they settled (Kelly 2011). Scots have played key roles in helping develop the modern world in disciplines such as science, education, literature and philosophy, to name but a few.

Scots have also entered the time-honoured professions of medicine, law, military and business. But one career which the immigrant Scot featured as a regular recruit was that of the peacekeeper: the policeman. A scan of the police records of the police departments in Chicago, New York, Boston, and the large Canadian cities reveals a long line of Scottish police officers – grandfathers, fathers and sons, who gave and are still giving loyal service to their communities. Even closer to home, the London Metropolitan Police Service has always had a significant number of Scots on their payroll and closer scrutiny also shows that many of the best detective officers in London and wider afield in the English counties were and are Scottish-born officers. Of the 5700 police officers in the Metropolitan Police Force between 1850 and 1869, 2.5 per cent were Scottish and 6.5 per cent were Irish, a mix that caused the Police Commissioner to be uncomfortable with deploying these officers in parts of London with high numbers of Scottish and Irish communities (Metropolitan Police 2010). The historian Michael Fry refers to the Scots abroad as the 'external history' of Scotland and believes it advances Scotland's 'internal history' which remains inadequate on many themes and fails to answer a number of questions about 'what Scotland is?' (Fry 2001: viii). The history and development of policing in Scotland are one such theme that has been neglected in academic dialogue with a few exceptions (see Barrie 2008a, 2008b, 2010a, 2010b; Carson 1984, 1985, Carson and Idzikowska 1989; Grant 1973; Golden 2003; Dinsmor and Goldsmith 2010; Dinsmor and Urquhart 2001; Goldsmith 2002; McGowan 1996; Walker 2000).

It is difficult to put a finger on what is distinctive about Scottish policing either in words or action or any other means. For example, Jane Brettle's exhibition of a series of photographic portraits of police officers across the eight Scottish forces is an attempt to show what constitutes the Scottish police service. This interesting compilation of photographs 'creates a dynamic between individual officers' allegiances to local forces and a wider collective occupational role, encouraging us to reflect on what it is that is distinctive about policing in Scotland' (Brettle 2007: 7). But photographs have their limitations as indeed does print when there is a lack of factual information to inform the reader. That said, as in many other theatres of life, the Scots people have been the first in so many things and policing is no different. The Scottish police were the first to introduce the police box; the first national computerised criminal record system and automated fingerprint system in the UK; the chequered police cap; and much more. Another first was revealed in 2008 as a result of a complaint made to the Advertising Standards Authority directed at a Metropolitan Police advertisement that stated: 'We're not just the oldest police service in the world. We're also the most modern.' The gist of the complaint was that the City of Glasgow Police was created in 1800 – i.e. 29 years before the Metropolitan Police (*The Times* 2008: 9). The complaint was upheld and a warning letter was sent by the Authority to the Metropolitan Police, who agreed not to claim they were the oldest force in the world. The main aim of this book is not to score points but to specifically focus on the 'police officer' in Scotland – past, present and future – with the aim of understanding the part played by these trained professional law enforcement officers in the Scottish police. Who is the Scottish police officer? As the reader will find out, there is no easy answer as there are many differing aspects to a police officer that have developed, in historical terms, in a relatively short space of time.

A brief history

Scotland's first constables were introduced in the seventeenth century in the reign of King James VI, with at least one man being appointed to each parish with limited duties being allocated and no real authority given. In towns and cities, the number of constables appointed was in proportion to the size of the settlement concerned. If the person chosen refused to accept the appointment of constable, he was liable to be fined and imprisoned. As time progressed, citizens in the old burghs of Scotland (the burgess) were obliged to perform the duties of 'watch and ward' within their own burgh and a burghal officer would pass from door to door when a watch was to be appointed by magistrates to be kept, and residents were summoned as were required to carry out watch duties. As always, anyone refusing to do duty was liable to a penalty. Duty commenced at the ringing of curfew and each watchman was issued with two weapons and instructed to carry out a watch until dawn. A form of municipal local government eventually emerged in the eighteenth century, and a number of attempts were made to introduce a small professional police force in Glasgow in 1779 and 1789 but it was disbanded after a short time due to the citizens' reluctance to bear the costs of running the force. As disorder and crime continued on the unlit streets and as a result of a citizens' petition, the first Glasgow Police Act was passed in 1800. As well as the inclusion of 'watching', the Act also allowed paving, cleansing and lighting of the streets, which was the main attraction of the Act for the citizens. The local magistrates were empowered to organise a police force paid out of a rate levied for the purpose, and it comprised three sergeants, nine day-officers and 68 watchmen under the command of a Master of Police, who also held the title of City Marshall. Representatives (commissioners) were elected by the citizens and sanitation departments were created. These changes significantly point towards policing in Scotland being more than just crime fighting and public order maintenance but one with a wider remit and responsibility for municipal welfare. This traditional police role in the well-being of the community has remained with the Scottish police officer to the present day and has underpinned the Scots' own brand of community policing.

It was not long before other cities followed the Glasgow example and police forces were established across the nation with burghs and counties being given the authority to establish a police system, recruit officers locally, fix salaries, and dismiss officers when appropriate. Records from this era highlight an extremely high turnover of constables, with low wages and poor working conditions, and only a small number staying in the service for more than a few weeks. The police service had to wait until the latter part of the twentieth century before they received proper remuneration and conditions of service.

Previously, Scotland's burghs and towns did have some form of permanent resident police force such as Perth's blue-uniformed 'police officers' who were armed with yellow batons (Whatley 2000: 209). But it was not until the passing of the Police (Scotland) Act 1857 that rules and regulations that hitherto had been optional in the towns, burghs and county areas were made compulsory, and pressure was brought on local authorities to maintain an efficient police force. Rules for the governance, pay, clothing and necessaries of the force were introduced, along with a system of inspection to ensure the efficiency of the police and police premises (Day 1918: 338). Prior to the 1857 Act, there were parts of rural Scotland without police coverage, for instance, in 1852, Orkney and Shetland had no police whatsoever and the total number of police in the crofting counties was 75. Those counties without their own police force were represented by sheriff officers and parish constables. The parish constable was a community member who, for a small retaining fee of a few pounds per year, carried out local but limited police duties. Suitably qualified men were difficult to employ due to the low rate of pay and the role fell to those of 'generally a very dissipated class, and no use either for the prevention of crime or the detection of offenders' (ibid.: 337).

The Scottish Highlands has a distinctive culture that withstood the political upheaval and social change in the eighteenth and nineteenth centuries, which witnessed a time of violence and modernisation. After the Napoleonic Wars, the Scots found the price of agricultural and farming produce was plummeting and the situation was made worse by the rising unemployment caused by soldiers returning from military service (Fry 2005: 189). Highland landlords sought profits through leasing land for sheep rearing and embarked on the now infamous 'Highland Clearances'. It was during this period that the police, militia and military personnel found themselves involved in violent confrontations and skirmishes with tenants during the ensuing evictions. Civil disobedience and refusal to pay rents were common during the period as in 1820 and 1821 clearances in Culrain, Rosshire and Sutherland 'were only effected with the use of guns and swords' (Whatley 2000: 293). In 1849, the people of Solas in North Uist resisted the police in their attempts to pull down the homes of those who refused to leave. In 1886, a naval ship with a contingent of police and marines was despatched to Skye to issue warrants for arrears of rents and arrests of those who failed to comply and the party was met with violence and arrests were made.

Accounts were also given of engineered emigration by the landlords in 1851 in South Uist and Barra with the assistance of the police. The account tells of people being forced to board a ship bound for Canada, although there were many passengers who embarked voluntarily, hundreds did not. When this happened, the Factor would order the police to pursue the people into the mountains and force them back to the ship. Some were 'seized and dragged aboard and men who resisted were felled with truncheons and handcuffed; those who escaped ... were chased by the police and press gangs' (Whatley 2000: 226, 283). Many of the clearances were done in an orderly manner though there were a number of episodes of violence whenever tenants resisted and in some cases homes were destroyed or set on fire to prevent tenants returning, with the police playing a central role.

> The idea that a landowner had the right to do with his property and tenants as he saw fit had supplanted the clan ideal of trusteeship, and bore the most poisonous fruit ever grown on the Atlantic seaboard. Emigration had become essential, but the way chosen for forcing it was barbarous. The islanders loved their homelands, were reluctant to leave, and were evicted.
>
> *(Murray 1973: 225)*

When the clearances were in full swing, the military and the police were used when resistance was likely to occur. As for constables being instructed by the factor to chase and arrest tenants, one observer at the time commented, 'had the scene been laid in Russia or Turkey, the barbarity of the proceedings would have shocked the nerve of the reader' (Mackenzie 1881: 29). Crofters who had been deprived of their grazing rights by the landowner refused to pay their rent and released their sheep on to the land to graze. The factor ordered eviction and initially the sheriff officers were prevented from serving eviction papers by the local people. The response from the sheriff was to call on a strong force of police officers normally from Glasgow to serve the summonses. On occasions police were mobbed and baton charges occurred with injuries on both sides and many arrests made. There was so much public outrage at these incidents that at a subsequent trial in Inverness the five accused received a fine which was quickly paid by the public. The Westminster government was so alarmed that a Royal Commission was set up to review the circumstances of what had been taking place. The Commission's final report disclosed 'a state of misery, of wrong-doing, and of patient long-suffering, without parallel in the history of our country' (Murray 1973: 231). The result was the Magna Carta of the Hebrides – the Crofters' Holding (Scotland) Act of 1886 which gave tenants a fixity of tenure and established a Crofters Commission with the power to fix fair rents.

It is not entirely clear as to the role of the police during the Clearances, as limited research has been carried out on this particular aspect of Scottish policing. Nevertheless, this period of history highlights the stark contrast in the role of the police officer at the time to that of the modern community police officer and the concept of community welfare and protection. Police officers were regularly called in to quell public disorder, for example, in the early 1770s, food riots occurred throughout most of Scotland, in particular, Dumfries, Tayside and Fife, and riots and protests continued across Scotland into the nineteenth century, and included disputes involving weavers, coal miners, cotton spinners, tailors and many other trades. Some of the worst riotous behaviour took place in Glasgow in 1819 and 1821 and in Greenock in 1847 the rioting was so ferocious that the neighbouring counties of Dumbarton, Renfrew and Stirling called for the creation of a 'rural police force' (Whatley 1997: 88).

What is policing?

Historically, policing is the second oldest profession (Emsley 2010). In his reminiscences of being a police officer in Aberdeen in 1873, Clark gave an emotional and simple account of his love of being a police officer – 'no part of the duties I had to perform gave me so much pleasure as directing a stranger who was lost in the city, or the recovering of a lost child to its sorrowing and anxious parents' (Clark 1873: 104). Even in modern times many police officers recounted their sadness at the cessation of police officers covering school-crossings when civilian patrollers took over the role. The reason they gave was that this particular duty offered a valuable interface with the youngest members of the community and their parents or guardians. That said, many of their colleagues would find it difficult to empathise with this reasoning on a cold wet and windy winter's morning. But what is policing in the modern day? Is it the prevention of crime, detection, the enforcement of society's norms or the non-crime duties and general control and surveillance of the population?

Traditionally, the police role has been to prevent crime and respond to it when it occurs, and deal with emergencies as they arise. Now this public protection service is celebrating over 180 years of existence and its definition has greatly expanded over the period. The additional responsibilities include cyber-crime, people trafficking, counter-terrorism, identity theft, social media crime, sex offenders, organised fraud, and much more. Police duties in the traditional areas of anti-social behaviour and neighbourhood disputes have been given a higher priority and more intensive policing tactics introduced, as a result of demands from the community. And with the advent of technology, the expansion of police support staff and the hiving-off of many non-operational police duties to other agencies, the modern police officer should, one would think, be closer to the 'purer' form of policing we have all strived to achieve – but that does not seem to be the case. According to the Scottish Police Federation, police officers 'perform a job like no other and are the service of last resort, and when other services cannot assist, we step into the breach' (SPF 2012a: 3).

We often hear the sound-bite – 'the public wishes more police officers on the beat' but what does this actually mean? In reality, most citizens have no real wish to have anything to do with the police, they just want to go about their everyday life unhindered and in relative security and are aware that an effective professional police service will enable this to happen. But most citizens rarely think of the police on a daily basis, even retired police officers will relate, if asked, that on retirement they are surprised to find how little policing is in the public mind-set. A closer examination of the origin of the 'officers on the beat' sound-bite shows that it is regularly used by politicians, senior police officers and police associations in their everyday discussions on policing for their own purposes and probably dates back to the 1950s and 1960s and the days of the iconic TV programme, *Dixon of Dock Green*. So is the phrase outmoded and should it be changed? Some leading academics have their own opinions of the police patrol officer based on research studies over the decades 'walking around in uniform is certainly not a particularly effective form of crime control' (Waddington and Wright 2010: 41). They and many others make the point that there is the 'reassurance gap' which means that when crime is falling and the public perception is one of rising crime, then there is a need to increase patrol officer numbers to fill the 'reassurance gap' as it reassures the public. But, in reality, it is mainly a symbolic gesture. One approach in recent times from the world of academia has been to ask how many other ways there are to achieve community safety, prevent crime, and ensure community well-being. Maybe the answer is more auxiliaries and community wardens, more social workers, better trained teachers, more accountable housing officers, more police support staff, better use made of technology, more strategic use of retired police officers, and increased partnership and accountability – the list is not exhaustive.

The police in Scotland have a history of being pioneers in policing and introducing innovative policing methods. The vast majority of police officers believe they should not be routinely armed and support a mainly unarmed police service. Unlike the majority of Scottish citizens, police officers do not have the right to strike or take any form of industrial action. However, at the time of writing, police officers in England and Wales are being balloted on the right to strike as they believe they are being treated unfairly by the UK Government over police reform.

Being a police officer

For most of the twentieth century, the police conditions of service remained relatively steady though the actual salary was fairly low until the Edmund Davis Review in 1978 when there was a marked increase in the basic police wage which also became index-linked annually to ensure the level never fell short again (Home Office 1978). At times of high unemployment, many recruits were attracted to life in the police because the organisation offered job security and other benefits such as rent allowance or rent-free police housing, a pension at the end of service, an incremental salary, free medical and ophthalmic prescriptions and access to good medical and welfare care, and boot allowance and plain clothes allowance when applicable. Most of these allowances do not exist in the present day. Other benefits of being a police officer were available to those interested which ranged from a good social life within the police family and sponsored sport facilities. Operationally a hard-working officer could earn regular overtime to supplement the basic income, and for those with the necessary attributes and inclination, promotion opportunities were a constant feature of police work. Unlike most other employers, police forces actively encourage members to interface with various force-appointed religious representatives. In recent times these have included Jews, Muslims, Sikhs, Pagans and many more.

Just like the military tradition of family members following a military career, the police service is no different. Family traditions ensure sons follow dads into the service and brothers and sisters do likewise. Many joined as police cadets as the police profession attracts recruits at an early age, and once in the cadets, these recruits normally progress to the regular service. However, there are those individuals who prefer to join the police at a later stage in their life believing they are too young at 18/19 years. There is also the category of citizens that we have all met who would have liked to join the police but had their own individual reasons why this did not happen. For example, dislike of unsocial hours, salary not good enough, family and friends put them off the idea, too much risk and physical danger, and those who would not be comfortable with enforcement duties. There are also those who have entered the police service and found that it was not what they thought it would be and promptly left. Unfortunately, there are many examples of police officers who have found that their 'heart' was not in the job but regardless of this and due to job security, remained working as a police officer, doing as little as possible, and in police jargon became a 'uniform carrier'. However, it must be said that it is difficult for this type of individual to remain in post in the modern police due to new monitoring and appraisal systems and procedures that focus on the individual and can deal more effectively with the non-productive officer – from re-training to the ultimate dismissal from the police service. Until fairly recently, this was difficult to do in the police organisation due to the lack of appropriate systems being in place. This topic will be discussed later in the book.

For most of the second half of the twentieth century there were other categories of police officers. For example, the police service was well known for retaining regular police officers in an array of non-police roles which covered many trades and professions, such as motor mechanics, technicians, pay clerks, housing officers, photographers, graphic designers, computer operators, lawyers, administrators and many more, much to the consternation of their regular colleagues who worked unsociable hours and involuntary overtime at the sharp end of policing. In the past, there were plenty of examples in the Scottish police service of police officers of all ranks going through their 30 years or more service outside the operational sphere of policing, making few or no arrests and rarely if ever giving evidence in court as professional police witnesses. Sadly, some wore this as a badge of pride, and one wonders if they had been put in the invidious position of a frontline operational officer, they would have seen out their full service. There is no doubt that until recently a common thread of unfairness prevailed in the police service because of these practices and many officers who suffered in silence had good cause for grievance. But even in the present day there is evidence of unfairness in the service as can be witnessed by the fact that officers who do not work unsocial hours receive the same salary as their colleagues who do. Surely, in the twenty-first century it cannot be just or reasonable for officers who do not work unsocial hours to receive the same remuneration as those who work all sorts of shifts which cause, among other things, family disruption and health issues. As will be seen later in the book, there is a growing awareness in political circles of some of these unfair practices and moves are afoot to tackle them.

The Police Service of Scotland

Prior to 1 April 2013, policing in Scotland was carried out by eight police forces whose boundaries were similar to the local government boundaries created in 1975. Now the demarcations have been removed and Scotland has a national police service for the first time in its history. The previous constitutional tripartite

TABLE 1.1 Number of recorded crimes in Scotland, 2007–2012

Force	*2007–2008*	*2008–2009*	*2009–2010*	*2010–2011*	*2011–2012*
Central	19,825	18,931	16,727	16,131	16,213
Dumfries & Galloway	8,391	7,509	6,950	6,770	6,036
Fife	25,362	24,075	21,120	18,668	17,848
Grampian	35,706	34,946	30,872	30,899	29,226
Lothian & Borders	70,619	70,925	64,862	60,178	57,466
Northern	16,134	16,117	14,152	13,584	13,556
Strathclyde	182,454	179,254	160,835	153,670	154,750
Tayside	26,904	26,047	22,759	22,385	18,996
Scotland	385,395	377,804	338,277	322,285	314,091

Source: Scottish Policing Performance Framework (SPPF) (2012: 26).

governance set-up of central government, local authority and the Chief Constable has now been changed and replaced by one Chief Constable and a newly created Scottish Police Authority (SPA) with the statutory responsibility of overseeing the police, and central government maintains its overarching role. The new Police Service of Scotland (PSoS), commonly referred to as Police Scotland, came into being on 1 April 2013 as a result of the Police and Fire Reform (Scotland) Act 2012 and is the biggest shake-up to policing in Scotland in a generation, and occurs at a time when crime is at a 37-year low and detection rates are at their highest levels in 30 years (Tables 1.1 and 1.2).

TABLE 1.2 Detection rates for recorded crimes in Scotland, 2007–2012

Force	*2007–2008*	*2008–2009*	*2009–2010*	*2010–2011*	*2011–2012*
Central	60	58	59	61	56
Dumfries & Galloway	61	66	71	69	72
Fife	55	55	55	55	60
Grampian	47	49	48	49	48
Lothian & Borders	44	44	43	44	44
Northern	63	63	62	63	67
Strathclyde	44	45	47	45	46
Tayside	56	58	58	57	58
Scotland	48	49	49	49	49

Source: Scottish Policing Performance Framework (SPPF) (2012: 27).

TABLE 1.3 Percentage of respondents who are confident in the police in six categories, 2008–2011

	2008–2009	*2009–2010*	*2010–2011*
Prevent crime	46	48	50
Respond quickly to appropriate calls and information from the public	54	58	61
Deal with incidents as they occur	58	61	65
Investigate incidents after they occur	64	68	71
Solve crime	57	60	64
Catch criminals	55	57	60

Source: SCJS (2011).

Violent crime is at a 30-year low and Scots are feeling safer in their communities than in previous years. Public respect and confidence in Scottish policing are increasing, according to the Scottish Crime and Justice Survey (SCJS 2011), the rolling social survey which asks people about their experiences and perceptions of crime in Scotland (Table 1.3).

One of the main driving forces for police reform is the expected £1.4 billion savings over 15 years. Police Scotland has a budget of £1.2 billion for 2013–2014 and is already facing a shortfall of £60 million in its first year, and £130m and £190m respectively in years two and three. As the Scottish Government has a policy promise to maintain police officer numbers at the present levels, a large part of the savings has to be found within the ranks of the civilian police support staff. The new police force is on record as being committed to voluntary redundancies and no compulsory redundancies, and according to its chief constable, 'the year one gap is doable, but after that it becomes more difficult – we're going to have to look to see how we can handle the budget gap' (House 2012). It is expected that the bill for these voluntary redundancies and early retirements will be around £60 million. Police Scotland will also face a VAT bill of £22 million which the previous police regime was not required to pay.

This is a major challenge for the new Police Scotland but one they can meet with some optimism as the Scottish police service has a good track record in recent years of successfully managing its budget. For example, in 2011–2012, the Scottish police service spent £890 million on salaries, 2 per cent less than the previous year. Operating costs were also reduced by 7 per cent for the same period to £156 million. Since 2008–2009, there has also been a significant reduction in capital expenditure from £36.2 million to £21.7 million (SPPF 2012: 79). This reflects the efforts made by the police to meet the required cost savings. However, there will be less opportunity to match these savings in the future as most of the easy options to do so have already been implemented.

One controversial issue arises out of the number of police officers and police staff presently suspended from duty, some for a number of years. The previous eight police forces have been paying out more than £1 million to around 25 individuals across Scotland – a bill that has been inherited by Police Scotland. This is on top of what is reckoned to be other debts amounting to £100 million handed over by the previous police regimes. The concerns voiced by politicians and members of the public centre on the fact that public sector organisations are already under exceptional financial pressures as a result of the present economic climate and find it difficult to accept what appears to be a blatant waste of public funds being paid out to persons not giving any return. The situation is exacerbated when you factor in the costs of other officers having to carry out their colleagues' duties in their absence. This does not include, however, those officers on sick leave or restricted duties through no fault of their own. The new oversight body, the Scottish Police Authority (SPA), has been working with the police in the run-up to the new single police force to quantify the problem and to seek some resolution. This will be one of a number of management challenges facing the new single police force in its transitional years.

The management structure of Police Scotland is expected to cost 50 per cent less than the previous wage bill, with the number of senior officers being reduced from 31 to 11. This entails a wage bill cut from £4.842 million to £2.083 million, a drop of 57 per cent. The previous eight chief constables, nine deputy chief constables (one on central service) and 14 assistant chief constables have been replaced by one chief constable, four deputy chief constables and six assistant chief constables. There are also three civilian Executives – a Director for Human Resources, a Director for Finance and Resources and an Executive Lead for Transformation. The four deputy chiefs have the following responsibilities – deputy designate, crime and operational support, local policing, and the Commonwealth Games and major events. The six new assistant chief constables have an individual remit for the following areas of policing:

- local policing East
- local policing North
- local policing West
- Major Crime and Public Protection
- Organised Crime and Counter Terrorism
- operational support.

These assigned areas of responsibility will enable the new single force to deliver services on a national basis. The responsibility of leading local policing in the new single police force falls to 14 newly appointed local commanders holding the rank of chief superintendent who will oversee:

- response policing
- community policing
- local crime investigation
- road policing

- public protection
- local intelligence.

Each local commander liaises closely with communities and elected members and develops localised policing plans for each council ward in Scotland. These local plans identify local priorities, address the issues of greatest local concern, and help maintain police performance. Local policing is to be the 'engine-room' of Police Scotland and in a support role the national and specialist police functions will be uniformly and equitably available across the nation to meet demands. The 14 local command areas are:

- Aberdeen City
- Aberdeenshire and Moray
- Highlands and Islands
- Tayside
- Forth Valley
- Edinburgh
- Lothian and Borders
- Fife
- Greater Glasgow
- Ayrshire
- Lanarkshire
- Argyll and West Dunbartonshire
- Renfrewshire and Inverclyde
- Dumfries and Galloway.

As Police Scotland moved towards its launch in April 2013, it identified seven high priorities for 2013–2014 based on consultation and cognisance of the Scottish Government's Strategic Priorities; the Scottish Police Authority's three-year Strategic Police Plan; the Police Scotland Annual Police Plan; 32 Local Policing Plans and 353 Multi-Member Ward Plans. They are as follows:

- reduce violence, disorder and anti-social behaviour.
- protect the public.
- increase road safety and reduce road crime.
- tackle serious organised crime and terrorism.
- effectively police major events and threats.
- maintain high levels of public confidence in policing.
- deliver equality and diversity outcomes.

Police Scotland also defines its purpose as: 'To improve the safety and well-being of people, places and communities in Scotland.'

The previous Central Scotland Police Headquarters in Stirling is to be the forward command base and interim headquarters for Police Scotland. Tulliallan

Castle, Kincardine, Fife, in the central belt of Scotland and home to the Scottish Police College, is to be the corporate headquarters of the new single force with its conference facilities, and the National Reform Team will remain there. Both locations are easily accessible to most parts of Scotland and convenient for the major hubs of Glasgow and Edinburgh and the Scottish Parliament, politicians and public officials. There was, however, initially much uncertainty around the introduction of a national police service in Scotland from politicians and senior police officers, but attitudes are now changing as the beneficial outcomes are becoming apparent. Even the Scottish Police Federation who were initially sceptical of a single police service in Scotland, are now of the mind that 'it provides the greatest opportunity to maintain a world-class police service' (SPF 2012a: 4). Further discussion on the governance and constitutional position of the new single police service and other pertinent issues will be covered in later chapters.

Police reform in England and Wales

To fully understand what is happening in Scottish policing, one has to be cognisant of the significant proposed and actual changes to policing in England and Wales. Some space has been given in this text to explain the growing differences in policing between Scotland and England and Wales. It is also worth mentioning at this stage that the police forces in England and Wales have received a 1.6 per cent drop in central government funding in 2013–2014.

The independent review of police officers and police staff remuneration and conditions in England and Wales, referred to as the Winsor Review, as the author was Tom Winsor, was commissioned by the UK Government in 2011 (Winsor Review 2012). The Review's recommendations are the most significant changes to police officers' work and police staff pay and conditions ever made, and not surprisingly, the proposed changes have been surrounded by acrimonious debate, involving Police Associations, politicians and government officials, and the review has been described as an attack on the 'office of constable'. Recommendations put forward include the introduction of unsocial hours allowance; changes to variable shift arrangements; the suspension of chief officers' bonuses; giving power of compulsory severance to chief constables; introducing a lower starting salary for recruits; a new national on-call allowance; abolition of the competence-related threshold payments; and a lot more. The UK Government also wish to push through significant pension reform in the police service.

The reforms are seen against the backdrop of the existing police pay system designed over 30 years ago. During this period police working practices have changed greatly but their remuneration and conditions have not. One example is that in the late 1970s, the vast majority of police officers regularly worked unsociable hours but in the present day only 60 per cent do. Significant changes have also been made in private and public sector pay systems over this 30-year period in order to recognise and reward skills. This has not happened to any great degree in the police service, and the contention is that skills, performance, and effective crime fighting are not rewarded enough. Traditionally, an officer's length of service and rank determined what they were paid. The Winsor Review is seen as a serious attempt at modernising police pay structures and many changes have already been agreed upon in England and Wales. How many of these recommendations will find their way into the new single Scottish police service will be a matter for the Scottish Government, as the majority of policing issues is a devolved matter. At the time of writing, Scottish ministers have made it clear they have no plans to implement most of the Winsor recommendations. That said, according to the Scottish Police Federation, the UK Government has unilaterally applied elements of the police pension reform to Scotland without the involvement of the Scottish police in negotiations. These changes should be viewed against the backdrop of political devolution and the forthcoming Independence Referendum in 2014.

In recent years, the UK police service, in particular in England, has been tested at all levels as never before. Tackling everyday and organised crime threats; ensuring a safe London Olympics 2012; meeting the continuous challenges of terrorism; expanding community policing initiatives; facilitating governance change with the introduction of Police and Crime Commissioners; and undergoing strategic structural changes and resource reduction against a backdrop of public service budget cuts. The fatal shooting of two police officers in Manchester while on a routine call in 2012 characterised the bravery and risks expected of police officers. All this is happening at a time of falling crime rates and increased public confidence in policing.

Single services efficiency

The Christie Commission (Scottish Government 2011a) was set up by the Scottish Government and has argued for a radical change in the design and delivery of public services in order to cope with the increasing demands on public budgets and to address the entrenched social problems which exist in Scotland. The Commission called for public services to be built around people and communities; increased collaborative working practices to achieve outcomes; prevention methods to be given a priority; and for all public sector organisations to continuously seek to improve performance, reduce costs and to be more transparent and accountable. The Scottish Government has already embarked on public sector reform along these lines and the recent police and fire reforms are good examples. In addition, the Crown Office and the Procurator Fiscal Service have also introduced a federation structure and the Scottish Courts Service is consulting on how the provision of courts at all levels can best be provided to meet future demands and challenges. The Scottish Government also plans to integrate health and social care to improve the overall quality of service. This is to be achieved through new Health and Social Care Partnerships with health boards and local authorities being jointly and equally responsible for delivering nationally agreed outcomes. Such a move will have an impact on criminal justice social work and policing at the local authority level. And, in 2012, a further Scottish Government consultation process was launched to redesign community justice (Scottish Government 2012a).

Three possible outcomes have been put forward: (1) enhancing the present criminal justice authority model; (2) local authority models; and (3) a single service model. Results of the consultation process will be known some time in 2013. The point being made in highlighting these exemplars of Scottish Government policy in relation to public sector reform is to show there is a sincere and meaningful momentum by politicians and others to bring about the much-needed modernisation and improvement to public services in Scotland. One thing is for certain, whatever the final outcomes of this reform programme, they are sure to have an impact on the new Police Scotland.

Police numbers in Scotland

As of 30 September 2012, the full-time equivalent police officers employed in Scotland reached an all-time high of 17,454, which is an increase of 1237 police officers (7.5 per cent) from 30 September 2006 and an increase of 189 officers (1.1 per cent) from 30 September 2011. Figure 1.1 shows the number of police officers in Scotland for 2006 to 2012 and includes officers on Scottish Police College training, secondment, central service, long-term sick leave and maternity/adoption leave, but excludes those on career breaks. Police officers employed by the British Transport Police, the Ministry of Defence Police and the Civil Nuclear Constabulary are not included.

These figures adequately reflect the Scottish Government's manifesto commitment to ensure there are 1000 extra police officers in Scottish communities. This is in direct contrast to what has been happening in the police service in England and Wales which has witnessed an estimated loss of 16,000 policing posts in a similar period.

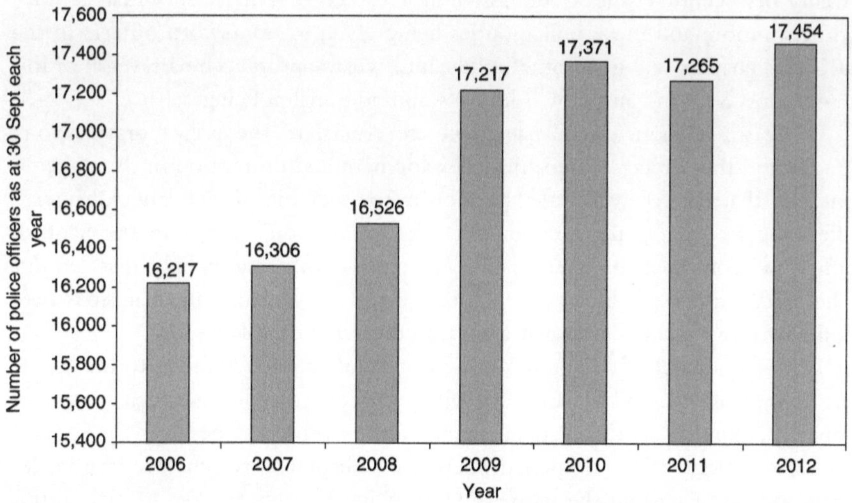

FIGURE 1.1 Number of police officers in Scotland (FTE), 2006–2012

Source: Scottish Government 2012b.

Overview of the book

The main books on Scottish policing focus on police history; police and the constitution; police and the law; police and crime; police management; and politics and governance. This still leaves a gap in the understanding of what the police actually do in Scotland. The general public and, to a degree, new recruits into the police service are not entirely clear as to what 'makes a Scottish police officer'. This book hopes to span this 'knowledge gap' by taking the reader through a set of basic topics and in so doing describe in simple practical language the 'Scottish police officer'.

Scottish policing is undergoing structural change and the profile of the police officer in the new century differs greatly from that of the past. Chapter 2 offers some explanation of the wider police tradition in Scotland rather than a discussion on police history in the central and western belt of the country, which is usually the case. As there are a number of training books and manuals available at present that cover criminal law and police procedures, Chapter 3 takes a more general informative approach and explains the initial recruitment of the police officer and formal training.

How the qualified police officer goes about his/her daily work policing Scotland is discussed in pragmatic terms in Chapter 4 and includes how this has changed over time as a result of organised crime, terrorism and the changing priorities of the public and politicians. Chapter 5 follows on from the previous chapter and focuses on highly trained and specialist units in Scotland such as organised crime, surveillance, security services and road policing.

The contribution of non-police officers such as police civilian support staff, auxiliaries, and the private sector, plays a key role in the policing of Scotland in the twenty-first century and is discussed in Chapter 6. The twenty-first century witnesses more and more police duties being given to non-sworn officers in the UK. This chapter will give some insight into what appears to be a reversal of this trend across Scotland and how it impacts on traditional policing.

Police supervision and management are crucial to the police organisation's success and the subject of personnel development and promotion in the police is one area that has received little attention from academics in Scotland. Chapter 7 offers the reader a general insight into the 'promotion' process in the Scottish police and comments on the suitability of the system in the twenty-first century. The appointment of chief police officers involves a separate mechanism where politicians have a key role to play and again this will be explained.

With the advent of devolution in Scotland policing has climbed to the top of the political agenda and the aspect of who 'oversees' the police is a regular topic of debate, both in the Scottish Parliament and outside. Who 'watches over' the Scottish police is explained in a simplified manner in Chapter 8, which gives the reader an introduction into all the parties and agencies who have a role to play in this increasingly key function of democratic policing. Some comparisons will be made with other UK systems.

Chapter 9 concludes the book with commentary on what lies ahead for the Scottish police officer and Scottish policing. General comparison is made with police colleagues and police forces in other parts of the UK and the European Union. Overall, the book takes the reader on a journey from the beginning of an officer's career through the processes of teaching and development and moulding the individual into the 'Scottish police officer'. In doing so, the reader is introduced to Scottish policing in the twenty-first century. The policing environment in Scotland is becoming increasingly political and in all likelihood the 'profile' of the police officer will undergo change in the coming years. What will happen to policing after the Independence Referendum in 2014 and in the next Scottish Parliament is difficult to determine at the present time. Nevertheless, this chapter pulls together the main themes of the book and offers some opinion as to what the 'Scottish police officer' will look like in the future.

This book has a dual role, first, as a general introduction to the Scottish police officer and, second, as an informative piece explaining how some of the key features of Scottish policing work.

2

THE POLICE TRADITION IN SCOTLAND

Introduction

Prior to 1707, Scotland had its own Parliament and made its own laws, and then, following the Union of the Crowns in 1707, the Scottish and English Parliaments were replaced by a United Kingdom Parliament, sitting in Westminster. Despite unification, the Scottish legal system and laws were left untouched and remained separate from the rest of the UK. So Scots Law retained its 'originality, determined by its distinctive history and its relationship with other legal systems' (Manson-Smith 2008: 1). The enactment of the Scotland Act 1998 resurrected the Scottish Parliament and the people of Scotland once again had their own devolved Parliament inaugurated in Edinburgh in May 1999. In Scotland, the Lord Advocate has overall responsibility for criminal prosecutions and the Office of Procurator Fiscal takes the lead in crime investigation and prosecution at the local level. Invariably, police officers or statutory agencies carry out these investigations and a mix of enforcement measures is available to prosecutors and police within the criminal justice system, in addition to arrest, report, charge, and court summons. These include – no action, warnings, restorative justice, mediation or reparation, a fiscal fine, fiscal work offer, and an array of fixed penalties.

Police reform in Scotland in the nineteenth century was closely allied to economic growth, commercialisation and industrialisation and it was during this period that local communities saw the need for a police force. This is supported by Barrie who has said that 'reform was essentially the result of the middle-class seeking to control and manage their cities more effectively in the face of rapid urbanisation and raised expectations of comfort and security' (Barrie 2008a: 262). It has to be emphasised that the definition of the police role in the eighteenth and nineteenth centuries by in large meant the regulation of orderliness, cleanliness and a general level of security in the community. One of the duties of the Edinburgh City Police included patrolling the streets in the early hours of the morning ringing a bell so the householders could deposit their rubbish onto the streets (Archibald 1990: 8). In Scotland, the concept of policing was for the public good and public welfare, which was as much to the fore as combating crime and public disorder (Carson and Idzikowska 1989: 270–1).

The government at the time tended to intervene only to regulate and was unwilling to tell people how to run their own lives because of the prevailing belief in 'individualism'. Nevertheless, during the nineteenth century the 'state' gradually got involved. In 1824, the government legalised trade unions and eventually took control of the gas, sanitation and water supply, weights and measures, food adulteration, patents and bankruptcy, reformed the Post Office and nationalised the telegraphs, telephones and broadcasting. Not surprisingly, and as a result of the growth in government intervention, the respective administrations of the civil service and local authorities increased in size. Against this background of social change emerged the need for a disciplined policing system to police the masses from within on a regular basis. This led to suspicion and unease among the populace who viewed the new police as an extension of government. It was around this time that the police took on a welfare role when it came to young children during the industrial upheaval of the nineteenth century. It was estimated that in the City of Aberdeen hundreds of children were surviving on the products of crime and begging, and a large number of them found themselves in the prisons. One police tactic would be to round the children up and march them off to the soup kitchens which gave the citizens some respite for a short period.

At the time, poverty was regarded as more of a fact of life than as a problem and since the system was run by the local parish, it led to corrupt practices and intimidation. Eventually the government was forced to do something about the poverty issue, which meant that Poor Relief was to become, for the first time in its history, uniform and centrally directed. The demands for education on political, moral, economic and social grounds were enormous and in 1870 legislation was passed that removed the major deficiencies in the education system. It is important to view the profile of the new police in the historical setting of this time, when in reality neither *laissez-faire* nor state intervention was the real engine of change throughout the nineteenth century. Instead, both were constant accompaniments to the basic force of industrialisation, with politics being the usual agent that society resorts to for profound and pervasive change. Industrialisation broke down old customs and the new entrepreneurs demanded additional freedoms and new services, such as a competent and efficient police service. And after nearly a century of libertarian resistance to government intervention, the idea of a uniformed constabulary was formally introduced across the nation around the same time that the Reform Act (1832) was enacted, which transformed the shape of politics and laid the foundation for the wider enfranchisement of the population with its accompanying freedom and democracy – epitomised by the police officer.

The police in Scotland have found themselves involved in many of the historical situations of the times. For example, in 1919, police found themselves embroiled in the industrial unrest of what was termed as the 'Red Clydeside' which had earlier been described by the Scottish Secretary as a 'communist revolution' brewing in Glasgow (Kerr 2010: 103). The confrontation culminated in January 1919 over pay conditions and hours worked and an estimated 90,000 people congregated in Glasgow's George Square. Major public disorder ensued and resulted in the police launching baton charges and running battles throughout the day which spread to other parts of the city. Eventually, over 1200 troops from England were brought in to restore order – a decision had been made not to use Scottish soldiers from nearby barracks due to the uncertainty they would not follow orders if called upon to use firearms against the crowds. Tanks and machine guns were also set up at strategic points in the city which had a calming effect on the strikers but it still took a week for the disorder to be brought to a close.

There have always been links between Scottish policing, Westminster and the English police. The story is told of the arrival in 1967 at the Westminster Parliament of Winnie Ewing, the second Scottish National Party MP, and the first person to greet her was a police officer born in Scotland called Manus 'Jock' Boyle, part of the police security contingent in the House of Commons. To some, it was a symbolic moment – 'the Glasgow solicitor (Ewing) dedicated to the dismantling of the British State at the gates of Westminster [met] by a British bobby on duty defending the Mother of Parliaments' (Stenhouse 2005: 89). To top it all, the 'bobby' was a Scot.

The fact is that the Scots influence on the Metropolitan Police originated with the contribution of Patrick Colquhoun, a former Lord Provost of Glasgow, who authored a Treatise on the police of the Metropolis in 1797. Colquhoun was a merchant who advanced the argument for a police service as essential to the protection of business and general community security. His vision also included improvements in the courts and magistrates system and the criminal law – founded on crime prevention rather than the incarceration of criminals. A second treatise by Colquhoun, *The Police of the River Thames*, in 1800 led to the introduction of the River Thames Police, a quasi-police force created to protect shipping on the Thames. The police reform of the times culminated in 1829 with the introduction of the Metropolitan Police and Robert Peel's Metropolitan Police Act 1829, designed to protect and regulate the sprawling metropolis of London.

The Scottish influence continued and in 1888 the first Scottish Commissioner of the Metropolitan Police, James Munro, was appointed and in the 1890s the force's Chief Surgeon was a Scot, Alexander MacKellar. The sourcing of police recruits for the Metropolitan Police has always been an issue, even into the twentieth century, and recruits were normally a mix of home-grown Londoners and those from the English counties. However, in the 1950s and 1960s, the Metropolitan Police had a specific policy of targeting recruits from Scotland in an attempt to introduce 'new blood' to combat endemic corruption in its ranks. and the London police even established a recruitment office in Glasgow in the early 1960s. Many police officers serving in Scotland were also encouraged to transfer down to the London police by friends and relatives who were already serving in the English force. The 1980s also witnessed the appointment of the first Scot in modern times, Sir David McNee, as Commissioner of the Metropolitan Police.

Pioneering police

Dating further back than Peel's Metropolitan Police Act of 1829, the history of the Scottish police is one of innovation. At the time of the publication of the Police Review's first edition in January 1893, the police in Scotland were well established, having been made compulsory throughout the nation's towns. Unlike other parts of the UK and long before the 1962 Royal Commission, Scottish policing was based on a system of tripartism, made up of the local police authority, comprising elected members; central government; and the chief constable who had the power to discipline, promote and appoint. Even going back to 1857, the Police (Scotland) Act of that year is looked upon as a turning-point in policing. The Act introduced procedures that remain with us to the present day, for example, the requirement of police officers to be exempt from jury service, the statutory requirement of chief officers to furnish criminal statistics to the Scottish Secretary of State, and the creation of the office of Her Majesty's Inspectorate of Constabulary.

Still there is much relevant comment to be made of the innovativeness of Scottish policing within an historic context, as reviewing police history helps us understand the modern-day police organisation. There are a number of landmarks in Scottish policing and organisation. For example, in 1927, the Scottish Police Federation agreed to represent policewomen 21 years before the Federation did so in England and Wales, and Glasgow was the first British police force to operate a Marconi police radio system. And in 1932, the internationally adopted police diced cap band was created in Scotland. As we will see throughout this text, Scottish policing is still at the forefront of many innovations in policing. One prime example was the introduction of the Scottish Criminal Record Office (SCRO) computer system in 1988, the first national computerised criminal records system in Europe. This was followed a few years later with the launch of the SCRO's national automatic fingerprint system – again, a first.

The SCRO computer system had a significant impact on Scottish policing and deserves much acclaim for doing so. The system centralises all Scottish criminal records and provides update and enquiry facilities at terminals spread throughout all of Scotland, down to sub-divisional level and is linked to other national information databases in the UK. The multi-search facility on the computer system allows the vast criminal information database to be interrogated at the local level during the course of criminal investigations. The SCRO computer system was the first piece of major technology to be made readily available to the patrol officer in support of frontline policing. The benefits to operational policing are immeasurable as officers have instant access on the street to a person's criminal convictions, marks, tattoos, aliases, pending cases, warning signals, and much more to assist their decision-making at the frontline.

Another illustration of pioneering police work in Scotland is very pertinent to present-day Scottish policing and deserves a mention. That is community policing which is discussed in Chapter 4, but a short historical input is needed here. To begin the story we have to go back to 1957, to the town of Greenock, situated on the south side of the Clyde estuary on the West coast of Scotland. At this time, the Greenock community was experiencing more than its fair share of poverty and unemployment, poor housing and amenities, and high crime levels. The then Chief Constable of Greenock Burgh Police, David Gray, started what was to become known as the Weir Street–Ladybank Project. Being particularly concerned about juvenile crime in the area, Gray suggested that concentrated attention be given to it by local authority services, the churches, teachers, police and others to produce a better environment for the children to play and grow up in. He posted three constables to the area with a remit to support the residents and the statutory agencies in the wide range of structural, environmental and sociological improvements. Gray believed that improving the neighbourhood environment through a multi-agency approach, with the police playing a central role, would increase the overall quality of life in the area and eventually reduce crime.

Gray, who was eventually appointed HM Inspector of Constabulary in Scotland, was undoubtedly ahead of his time; for example, his Ladybank Project was a forerunner of what Wilson and Kelling eventually espoused as 'the broken windows' syndrome in their renowned *Atlantic Monthly* article of 1982[1] (Wilson and Kelling 1982). His appointment of a group of dedicated police officers with specific instructions to develop useful and constructive relationships with local people is the obvious prototype of community policing. These issues were being discussed in Scotland long before some police contemporaries were credited with originating comparable ideas, and more specifically, 20 years prior to similar findings and recommendations of the Scarman Report in 1981 (Home Office 1981). Such understanding of the police, community links and partnership working reflects the best in traditional Scottish policing.

Characteristics of a good police officer

The Scots have always had an aptitude for police work and have held police posts across the world, particularly in the British Commonwealth in India, Hong Kong and Canada. We are all aware of the stereotypical Scot mainly marketed by the media and tourism pundits, but what of the real Scots persona and what makes the good police officer? Many of the likely traits can be found in lots of other cultures but history shows they do exist in plentiful supply in the Scottish people and specifically in their scientists, engineers, teachers, academics, doctors, and of course their police officers. Here are some of the characteristics that make policing an ideal occupation for the Scots:

- tough, stubborn and argumentative;
- intelligent and independent thinker;
- serious and not easily discouraged;
- unafraid of hierarchy and perseveres;
- innate feeling that every person is equal and deserves respect;
- original thinker with enquiring mind;

- patient when required and sanguine;
- inventive and not easily fooled;
- well liked socially and hard-working;
- loyal and patriotic;
- pragmatic with common sense.

Many of the characteristics are reinforced in the 'constable's declaration' which has to be made by every new police recruit before they obtain the legitimacy to act as a police constable. The declaration is made before a sheriff or justice of the peace in the following terms:

> I do solemnly, sincerely and truly declare and affirm that I will faithfully discharge the duties of the office of constable with fairness, integrity, diligence and impartiality, and that I will uphold fundamental human rights and accord equal respect to all people, according to law.
>
> *(Police and Fire Reform (Scotland) Act 2012, Section 10(1))*

As to what level and degree these characteristics are present in the individual is for the reader to decide.

The making of a police officer

A public information documentary film released in 1945 made it clear in simplistic terms that in order to be a police officer you had to have good character, strong physique, appropriate height, good health and good eyesight, and be intelligent. After three months training, the public expect you to look the part in uniform and handle situations as they arise, despite most probationary constables feeling a bit unsure and self-conscious at the beginning of street duty in their pristine uniform and carrying 'a shiny new truncheon, a whistle never blown and an empty notebook' (British Council 1945). The point made by the film nearly 70 years ago that still has relevance today, is that the police officer is not and never has been an 'instrument of oppression' and that traditionally there has been a mutual trust between police and the public. Remember that one of the main reasons for the creation of the police in Scotland was to assist people and improve the well-being of individuals, in addition to their crime prevention and detection roles. The police officer is born out of the common law duty of all citizens to play a part in the maintenance of law and order, be a witness, give statements and attend court. In many ways police officers do the things we ourselves would have to do if there were no police, such as report a road accident, administer first aid, or look after a lost child. The difference is that traditionally the police officer does it more efficiently since he/she is a trained specialist in a wide variety of skills. The police officer enforces rules made by the community but remains a member of the community he/she serves.

Thirty years after the public information film was released, Scotland was going through police reorganisation in 1975 and another film documentary entitled

The Making of a Policeman was broadcast on television. In the film it was emphasised that the officer is

> bounded by discipline and is an upholder of the law not its interpreter and the discipline which must come from within manifests in these outward gestures on the drill parade – the public are the first to demand a disciplined police force.
>
> (Scotland Today *1975)*

However, a police officer must also be tough but restrained and has to be trained in more than the niceties of 'square-bashing'. In the same programme, the first chief constable of the Strathclyde Police Force, Sir David McNee, commented that he believed what attracted the police officer to the job is challenge and on arrival at the Scottish Police College for the first time they have no real idea of what lies ahead of them in their career. The Police College strives to give officers confidence and common sense and in the 1970s there was a strict regime of discipline that all new recruits had to go through in order to achieve self-discipline. As one probationer noted in the film, 'they take your personality away from you and substitute it with a number'. The conventional wisdom of the time was that when leaving the College, students should have an idea of how to tackle basic problems in the community. One should not forget that the public have a clear image of what a police officer should look like – a generic model which the College endeavours to attain. And as police operational work is under constant scrutiny by the media, according to Sir David McNee, this meant police officers having to be 'intelligent, well-trained and have an abundance of good-old common sense'. The police officer of the time also carried out the role of the untrained social worker, delivering messages of death, dealing with the mentally ill, protecting and caring for the weak and infirm – within a construct not so much of a police force but a police service. The career of the Scottish police officer in the mid-1970s is succinctly described as two years footslogging, then maybe specialisation; then for the few, promotion to Sergeant after seven years though no guarantees. The statistics at the time revealed one in five officers attained the Sergeant rank and one in twenty made it to Chief Inspector or above. For the majority of officers who remain on the beat for most of their career, they can expect to cover 4536 miles a year on foot.

A few years later, when commenting on community policing in the Strathclyde Police in the early 1980s, the then Chief Constable Pat Hamill said, 'It is intended to involve people in crime prevention, to encourage public participation in reducing disorder, and to improve understanding of the police through consultation and liaison' (*Glasgow Herald* 1983). This is the traditional notion of the Scottish police officer encouraging and facilitating the community to participate in their own community safety and has been the bedrock of policing in Scotland for over a century, and as we will see in later chapters, this has been honed and intelligently refined in recent decades.

The media and the police officer

Police officers are easy targets for the media, both professionally and in their private life and regularly attract attention in the press and television far in excess of any other profession apart from actors. In addition to the usual suspects involved in complaints against the police in the normal course of an officer's duties, police officers are also vulnerable to threats of being reported or complained against by spouses, neighbours, relatives, colleagues and even friends, for a wide variety of misdemeanours that would not warrant similar action elsewhere. For example, police officers can find themselves in difficulties with their police bosses if they fall behind in any financial payments such as loans, mortgages, and council tax payments. Traditionally it has been frowned upon for officers to be in debt and this could be construed to be a discipline offence. As a result, police managers regularly receive letters from lawyers, banks and other financial organisations bringing an officer's transgression to the attention of his boss, usually seeking some kind of reimbursement from the individual's salary. In the vast majority of cases such approaches to employees would never have happened if the person was in another occupation. In the 1990s, police forces were inundated with correspondence seeking redress from an officer as a result of failure to pay poll tax or child maintenance allowance. Police officers are also prone to be complained against by a neighbour in the aftermath of a dispute or fallout along the lines of 'behaviour unbecoming a police officer', knowing that it can make things difficult for the officer. Traditionally, it has always been easy to complain and report police officers to their bosses with allegations relating to off-duty conduct. Fortunately, most police managers deal with these issues in a sympathetic and understanding manner.

In the second half of the twentieth century the television media was responsible for a relentless portrayal of numerous genres of police officers which influenced people's thinking of the police: *The Sweeney*, *Dixon of Dock Green*, *The Bill*, *Heartbeat*, and many more, including comedies like *The Thin Blue Line*. The Scots had their own distinctive brand of police officer in Rebus, Laidlaw, Taggart and Hamish Macbeth. The fictional character of police constable Macbeth first appeared on television in 1995 and could be described as the George Dixon of the Highlands, and was always accompanied by his dog, Wee Jock (until its demise) on patrol in the small town of Lochdubh, keeping the peace in his own way without an over-dependence on the law. Although the Macbeth storylines exaggerate reality, the TV series was successful in depicting rural policing in the Highlands and islands of Scotland and allows for a comparison of the 'hard' policing depicted in Scottish cities by Rebus, Laidlaw and Taggart. Policewomen were not ignored either, as a number of TV programmes depicted their role in policing and how it has changed in the past century, from those in the more traditional police genre of *Juliet Bravo* and *The Gentle Touch* to the tougher models of *Cagney and Lacy* and *Prime Suspect* (Heidensohn and Brown 2011: 111–34). These offerings are mainly set in England and there has not been a Scottish equivalent that portrays the distinctiveness of the contribution made by Scottish policewomen to both uniform policing and criminal investigation. There have been and currently are a number of middle- and senior-ranking women police officers who have played a key role in helping to shape the present model of Scottish policing – TV producers, please note. In addition, the television moguls should take time out to read some of the non-fictional accounts of real-life policing from retired Scottish police officers depicting their police careers and experiences – mostly male detective officers, as they seem to have the more interesting stories to tell from the reader's perspective (Brown and Jeffrey 2007; Gallacher 2011; Jackson 2008; McLaughlin and Smyth 2012; Pearson and O'Hare 2008; Scott 2003). These are enjoyable reads that young police recruits would benefit from browsing through to gain an insight into what to do and, more importantly, what not to do.

The Scots never managed to match the most successful of the TV 'cop' series, *The Bill*. Even the well-respected ex-Deputy Chief Constable of Greater Manchester, John Stalker, made the following observation of *The Bill* :–

> [I]n a class of its own [giving] an accurate view of what modern policemen do – one minute they're fending off mad dogs, the next they're dealing with lost children. What it loses in car chases, it gains in accurate detail, right down to the relationship between officers, and all the paperwork. It's by far and away the best.
>
> *(Lynch 1991: 5)*

Though situated in London, this popular programme was a great hit with serving officers of the time who regularly watched the series and believed it to be the most authentic on offer.

The police welfare role

Prior to the Second World War, the police still had a role to play in the Parish Relief System, when poorer families in Edinburgh could attend the High Street police office and pick up free clothes and shoes, which led to the stigma of wearing easily identified 'polis boots' with holes punched in the ankles to prevent them from being pawned or sold (Clark and Carnegie 2003: 152–3). But the police organisation should have been looking more to improving the welfare within its own ranks. Even by the 1960s the police service across the UK was still operating in the Dark Ages as portrayed in an ex-chief constable's autobiography. When explaining his early career, he described officers having to parade on a weekly basis to collect their salary in cash as they saluted, and duties for the forthcoming week were also issued at the same time. Officers had to work the shifts they were given, regardless of how it impacted on family or social life and permission to take leave, change shifts and have time off was regularly refused – 'your life was not your own, it belonged to the police' (Hellawell 2002: 39). Authorisation was also required to live in a particular location and to get married, and on occasions the future spouse had to be interviewed by a senior officer who would decide if she was a suitable person to marry a police officer. It was only in the 1980s that most of these practices were phased out, particularly in Scotland due to the relentless lobbying from the Police Federation.

The Scottish Police Federation (SPF) was a product of the police strikes of 1919 with the aim of ensuring police officers had a voice on all matters pertaining to the welfare and efficiency of officers. The SPF represents over 99 per cent of the police officers in Scotland and has a remit which covers the welfare and efficiency of its members. The SPF is the only statutory consultation body for the police services in Scotland and regularly contributes to police policy-making. As Grant points out, police officers are neither 'employees' nor workers but 'office holders' and while statutory employment rights do apply to all 'employees', they do not necessarily apply to 'workers' such as the self-employed, home-workers, agency workers, freelancers, sub-contractors and casual workers (Grant 2010: 145). Police officers' rights and duties are independently defined by their 'office' rather than the individual, unlike an employee's rights and duties as defined by employment contract. The work of the SPF has expanded considerably over the past 94 years but in principle has maintained its original objectives as stated above.

Disability, ethnicity and gender

I wonder what Hellawell and his contemporaries would have made of the current situation in the world of policing with public organisations such as Police Scotland being statutorily bound by the Equality Act 2010 to do what it can to eradicate unlawful discrimination in the workplace and advance equality of opportunity and diversity. I dare say he would have approved and supported the police who have made great efforts to be more transparent in the area of diversity and regularly produce data that measures the level of disability, ethnicity and gender in the organisation. Tables 2.1, 2.2, 2.3, 2.4 and 2.5 are contained in the Scottish Police Performance Framework (SPPF) for the period 2011–2012.

As can be seen from Table 2.1, 3 per cent of officers and 6 per cent of police staff employed by the Scottish Police in 2011–2012 declared that they have a disability. The previous Strathclyde Police force, which covered half of Scotland, employed the largest percentage of police staff with a declared disability, around 9 per cent.

Table 2.2 reveals around 1 per cent of police officers and staff stated they were from an ethnic minority group. The figure for Special Constables was 2 per cent nationally and 4 per cent in Strathclyde.

The ratio of female officers in the Scottish police has been rising over the years and for the period 2011–2012 the figure was just under 28 per cent (Table 2.3).

The percentage of male and female police staff employed by the Scottish police has remained fairly static over the years with most forces employing around twice as many female staff as male staff (Table 2.4).

Unlike the 28 per cent figure for the regular police force for the period 2011–2012, the percentage of female officers in the ranks of the Special Constabulary is just under 37 per cent (Table 2.5). The lower numbers of female police officers in

TABLE 2.1 Percentage of police officers, police staff and Special Constables by declared disability, 2011–2012

Force	*Police officers*		*Police staff*		*Special Constables*	
	Yes	*No*	*Yes*	*No*	*Yes*	*No*
Central	2.9	91.5	4.2	91.6	*	68.8
Dumfries & Galloway	1.7	90.0	5.0	90.0	*	62.6
Fife	0.5	93.2	1.7	94.2	0.0	84.4
Grampian[2]	6.5	0.0	8.2	0.0	0.0	0.0
Lothian & Borders	2.5	97.5	5.8	94.2	0.0	100.0
Northern	1.4	90.5	3.4	93.7	0.0	18.5
Strathclyde	3.8	92.8	8.6	90.6	*	75.2
Tayside	1.4	85.5	2.4	76.4	*	26.3
Scotland	3.2	84.8	6.3	80.4	0.7	57.8

Source: Scottish Policing Performance Framework (SPPF) (2012: 75).

Notes:

1 The data presented do not include the unknown response to disability declarations, so the data do not total to 100.

2 Grampian data return only completed the disabled and unknown categories.

An asterisk (*) indicates some data has been suppressed in the interest of individual confidentiality.

TABLE 2.2 Percentage of police officers, police staff and Special Constables by declared ethnicity, 2011–2012

Force	*Police officers*		*Police staff*		*Special Constables*	
	White	*Minority ethnic*	*White*	*Minority ethnic*	*White*	*Minority ethnic*
Central	96.1	1.0	96.7	*	80.6	*
Dumfries & Galloway	93.6	*	94.2	0.0	75.7	*
Fife	86.2	0.9	79.9	*	70.6	*
Grampian	86.9	*	74.7	*	52.6	0.0
Lothian & Borders	96.1	1.4	98.4	1.0	97.8	*
Northern	92.7	0.8	94.4	*	84.6	*
Strathclyde	93.2	1.5	97.2	1.4	84.3	3.8
Tayside	94.4	1.1	96.1	*	67.1	*
Scotland	92.9	1.2	93.2	1.0	78.2	2.1

Source: Scottish Policing Performance Framework (SPPF) (2012: 76).

Note:

1 The data presented in these tables do not include the unknown response to ethnicity declarations, so the data do not total to 100.

An asterisk (*) indicates some data has been suppressed in the interest of individual confidentiality.

TABLE 2.3 Percentage of police officers by declared gender, 2011–2012

Force	*2008–2009*		*2009–2010*		*2010–2011*		*2011–2012*	
	Male	*Female*	*Male*	*Female*	*Male*	*Female*	*Male*	*Female*
Central	73.9	26.1	72.7	27.3	71.7	28.3	70.8	28.7
Dumfries & Galloway	–	–	73.4	26.6	72.2	27.8	71.5	28.5
Fife	–	–	–	–	73.5	26.5	71.6	28.4
Grampian	–	–	73.6	26.4	73.2	26.8	72.9	27.1
Lothian & Borders	76.9	23.1	75.7	24.3	75.1	24.9	74.5	25.5
Northern	76.7	23.3	74.8	25.2	74.3	25.7	74.0	26.0
Strathclyde	74.2	25.8	72.7	27.3	72.1	27.9	71.5	28.5
Tayside	–	–	73.2	26.8	72.4	27.6	71.1	28.9
Scotland	–	–	–	–	72.9	27.1	72.2	27.8

Source: SPPF Annual Report 2011–2012 (2012: 76).

the regular service may reflect the physical nature of policing and the need to retain a substantial number of male officers. One would imagine rising concerns if the percentage figures for female officers rose to 60 per cent or more of the regular force. The figures suggest it is much easier to recruit higher numbers of female officers for the Special Constabulary.

TABLE 2.4 Percentage of police staff by declared gender, 2011–2012

Force	*2008–2009*		*2009–2010*		*2010–2011*		*2011–2012*	
	Male	*Female*	*Male*	*Female*	*Male*	*Female*	*Male*	*Female*
Central	31.8	68.2	32.5	67.5	33.4	66.6	31.6	68.4
Dumfries & Galloway	–	–	30.9	69.1	28.5	71.5	29.7	70.3
Fife	–	–	–	–	30.4	69.6	29.8	70.2
Grampian	–	–	32.9	67.1	32.8	67.2	32.9	67.1
Lothian & Borders	39.2	60.8	39.9	60.1	40.1	59.9	39.1	60.9
Northern	26.3	73.7	25.4	74.6	25.2	74.8	24.6	75.4
Strathclyde	34.6	65.4	35.4	64.6	36.9	65.6	35.9	65.7
Tayside	–	–	35.4	64.6	35.0	65.0	35.9	64.1
Scotland	–	–	–	–	35.1	65.8	34.5	66.1

Source: Scottish Policing Performance Framework (SPPF) (2012: 76).

TABLE 2.5 Percentage of Special Constables by declared gender, 2011–2012

Force	*2008–2009*		*2009–2010*		*2010–2011*		*2011–2012*	
	Male	*Female*	*Male*	*Female*	*Male*	*Female*	*Male*	*Female*
Central	56.0	41.0	59.8	40.2	58.9	41.1	53.8	46.2
Dumfries & Galloway	–	–	66.4	33.6	69.2	30.8	69.6	30.4
Fife	–	–	–	–	59.4	40.6	59.6	40.4
Grampian	–	–	65.9	34.1	64.5	35.5	62.0	38.0
Lothian & Borders	–	–	–	–	65.9	34.1	65.7	34.3
Northern	–	–	–	–	–	–	60.0	40.0
Strathclyde	–	–	64.2	35.8	64.0	36.0	63.9	36.1
Tayside	–	–	59.1	40.9	65.7	34.3	65.1	34.9
Scotland	–	–	–	–	–	–	63.1	36.9

Source: Scottish Policing Performance Framework (SPPF) (2012: 77).

Policewomen

Traditionally, the police officer was a white male, normally with a working-class background. Now the profile has evolved into a gender-mixed occupation regulated by strict equality and human rights employment legislation. In the twenty-first century the number of policewomen serving in the Scottish Police is at its highest level and as Table 2.3 shows, women make up over a quarter of the police total numbers. This shift in the gender balance of the police has helped to bring about a change in perspective to policing and how traditional duties of the police have been modified. For example, improvements in the way children and female victims of crime are dealt with and a softer approach to community liaison.

But this was not always the case, the Great War of 1914–1918 witnessed a sea-change in the role women played in society. Prior to the First World War a woman's place was viewed as being in the home, but through necessity this image changed during the war years. Women carried out work previously done by their menfolk, which included service in the police and they played a vital part in the war effort and helped keep the country operational during the war. By the end of the 1920s, women were rewarded for their war efforts and were given equal voting rights with men, but most women returned to domestic services, child-minding and housework, similar to before the war.

Around this time the idea of women in the police service attracted much opposition. In the Foreword to *The Women Police Question*, author and social commentator Livesey talks of the police role during the General Strike of 1926 and the need for organised physical force which he hopes will sway public opinion to 'firmly reject any further proposal to squander money upon such fantastic futilities as female police officers' (Livesey 1927: Foreword). Livesey was not one for holding back as he continued his diatribe on women in the police describing them as:

> a war product, the relic of a time when abnormal conditions reduced the total strength of the manhood of the country; the conditions under which her very limited efficiency was of value to the State have passed away, her now unjustifiable existence is being prolonged in deference to the clamour made by a small group of totally unrepresentative women.
>
> *(ibid.: 16)*

The concept of motherhood and keeping a home was to many much preferable to women following males into policing. It is important to give space to these comments from an age gone by in order to highlight the misdirected opposition to the introduction of women into the police service at the time. Even the Police Associations are not blameless, in their *Report on the Question of Police Women*, the Federation of Police Officers in 1924 revealed their entrenched views on the subject:

> Police duty requires men, and then only men who are specially fitted and adapted for it . . . We are unable to conceive of a woman who could be so fitted. She would be an unnatural product. Police work is men's work.
>
> *(Police Federation 1924)*

Fortunately, a counter-argument was made at the same time which emphasised the important role of policewomen in the prevention and protection of young girls in their teens and the taking of statements from girls and children. The report recommended the increased employment of women police officers (Bridgeman Report 1924).

A more up-to-date account of women in the police by Carrier explains that women are an integrated part of the nation's police service and for many of today's generation it may be difficult to understand why the introduction of women into the police service was bitterly resisted in the first half of the twentieth century. According to Carrier, even 'chief constables suspected the women of feminism, the police Federation were openly hostile towards them, and the Home Office abstained from encouraging their employment' (Carrier 1988: xvii). How times have changed, as in 2012 two of the eight Scottish chief constables were female and as of 1 April 2013, three out of the 25 senior police posts in Police Scotland have been awarded to females – one deputy chief constable and two chief superintendents. It is expected that further appointments of female officers in the chief superintendent and superintendent ranks will be made during 2013. The modern view in police circles is that those appointed have the necessary balance of skills and experience to lead the service and build on the existing successes of Scottish policing, and are not appointed on the basis of gender.

Scott's (2003) book, *A Fair Cop*, gives a good account of the period of change that faced policewomen in the transition from chauffeur/tea-lady/policewoman department of the 1960s to the fully operational policewoman of the 1980s: a practical account of a Scottish policewoman's career. Coincidentally, a forthcoming TV series due in 2013 is set in the 1950s and tells the story of a young policewoman just newly arrived on the job in a rural police station in England. A preview of the first episode sums up the police working environment at the time and what female police officers had to endure from their colleagues. On the first day on the job, she meets her Inspector boss who says 'Your timing couldn't be better, do you know where the teapot is?' By the end of her first day, she has been given an office in a broom cupboard with no phone, 'Can't give you a phone! We'd never get you off it!' Told to sit in a van during a raid and informed by her Commander that her job is to support the men so that they can get on with the job of 'real policing!' And this is all before they get to the initiation ritual, involving bare flesh and the office stamp (BBC 2013)!

New campaigns still await the modern-day female recruit as the new single police force reviews how best to test police officers for fitness. Calls are being made from within and outside the police service regarding claims that some of the physical tests are too demanding and unfair to women police. Individuals who fail the fitness test have no option but to leave the service. The attrition rate for women is around 47 per cent and 39 per cent for male officers. Of the female failures, 74 per cent is due to a physical running test called the 'shuttle run' in which candidates continually run between two fixed points at an ever faster rate to a quickening electronic beep. The point being made by opponents to the fitness test is that it places females at a disadvantage even though the pass criterion is lower than that for men. Another factor in support of the discontinuation of the test is that the police service does not test the fitness of officers again after their probationary period ends. The concern is that Police Scotland could be taken to an employment tribunal over the issue.

Bread and butter policing

Although the Scottish criminal justice system and the police have made great strides in combating domestic violence, it was not always that way. In Conley's (2007) historical account of violence and homicide in the nineteenth century, she refers to an account in the *Glasgow Herald* on 26 October 1886 and reminds us that victims of violence may have looked to the police and courts for protection but that was not always forthcoming: 'in Glasgow when a witness reported that a neighbour was beating his wife with a hammer, the policeman replied that "it wasn't his beat"' (ibid.: 130). Members of the public were also reluctant to intervene in domestic violence, afraid of being attacked themselves. One story relates to a minister testifying in court that 'he had heard a woman screaming on the night a tinker murdered his wife . . . and that he had not interfered because he was afraid of the tinker' (ibid.: 130–1). The police themselves often declined to get involved in family quarrels and violence which in many instances resulted in an escalation of the violence with fatal consequences. This is depicted in a report in the *Glasgow Herald* of 20 November 1871, that told the story of a brother who approached a police officer for assistance to get his unruly brother home and was told by the officer that it was not the role of the police to interfere in a family quarrel. When the officer left the scene, the individual was again attacked by his brother who in retaliation attacked and killed his brother and was charged with murder.

History portrays Scotland as a violent nation and in the twentieth century violence became a major societal issue with the number of homicides rising significantly as the century progressed. Homicide figures stood at 60 in 1925, falling to 35 by 1950, then rose to 84 in 1985 and 137 by 1995. As a reflection of the increase in crime, the Scottish prison population steadily increased throughout the century, from around 2800 for the period 1900 to 1910, falling to an average 1800 between 1920 and 1950 and then rising steadily to 2700 by 1960 with a sharp rise in 1970 to 4900. Prison numbers stayed steady till the late 1990s when the total escalated to 5900 by 2000 (Abrams and Brown 2010: 45). Violent crime in Scotland at the present time is at a 30-year low and will be discussed later in the text.

As well as crime, many Scots experience social disturbance and anti-social behaviour on a regular basis and in 1999–2000 around 8 per cent of households experienced disturbance and/or noisy parties as a regular occurrence, rising to a figure of 14.4 per cent for those living in social rented accommodation. When it comes to regularly experiencing alcohol and drug abuse, the figures rose to 23.5 per cent of households, with 34.6 per cent for those in social rented houses, and for those who own their own home the figure was 12.2 per cent (ibid.: 45).

Improving the quality of life in communities and neighbourhoods has always been a major objective of Scottish politicians, and the police service has a key part to play in this. Public perception of the prevalence of anti-social and neighbourhood problems is inextricably linked to what makes a community and a neighbourhood a good place to live. Continuing research by the Scottish Housing Survey has identified nine main anti-social problems which the public perceive to have a negative impact on the quality of life in a neighbourhood and which traditionally the Scottish police officer has had to deal with on a regular basis. These nine problems are:

- vandalism, graffiti and damage to property;
- groups or individuals harassing others;
- drug misuse or dealing;
- rowdy behaviour;
- noisy neighbours and loud parties;
- rubbish or litter;
- animal nuisance and dog fouling;
- abandoned or burnt-out vehicles.

(Scottish Household Survey 2012: 26)

Responding to these issues was and is the 'bread and butter' of policing. The most prevalent are noise, dog fouling and rubbish and litter with 25 per cent saying the problem is a regular occurrence. Anti-social and rowdy behaviour comes next at around 14 per cent. The SHS data shows that up to 2010 the trend has been one of gradual improvement in public perceptions of their neighbourhood problems. However, indications are that in 2011 there is a slight increase in most of the problem areas, particularly noise and dog fouling increasing by 2 percentage points. One important finding is that the perception of vandalism and graffiti is around 11 per cent and continues to decrease year on year.

When comparing perceptions of safety or fear of crime in the most deprived areas of Scotland, 65 per cent of people say they would feel very or fairly safe when walking alone, compared with 81 per cent of those living elsewhere. Evidence also suggests 6 per cent of those in deprived areas feel less safe in their home alone compared to 2 per cent in the rest of Scotland (SHS 2012: 35). Overall, 56 per cent rate their neighbourhoods a very good place to live, which shows a rising trend in recent years. In the more rural areas of Scotland, the figure is 75 per cent. Not surprisingly, the figures decrease as the level of deprivation increases. More up-to-date data from the Scottish Household Survey shows that the strategic targeting of resources by the police and other agencies has had a positive impact on these perennial problems in recent years.

The persistent and growing problem of mental health in our modern society continues to be met by the frontline police officer, as in addition to normally being the guardian of the criminal justice system, the police officer is usually first on the scene of an incident involving someone suffering from mental illness. In some instances the officers are confronted with violence that can have dire consequences. For too long the police have been left to deal with the mentally ill on a 24-hour basis when in reality it is more a health issue for medical practitioners and specialists to deal with in a hospital environment. There are parallels here with individuals who are drunk and incapable through alcohol consumption who get picked up by the police and spend the night in a police cell solely for their care and protection. Senior police management have been in agreement for some time that persons who fall into these categories have traditionally found themselves in police custody simply because there is no alternative. There are many sad stories of suicides and accidental deaths in police custody as a result and in the majority of cases through no fault of the police. The Police service is usually the only agency to hand to render assistance and have a reputation of handling these awkward situations in a common-sense and practical manner, as many a sheriff or High Court judge will testify. Surely this is one police tradition that needs to be changed in the twenty-first century.

Conclusion

Traditionally, police officers in Scotland have been a talented bunch with a wide variety of interests, skills and other attributes, for example, there have been many officers who have had a successful parallel career as professional sportsmen and women. Not to forget those who were musically inclined and held key positions in many of the police pipe-bands. The book, *Fuzz to Folk*, published in 2011 by a retired police inspector from Edinburgh, Ian Green, is a case in point. The book chronicles his life from being drafted into the army to serve in the Korean War to being a mechanic, footballer, 30 years as a police officer, angler, music organiser, concert promoter and owner of the most successful small record label in the UK, while also playing a significant role in the resurgence of traditional folk music in Scotland, culminating in him being conferred an honorary degree by the RSAMD 'for his tireless work on behalf of Scottish traditional music and the musicians who sing and play it' (Barrow 2011: 11). This is just one of the many remarkable and varied lives of police officers.

As far back as 1963, one respected commentator on the Scottish criminal justice system wrote that 'In a free and open society such as ours aspires to be, it is desirable that the police should be humanly efficient, locally controlled, known as individual persons, and be part of the community' (Mack 1963: 375). That still stands today even with all the upheaval society is going through and is in the best tradition of the Scottish police.

Scottish towns had a variety of local officials in the late eighteenth and early nineteenth centuries, with the most important being the office of constable that dated back to the early seventeenth century. This was not a salaried position but was looked upon as an individual's contribution to the community, and constables were allowed to claim fees from the amount raised from fines and rewards. Middle-class householders would on occasions employ a substitute to take their place of what was 'a time-consuming, unpaid and burdensome work' (Barrie 2008a: 27). What a difference a few hundred years makes, police work is still time-consuming but less burdensome and more interesting for most, and since the 1980s the police officer has been relatively well paid with good job conditions – though that may change in years to come, as we will discuss in later chapters.

This chapter has introduced some police traditions that are still relevant today, such as the need for discipline, fitness and sound personal characteristics. These positive traditions can be compared to the earlier negative approach to having female police officers in the police service and the poor police response to domestic violence. Future chapters will discuss how these negative traditional elements of policing have been progressively replaced by the positive attitudes of today. This is due in no small way to the efforts of the Scottish police officer.

Note

1 The image of the 'broken windows' environment is used to explain how communities descend into incivility, disorder and criminality if cognisance is not taken of their maintenance and upkeep.

3

HOW ARE POLICE OFFICERS RECRUITED AND TRAINED?

Introduction

In the nineteenth and early twentieth centuries, the police role was looked on as a low-paid but secure job with poor conditions – officers were not entitled to a day off and had to pay for their own equipment. Prior to the Police Act of 1919, there was little attempt at any formal recruiting or training in the police service. An *ad hoc* system existed which relied heavily on a short interview, a height and eyesight test which, if satisfactory, would endorse the recruit into the police service. As for the training of recruits, there was a great reliance on seasoned police officers giving tuition and the 'university of life' also played a part. After both the World Wars, ex-military personnel joined the police as there was little else employment for them and the disciplined life of the police was similar to what they had been used to in the military services. Nowadays there is a whole industry geared up to support those aspiring to a career in the police service. The UK and Scottish Governments have their websites full of a plethora of information on what candidates have to do to fulfil the basic application criteria and the police themselves have similar information links and recruitment departments with an enthusiastic staff always on hand to assist. For those contenders keen to research and prepare for all eventualities, there are a number of comprehensive guides and books packed with the latest recruitment information and advice on how to prepare specifically for police entrance exams, psychometric testing and interviews. The following are only a selection (Clabby 2004; Cumming 2010; Malthouse and Barentsen 2010; McMunn 2011; McTaggart 2010; Ricketts 2008; Tolley *et al.* 2010; Tozer 1996; Walmsey 2007).

The abundance of literature and advisors to assist prospective candidates seeking a career in the police highlights how police entry standards have risen, reflecting an increasingly competitive environment. Modern society also demands higher ethical values and tougher screening of potential candidates to test for racist attitudes, drug misuse, credit and fraud history, and for inappropriate attitudes not suited to the role as a police officer. The risk of not recruiting the right person is too high in the modern day, as this will eventually come to light and have a detrimental effect on the police organisation and in all probability have a negative impact on public–police relations.

There are many examples of individuals going to great lengths to get recruited into the police. The story is told of one keen female recruit who, having failed the initial entry due to being 5 feet 5 inches when the regulation height was 5 feet 5½ inches, she went to a clinic that specialised in stretching people. After a short course she re-applied and was accepted after making the regulatory height (Scott 2003: 6–7). Other individuals who have been unsuccessful in their attempts to join the police have entered the armed services or the military police to gain experience in a disciplined service and have re-applied to join the police on leaving military service with a fair degree of success. Other candidates unable to gain entry into their local force have been so keen on a career in law enforcement that they have travelled to another force such as the Metropolitan Police to gain entry and in many cases have applied to transfer to their chosen force after the completion of their probationary service. This has always been a sore point with the larger forces that see themselves as paying for the initial training effort and costs for an individual recruit only to see them transfer to another police force.

In his autobiography, the former Metropolitan Police Commissioner, Sir Robert Mark, explained his reason for joining the police service in 1937 as down to choosing an occupation which was not greatly popular in the public eye at the time and offered little competition for an ambitious individual who was 'well built, fit, good at games and not entirely stupid' (Mark 1978: 16). To get his point across, Mark offers quotes from the title of one of H.G. Wells' short stories '[in] the country of the blind, the one-eyed man is king' (Wells 1904) – or, in other words, a person with mediocre capabilities may achieve significant advancement in an organisation if its members are less capable. This is true of many senior police officers who aspired to reach the top levels in the police.

This chapter offers general comment on the recruitment and training of the modern police officer and examines the profile of police recruits in Scotland. It also includes comment on the Special Constabulary and Police Cadets, and the role of central training at the Scottish Police College. Various aspects of initial police training are also discussed.

Recruitment

Prior to the introduction of Police Scotland, the eight police forces had the responsibility for recruitment of police officers at the regional level. Although there were some local variations in assessment methods, the recruitment and selection procedures were mainly similar. To maintain the highest standards in the police service, applicants have to meet essential criteria at the first stage as follows:

- be 18 years of age;
- be a British citizen or EU/EEA national, Commonwealth citizen, or foreign national with indefinite leave to remain in the UK;

- there is no minimum or maximum height requirements;
- meet the mandatory national eyesight standard;
- there is no formal education requirements but you will have to pass written tests;
- be of good character and although you may still be eligible to join the police service if you have minor convictions/cautions, there are certain offences and conditions that will make you ineligible;
- be physically and mentally able to carry out police duties, the initial fitness assessment will be based on the Scottish National Fitness Standard;
- must have a full current UK driving licence;
- cannot apply if you have submitted an application that is still being considered by any other police force;
- cannot apply if you have been rejected for any reason in the past 12 months by any police force.

Potential police officers are assessed from the moment they submit their application to join the service, so what a candidate has to remember is that the information provided in response to the competency questions is all the assessor has to go on when considering the individual for the next stage of the process. The overall quality of a candidate's communication skills is being evaluated even at this early stage and may be grounds for rejection.

More than ever before, prospective police officers have to demonstrate an understanding of the wider role of the modern police officer and the unique relationship with communities, partners and customers. Being an effective communicator with good problem solving skills is essential, as is having a high level of integrity and honesty. Future police officers must also be effective team players with sound temperament and a desire for continual personal development. Those thinking of a career in the police must also appreciate a police officer's accountability to the public in all its guises, who expect high standards of conduct at all times, both on and off duty. Police recruitment departments will also encourage applicants to reflect on how being a police officer will impact on their personal lives and put forward a list of questions – the answers to which should be considered carefully and assist the individual's decision as to whether they are suitable for a career in the police. The following are sample questions to be considered:

- Can you act with resolve, tolerance and restraint – even in the most demanding situations?
- Are you willing to accept responsibility for your own decisions and actions?
- Do you behave in a professional, honest and trustworthy manner – at all times?
- Do you understand that the misuse of drugs is illegal and is never acceptable?
- Do you understand that as a member of the police service, officers cannot misuse their position?
- Do you treat everyone with respect and courtesy?
- Can you demonstrate sound judgement in your relationships, friendships and associations?

- Are you able to demonstrate sound judgement in relation to your financial obligations?
- Are there any factors that make you susceptible to corruption or compromise?
- Are you aware that police resources and information can only be used for policing purposes?
- Can you maintain confidentiality in relation to all information that you will have access to?
- Do you have cause for concern about your own criminal history record?
- Do you realise that the Chief Constable reserves the right to reject any applicant without giving a reason?

(Strathclyde Police Force 2012)

The recruitment process in the new single police force is the same for everyone. At the time of writing, the new recruitment and selection system for Police Scotland was still being finalised but is expected to assess the same competencies and attributes as the previous system and will include personal and family security vetting and physical fitness. Existing assessment tools are also currently being looked at with the likelihood that the present Standard Entrance Test may be replaced in the future. Wherever possible, Police Scotland will take account of new recruits posting preferences when placements are being decided. However, as the new single police force needs to ensure all the communities within its domain are effectively policed regardless of geography, new recruits will have the opportunity to work at any location in Scotland.

Recruitment competition

Even for an experienced police officer from outside of London, the size and diversity of the Metropolitan Police Service (MPS) have always offered unique professional challenges and rewards with a wide range of potential career paths. A major recruitment drive by the MPS in 2012 to attract police officers from across the UK who had completed their probationary training highlighted some of the benefits. MPS officers receive London Weighting Allowance on top of the national pay scales. In 2012, this stood at £2277 per year for London Weighting and £1011 for London Allowance. In addition, experienced officers presently in receipt of rent or housing allowance could be eligible for rent of housing allowance up to a maximum of £5126 per annum housing allowance or if in receipt of transitional rent allowance, £5863 per annum. Officers can also expect to have 25–30 days annual holidays depending on length of service on top of normal public holidays and an average two rest days per week. And in line with national agreements there are many forms of leave, including maternity, paternity and adoption, special leave, and career breaks of up to five years. MPS officers also receive a wide range of discounts and special deals with major high street stores and retail outlets.

The MPS selection procedure is along similar lines as other police forces with candidates being invited along to an assessment centre for interview and standard medical and fitness tests. There is also a full vetting procedure and applicants have the opportunity to nominate three choices of working locations. What is not clear at the time of writing is how the ongoing police reforms in England and Wales will affect the MPS' recruitment package.

Profile of recruits

The previous eight Scottish police forces recruited candidates for the police at the force level and as a consequence there is a lack of centrally held information on the profiles of police recruits joining the Scottish police service. However, in order to gain some insight into the recruiting profile of police in Scotland data was obtained from the Strathclyde Police force for the two-year period October 2008 to October 2010 which contains the profile information of 1539 recruits appointed by the force during this period. During its existence the Strathclyde Police force accounted for 50 per cent of the total complement of police officers in Scotland and this large sample cuts across rural and urban areas and gives some insight into the profile of candidates applying for the police service in Scotland. The available information relates to previous occupation, gender, age, ethnicity and the number of graduates.

Using the job classification from the Office of National Statistics (ONS 2012), the large number of previous occupations were appropriately categorised to facilitate analysis. This was reduced from an inventory of hundreds (see Appendix A) to around 40 key job titles each held by at least two individuals (Figure 3.1). This creates a slight discrepancy in the total numbers which is negligible.

The data reflects a cross-section of the previous occupations of recruits prior to joining the police and reveals a weighting towards admin, sales, customer service roles, etc. Interesting to note is that the types of skills and competencies required of these roles, such as managing people, communication skills, interpersonal skills, influencing and negotiation skills, and being computer-literate, are very much sought after in the police service. The data raises the question as to whether the police selection process is selecting people who have the skills and competencies associated with these jobs and is not recruiting from manual and tradesmen jobs as was the case in the past. In other words, the demands and complexity of the role of the twenty-first-century police officer requires more use of brains rather than brawn. Alternatively, it may just be that there is a surplus of people in these types of roles, for example, there are a high number of leaders and managers, and people who have experience in supervision and management. The number of recruits previously employed in the 'protective services' is high too, which is to be expected.

There is also a high proportion of business, finance and IT professionals, many of whom will have been through higher education with various degrees. In fact, out of the total number of 1539 recruits examined, there were 414 graduates – nearly 27 per cent of the sample. The unemployed figure of 62 is significant too and it would have been interesting to know which job they used to hold. Individuals from sports and fitness backgrounds also feature high on the list and this is expected, given the physical nature of the police officer's job.

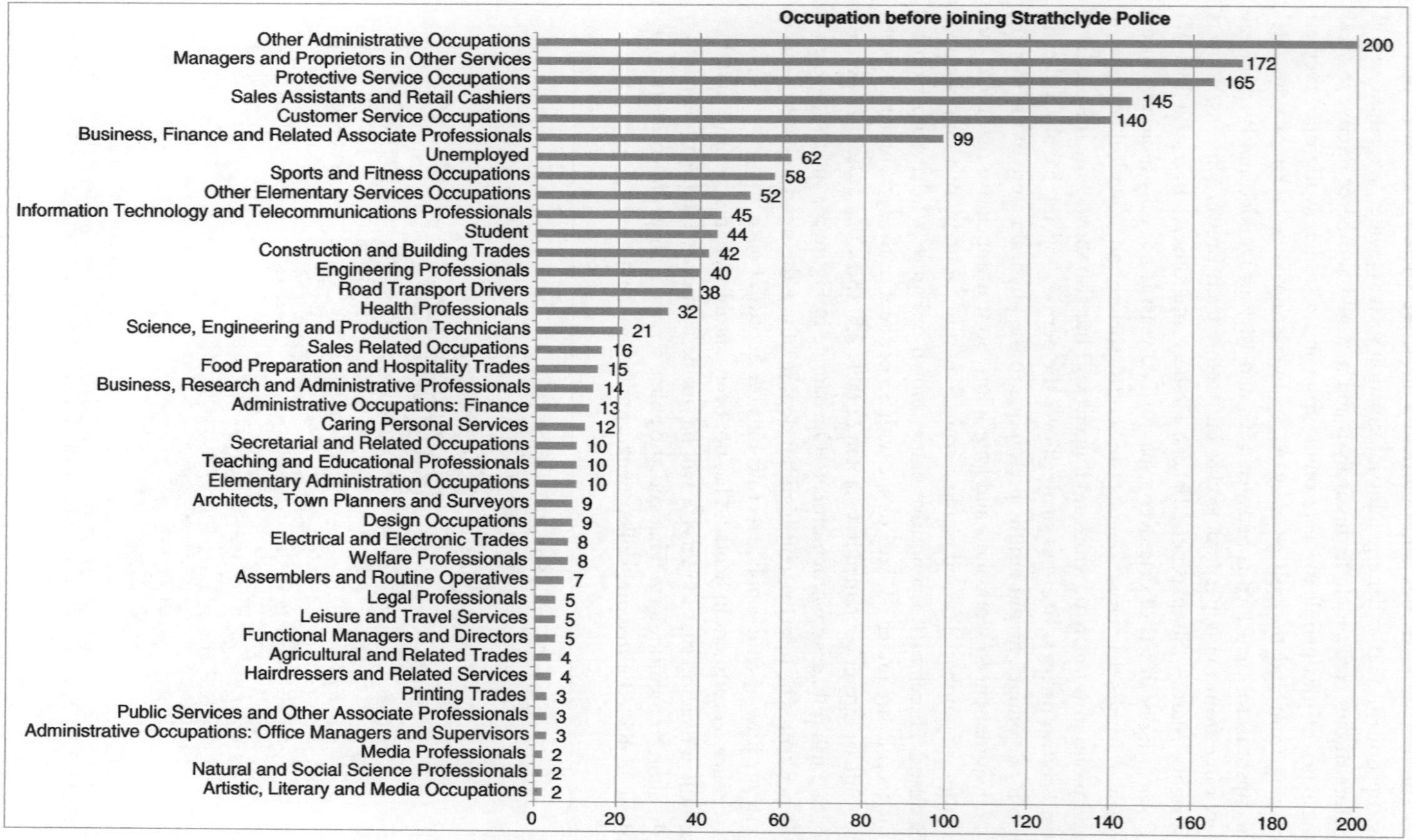

FIGURE 3.1 Occupation of recruits before joining Strathclyde Police Force (October 2008 to October 2010)

Source: Police Recruit Profile Information (Strathclyde Police Force 2010)

The limitations of this study prevented any cross-reference between previous occupations and other demographic information such as gender, age, ethnic origin. Future studies could include this analysis and it would also be of interest to show the types of jobs people are *not* coming from just as much as the ones they are coming from and the reasons why. As an interesting aside, a list of constable's occupations for the 21 years between 1794 and 1815 in Dundee and Perth reveals few came from the upper middle class but mainly from Brewers, Smiths, Weavers, Wrights, Masons, Shopkeepers, Bakers, Fleshers and others (Barrie 2008a: 27). Comparing both sets of data over a span of 200 years is not only indicative of the massive changes that have taken place in Scottish society and individual occupations and professions (many of which no longer exist) but also shows how the profile of the Scottish police officer has changed over the period. Policing has always been a job for a younger, fit and healthy person due to the physical nature of the role and the requirement to work shifts and long hours. So it is imperative that there are a significant number of fit and young recruits to ensure a sound future for policing in Scotland. Therefore, it is a positive sign as shown in Figure 3.2 that 86 per cent of the recruits are under 34 years of age with 35 per cent of the total under 24 years.

Official figures contained in Chapter 2 (Table 2.3) show that around 28 per cent of Scottish police are women officers. Our sample in Figure 3.3 suggest a figure of 34 per cent which seems a bit high but does reinforce the trend in recent years of a steady flow of female police recruits into the Scottish police.

Police recruitment in Scotland has not been a problem in recent times and there is little indication that the service will be unable to meet recruitment demands in the short to medium term. That said, the police service is always in competition for those highly educated and skilled workers who have above-average potential.

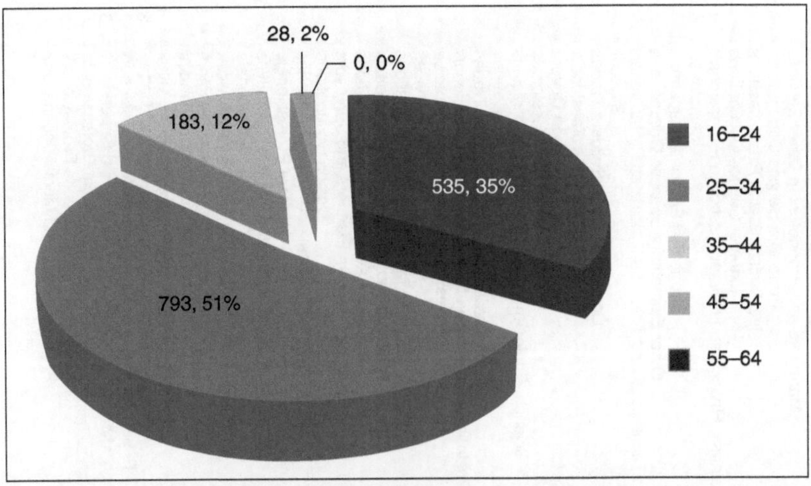

FIGURE 3.2 Age of police recruits in the Strathclyde Police Force (October 2008 to October 2010)

Source: Police Recruit Profile Information (Strathclyde Police Force 2010)

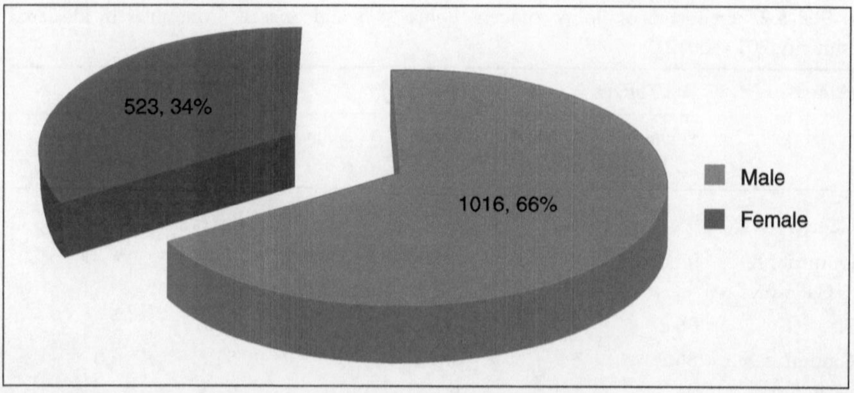

FIGURE 3.3 Gender of police recruits in the Strathclyde Police Force (October 2008 to October 2010)
Source: Police Recruit Profile Information (Strathclyde Police Force 2010).

Out of the 1539 Strathclyde recruits, only 32 declared themselves in the Black and Ethnic Minority (BEM) category which is 2.0 per cent (see Table 3.1). This is a higher figure than that for national recruitment in 2007–2008 and 2008–2009 which was around 1.0 per cent. The figures for BEM recruits have been fluctuating

TABLE 3.1 Ethnic origins of recruits joining Strathclyde Police (October 2008 to October 2010)

Ethnic origin	*Number*
White Scottish	1440
White English	33
Polish	2
Chinese	4
African	4
Pakistani	13
Finish	1
Greek	1
Italian	1
Asian	3
Other White British	9
Mixed	3
Indian	5
Australian	1
White Irish	17
White Welsh	2
TOTAL	1539

Source: Police Recruit Profile Information (Strathclyde Police Force 2010).

TABLE 3.2 Percentage of police officers, police staff and Special Constables by declared ethnicity, 2011–2012

Force	*Police officers*		*Police staff*		*Special Constables*	
	White	*Minority ethnic*	*White*	*Minority ethnic*	*White*	*Minority ethnic*
Central	96.1	1.0	96.7	*	80.6	*
Dumfries & Galloway	93.6	*	94.2	0.0	75.7	*
Fife	86.2	0.9	79.9	*	70.6	*
Grampian	86.9	*	74.7	*	52.6	0.0
Lothian & Borders	96.1	1.4	98.4	1.0	97.8	*
Northern	92.7	0.8	94.4	*	84.6	*
Strathclyde	93.2	1.5	97.2	1.4	84.3	3.8
Tayside	94.4	1.1	96.1	*	67.1	*
Scotland	92.9	1.2	93.2	1.0	78.2	2.1

Source: Scottish Policing Performance Framework (SPPF) (2012: 76).

Note: The data presented does not include the unknown response to ethnicity declarations, so the data does not total to 100.

between the 1–2 per cent mark in recent years and this is despite major efforts by the Scottish police and politicians and ethnic group representatives themselves.

If we compare these recruitment numbers for BEM to the ratio of those serving in the Scottish police for the year 2011–2012 in Table 3.2, we see a figure of 1.2 per cent nationally and 1.5 per cent for Strathclyde Police.

There is no doubt the figures are disappointing, considering the genuine efforts being made to increase the numbers, and senior police management are concerned that low recruitment of ethnic minorities will have a negative impact on efforts to police Scotland's growing multicultural communities. There is a need for community police officers to have a fundamental understanding of cultures and languages when tackling crime in minority communities and particularly when dealing proactively with terrorism. The benefits that would accrue from a more diverse police service is self-evident as it would introduce better communication and understanding between police and communities which inevitably lead to increased trust, which is essential to democratic policing. It is hoped that the arrival of Police Scotland will facilitate a more comprehensive and focused approach to encouraging BEM members to join the police.

The militaristic and disciplined nature of police work with its impact on officers' personal lives has always discouraged a particular section of society from seeking a police career. Modern generations view the life restrictions of police officers and the adherence to expected behavioural codes on and off-duty as a disincentive to a police career, and the lack of flexibility in organising social arrangements due to unsocial working hours does not help.

Police recruits are still comprehensively vetted and expected to be of good background and in excellent health and fitness. With policing becoming more community-oriented, there is a requirement for candidates to have additional skills as they will regularly interface with a wide range of people from diverse backgrounds and cultures with differing needs and expectations. A modern police officer should possess good communication skills, be analytical and strategic, a good problem-solver and technically and culturally competent.

Recruitment challenges

A review of police staffing and recruitment literature in England and Wales in 2012 suggested that police recruitment faces three main challenges in the future. These challenges are just as pertinent to Scotland in the twenty-first century and worthy of inclusion:

> *Increase in attrition*: baby-boom generation retirements; generational change which view a police career as less attractive and inflexible and probably do not have the required commitment; the era of austerity having a negative impact on police salaries and conditions of service.
>
> *Recruitment sources*: a decrease in qualified applicant pool as a result of potential recruits with criminal records, debt, and lack of fitness; and those who seek a non-militaristic career with more flexible working arrangements; increased competition from other agencies such as the military or private security; an increasing set of skills required in modern policing; competitive benefits and opportunities in other careers; image of the police officer less attractive.
>
> *Increased policing responsibilities*: exacerbates the supply and demand model of police recruitment, for example, the explosion in community-oriented police work; increased use of intelligence, surveillance, counter-terrorism duties, coupled with newly emerging crimes such as intellectual property violation, identity theft, cyber-crime, human trafficking and serious fraud, further complicates the recruitment and retention position of police agencies.
>
> (Wilson 2012: 342)

Suggestions are put forward that, in order to ease potential recruitment difficulties, a broadening of the recruitment market could be achieved by 'relaxing age, education, or residency requirements and becoming more tolerant of experimental drug use, bad credit history, and minor arrest records' (ibid.: 343). Opposition to such moves is mainly based on the risk of reducing the quality of recruits and the potential impact on police performance. Police officers are expected to be law-abiding citizens themselves and it is imperative that the public hold them in respect.

However, these concerns can be reduced by improving recruitment procedures, screening, interview methods, and introducing more comprehensive background checks.

A liberal approach towards police officers with criminal convictions is evident in Scotland, as shown by the fact more than 333 serving police officers have criminal records for vandalism, drug offences, domestic abuse and serious assault. A significant proportion of these convictions happened while the officer was serving in the police.

Having a national police service in Scotland should facilitate the gathering of personnel and recruitment data for better analysis of future demands and pressures on recruitment. Included in any study should be the identification of the type of police officer required by communities, the skills needed and the likely demands being asked of them – rather than just adopting a number-based system of recruitment and retention.

Training

It became apparent by the 1960s that society was changing and along with it demands on policing were becoming more complex and the traditional police officer required more knowledge, skills and a broader education, particularly for those who would aspire to be future leaders. As a result, the 1960s saw the introduction of training programmes for all officers, especially the middle to higher ranks. This 'higher training' involved Sergeants and Inspectors attending courses at the Scottish Police College (SPC) where they were introduced to management and organisational teaching as well as law enforcement. It was around this time that the Aberdeen City Police, which was renowned for support of further education for its officers, sponsored a number of police officers on a Business Management Course at the local college. This was followed by the first Accelerated Promotion course in Scotland in 1964, which was a move to identify and develop officers with above-average potential for leadership. And for those officers who had passed their police promotion exams and wished to continue with further education, a new Higher National Certificate in Police Studies was introduced in 1968 which consisted of short 'block release courses' over a two-year period. The reality was that in the spirit of Scottish education the police service was playing 'catch-up' as for far too long the police had relied on the traditional profile of a police officer for its recruitment. This was inadequate in a rapidly changing world where criminals were becoming more sophisticated and crime more complex.

One example of change was the appointment of a new chief constable in the Aberdeen City Police in 1970, Alexander Morrison. A native of the Outer Hebrides, Morrison began his police career in London where he gained rapid promotion and at the age of 36 years he became the youngest police officer to attend the Senior Command Course at Bramshill, Hampshire, and on his arrival at Aberdeen he was the youngest Scottish chief constable (Irvine: 1972: 125). It was time for change in the Scottish police.

The Scottish Police College

The Scottish Police College is situated in the Central belt of Scotland and caters for around three-quarters of the police and support staff training needs from basic probationary training to senior command training. The College also caters for most of the specialist training such as road patrol, crime prevention, crime investigation, supervisory and leadership courses. Specialist and developmental courses offered by the SPC will be discussed in later chapters.

The SPC is an award-winning centre of excellence and provides formally recognised courses and programmes through the Scottish Credit and Qualifications Framework (SCQF), universities or professional bodies. The SPC goal is to offer a range of training, assessment, qualifications and professional development opportunities to enable students to advance their professional competence throughout their career. This is achieved through offering centralised police training to the police service in Scotland; specialist police training; leadership and management courses for police and non-police organisations; conference and training facilities; and recreational and residential facilities. It is the only central police college in the UK that provides all the training elements in one establishment.

The delivery of training is only one part of the story, how effective the training is has always been a priority in the Scottish police in modern times. So in order to assess this aspect of the training of police officers, the Scottish Police Service regularly measures the degree to which officers and police staff have made good use of the knowledge learned from the SPC in the workplace. This is normally carried out six months after the completion of the training course. The latest evaluations for the period 2011–2012 revealed that out of 193 surveys, 170 (88 per cent) officers and staff had made use of the training received (SPPF 2012: 72).

Probationary training

Probationary officers attend their first Module 1 training at the SPC which is specifically designed for probationary officers to receive the necessary knowledge and to develop an understanding required of a police officer in Scotland. The student is taught six subject areas:

- Police and the Community
- Evidence
- Crime
- General Police Duties
- Road Policing
- Writing Skills.

Included in the training are many simulated exercises run by experienced police supervisors who have been seconded to the SPC for a two- or three-year period to train probationary officers and run a variety of other courses. These police trainers are professionally qualified tutors who work alongside a number of similarly qualified civilian trainers to deliver the probationary training programme. This approach to training ensures all students receive a high standard of classroom and practical exercise work by operationally experienced police officers who are also nationally qualified trainers – police training has always been based on this concept.

On return to their force, the officers undertake work-based training, with guidance and the supervision of a tutor constable and force supervisor, to assimilate their learning in an operational setting. Tutor constables are hand-picked experienced police officers who have undergone a level of instruction in how to tutor a probationary officer and ensure he/she is exposed to as much varied police work as possible. The role of a tutor constable is vital to the initial training of a police officer, as what is learned in the first formative years will dictate a recruit's attitude and performance for the rest of his/her career. Police officers always recollect how they were initially trained and which officer(s) they were 'paired' with during their probation and whether it was a good or bad training experience. Unfortunately, police officers can teach new recruits bad habits just as easily as good habits, but with the present formal tutor constable system, there is less chance of that happening.

Probationary officers are required to complete a minimum of 320 hours operational policing and are expected to maintain a log of their experiences and learning. Officers also complete an Evidence Validation Report outlining their performance against prescribed behavioural competences. Officers return to the SPC for a three-week assessment phase when they are given the opportunity to reflect on their training and operational experience to date, and thereafter be assessed on their knowledge, understanding and skills, through course exams and oral examination. Probationary officers then return to their own force and continue to develop their knowledge and understanding in the operational environment with full supervisory support and guidance from tutor constables. As the probationary officers regularly update training logs which are checked by supervisors, it is easy to spot an area of police work an officer has not been involved in and where they are lacking experience. Appropriate action will then be taken to address the matter. For example, through no fault of the officer, he/she may not have been involved in a drink driving case, serious road accident report, a drug case, and so on. Probationers also get the opportunity to do work experience in other local divisional departments, such as the CID and have a spell with a community police officer. Officers are also expected to complete nine Open and Distance Learning packages:

- Road Policing
- Management of Police Information
- Animal Health and Welfare
- Dangerous Dogs
- Dogs
- Human Trafficking
- Firearm Certificates
- Foreign Drivers
- RIPSA (Regulation of Investigatory Powers).

Officers are required to sit a final exam on reaching between 12 and 16 months service. Probationers continue to attend incidents as directed in order to gain experience under the supervision and assistance of their colleagues and are assessed for the remainder of their probationary period. At which time the chief constable may confirm the officer in the rank of constable.

By the end of a two-year probationary period an officer will have gained a wide range of operational experience supported by theoretical and legal knowledge. The new 'graduate' should now be confident enough to meet the challenges in the world of policing. In reality, though, successfully completing the probationary period can be compared to passing the standard 'driving test', it is only when you have passed the test that you really learn to drive – when you are on your own making the decisions!

Early training

Police training does not stop at the two-year point but continues throughout an officer's career, regardless of the career path taken. For example, police officers undergo a wide variety of training during the early stages of their service. The following are two examples that give some indication of the challenging environments that officers and support staff work in. First, is born out of the duty of care that all police managers have in relation to blood-borne viruses in the police environment when police officers, police staff and prisoners are at risk. Second, is to emphasise the crucial role the police have in gathering and preserving evidence during criminal investigations.

Blood-borne viruses

Police officers, along with other members of the emergency services, are regularly at risk from blood-borne viruses (BBVs), particularly from persons in police custody. Police management is duty-bound to ensure police officers and support staff are fully aware of the dangers of hepatitis B, hepatitis C and human immunodeficiency virus (HIV). Specifically, those police personnel with responsibilities for prisoner custody and care require basic infection control guidance in order to maintain a safe prisoner custody environment. Although police surgeons have the main responsibility for the medical care of persons in police custody, it is essential that all persons within the police custody environment have an understanding of infection control; handling and disposal of needles and sharp objects; managing blood and body fluid spillage; routine cleaning of prisoners' cells and, when required, specialised cleaning; and the handling and disposal of clinical waste. An additional precaution is the vaccination of police personnel who are likely to come into regular contact with at-risk groups. Police custody staff also have a duty to protect detainees from being infected by other detainees and precautions have to be taken accordingly. The reality is that in today's modern society with significant drug misuse, there is a constant flow of detainees in police custody who may carry a variety of infectious diseases. This places police officers and police support staff members continually at risk and emphasises the need for regular training and awareness of the dangers in the prisoner custody environment.

Scenes of crime procedures

Scientific support in criminal investigations is a regular feature in solving crimes and the police officer attending the initial crime scene and the crime scene examiner have a crucial part to play in a successful outcome. All police officers are tutored on the importance of preserving a crime scene from the first day they join the police service. Officers are left in no doubt as to the importance of preserving fingerprints, crime scene marks and impressions, blood and body fluids, photographing and videoing individual loci, and many more simple crime scene methods. The critical nature of 'best evidence' is repeatedly emphasised to police personnel along with the importance of controlling a crime scene. So much so that anyone breaching guidelines or adopting a haphazard attitude to these duties faces disciplinary consequences. Crime scene management is so crucial to a criminal investigation that a dedicated crime scene manager (CSM) is appointed to ensure liaison and control of all parties involved in an investigation. To ensure a nationwide professional approach to crime scene management is universally adopted, a number of dedicated training courses have been developed by the police and other specialists over the years in the crime scene discipline.

Cumulative experience has identified a list of the most common actions by police officers at a crime scene that have destroyed or contaminated potential evidence. The main examples are presented in Table 3.3.

Foreign recruitment

Foreign recruitment as direct entrants to the rank of superintendent from countries such as Australia, Canada, New Zealand and the USA, is being seriously considered by the UK Government for England and Wales and is fiercely opposed by police associations. The move is on the back of regular comment from the UK Government on the lack of leadership quality in policing ranks. The initiative which hopes to bring in foreign nationals is seen as complementary to other direct entry schemes to fast-track graduates into the rank of inspector without having served in the lower ranks. The idea of individuals joining the police as superintendents with no police experience is a concern shared by many operational police officers. For those who know, the rank of superintendent in the modern police service is one of high responsibility, and any person with limited experience and background in the role of taking the lead on major crime investigations or of being an incident commander in charge of serious incidents, sporting events and public disorders, will have many hurdles to overcome, regardless of personal abilities and talent. The response from the UK Government is that only applicants with the right skills and expertise to manage at the highest levels of policing would

TABLE 3.3 Crime scene contamination

Action	*Consequence*
Use of telephone	Addition/obliteration of fingerprints
Use of washing facilities	Obliteration of blood-stained fingerprints on and around basins; flushing of possible evidential material from sink trap
Use of toilet facilities	Flushing of possible evidential material from toilet; and addition/obliteration of fingerprints
Use of towels	Cross-contamination
Smoking at scene	Addition of cigarette stubs and ash
Unnecessary handling of weapons	Addition/obliteration of fingerprints/DNA; possible injury
Use of bare hands to open doors	Addition/obliteration of fingerprints/DNA
Careless use of glove hands	Obliteration of fingerprints/DNA
Standing on footwear/tyre impressions	Obliteration of marks
Standing on wet blood	Additional footwear impressions
Moving the body/clothing of deceased	Photographs should be taken first
Covering body with blanket	Introduction of extraneous fibres
Entering crime scene without protective clothing/footwear	Cross-contamination

Source: Hogg (2009: 172).

be considered; the aim is to attract people with varied backgrounds and different perspectives. A laudable concept but modern policing is a complex mix and in order for police managers to successfully lead and interface with their workforce and, indeed, communities, they must understand the tradition and culture of the internal police organisation and the nation's communities. This has to come as second nature to a police leader and can only be obtained as a result of a long apprenticeship in the police organisation. Security concerns are also an issue with such appointments as chief police officers have a crucial part to play in counter-terrorism and have close links with the security services and high level intelligence. Having a foreign national with a different background brought in to be in charge of a police force in the UK with access to sensitive information will inevitably give rise to questions of national security. There are no plans to introduce a similar policy in Scotland at the present time.

Special Constables

Volunteering in the public sector is not new and has been crucial to the survival of many organisations, such as the Salvation Army, Oxfam, Victim Support, the

Samaritans, and certain sections of hospitals and schools. Volunteers bring a wide range of skills and experience to their local police and can even enhance customer service. To date, throughout the UK, volunteers have proved successful in assisting the police at public counters, press office support, general administration, helping with police training, updating databases information and getting involved with Neighbourhood Watch. Enlisting as a Special Police Constable is a more formal way of volunteering to do regular police work. By volunteering their free time, Special Constables and other police volunteers provide a tangible way for citizens to make a difference in their communities. Specials have a long history in the UK and have played a significant role in supporting the police and military during major periods of public protest.

The Special Constabulary is viewed as great value for money and cost-effective and reflects a credible cross-section of the local community, more so than some other methods of police service delivery. They offer a wide array of skills and do a great deal to enhance communication and understanding between the police, communities and local businesses. More use is made of Specials in England and Wales than in Scotland, as they assist and support the regular police in a number of ways – foot and mobile patrol; performing administrative duties and computer interrogation; community interface and anti-social behaviour tasks; minor crime investigation; major incident support and road traffic duties. Specials wear the same uniform and have the same powers as the regular police. The aim has never been to replace the core group of police but to enhance support and add value and in the new age of specialism in the police, these skilled volunteers can be employed anywhere in the police organisation. Indeed, some research has shown that those volunteers employed in the more demanding specialist posts remained longer in the organisation and even increased their hours worked, as opposed to those given the less demanding and mundane tasks.

In 2012, there were 1468 Specials in Scotland which was around 8 per cent of the regular force and they worked 228,374 hours in the year which equates to an average of three hours per week. The numbers of Specials volunteering in recent decades go up and down but in the last year or so the number has declined, as shown by the following figures for the past five years (Table 3.4).

TABLE 3.4 Numbers of Special Constables, 2007–2011

Date	*Number*
2007–2008	1408
2008–2009	1678
2009–2010	1849
2010–2011	1863
2011–2012	1468

Specials receive expenses and those who manage to work 45 four-hour shifts in a 12-month period qualify for a £1500 reward. There is a nationally agreed minimum requirement for Specials to work 60 hours per year. Applicants go through a vetting procedure similar to that for regular police officers.

The selection process for Special Constables who join Police Scotland includes a mandatory requirement to sit and pass the national Standard Entrance Test. Successful applicants then undergo a standardised training programme aligned to that offered on the initial training for probationary constables and the early induction phase prepares them for operational duties alongside their regular colleagues. The second phase of training covers legislation, processes and procedures. Training can be delivered at the weekends over 15 weeks or so but on occasions can be a block training Monday to Friday. All candidates must be able to meet this training commitment. Training for Specials covers similar topics taught to full-time officers such as Police and the Community, Evidence, Crime, General Police Duties, Road Policing and Investigative Skills. In addition, training is given in officer safety techniques, police powers, scenes of crime, radio procedures, powers of arrest, detention and search and community issues. All Specials receive a certificate of achievement on completion of the course. Special Constables who have obtained this certificate and go on to become regular police officers would attend the Scottish Police College to complete a shortened initial Probationer Training.

An applicant for the Special Constabulary must be a British citizen, a member of the EU or other states in the EEA, a Commonwealth citizen or a foreign national free of restrictions. They should also have been resident in the UK for three years immediately prior to application. It is a requirement not to have a conflict of interest such as being a member of the Fire Service who are regularly called to work unexpectedly. They would be unlikely to be considered if they were an employee of a security organisation, manager or staff of licensed premises and betting offices, or serving member of the armed forces.

The new Police Scotland is considering plans to introduce a ruling that potential police recruits into the regular police will have to spend a year as a Special Constable before being eligible to join the regular police service. The idea is to give would-be police recruits some experience of police work at first hand and a way of giving individuals some training prior to joining the regular force, and to test the person's suitability for a career in the police. Some view this move as cheap labour while others see it as an opportunity to return to traditional policing. In simple terms, the police service is asking potential candidates for the regular police to work for a year for free, bar expenses and rewards before applying for the regular force. There is a high risk that this requirement may put many high quality candidates off a career in the police as not everyone will be in a position to devote the time and the effort to complete the conditions as a Special Constable, while other less able individuals may be in a position to do so with ease.

There may be advantages to the police having an apprenticeship to evaluate individuals as to their suitability for the police, but in reality this is already happening with probationary officers who work full-time on shifts with their colleagues and supervisors, sharing the trials and tribulations of policing on a continuous basis. Carrying out a similar assessment with Specials would be difficult to achieve when the individual works an average of three hours per week. It would not be a fair evaluation and good candidates face the risk of rejection.

This ruling has already been introduced into the London Metropolitan Police who only recruit regular police constables from serving MPS Special Constables and Police Community Support Officers (PCSOs). This is the only formal route into the MPS at the present time. This means a two-year term as a Special in order to become eligible for entry to the regular MPS. In July 2012, the MPS had its largest 'passing out parade' with 567 new regular officers – all former Special Constables or PCSOs (Donnelly 2013: 101–2). This raises a number of issues – not least that the Police Federation would have to represent unpaid volunteers if Specials were admitted to their ranks.

Cadets

Prior to the introduction of Police Scotland, the previous Grampian Police force was the only Scottish force recruiting police Cadets after re-introducing them in 2006. Enthusiasm for running Cadet programmes waned in the late 1990s as a result of the need to direct resources to meet the demands for regular patrol officers. Recruitment campaigns were again launched in the early part of the twenty-first century with most forces employing Cadets. However, as the Scottish Government's policy in recent years has been to maintain the numbers of regular police officers, most forces felt it unnecessary to bring Cadets on board as there was an adequate pool of good quality candidates for the regular service. To some, this is a pity as the Cadet system offered young people an opportunity to develop themselves with a view to having a career as a regular police officer. There was never any guarantee that a Cadet officer would automatically be accepted into the regular police but they do proceed to the final selection process including a medical and fitness test. As it stands at present, there are a number of young people employed as Cadets at various stages of development in Scotland. Cadets do not do beat duty but do get involved in many aspects of policing. They have to be at least 16 years of age and pass a fitness test but do not require formal qualifications. Training is given that forms part of an accredited Scottish Qualifications Authority qualification and on successful completion of the course a nationally recognised qualification is awarded. Cadets also get the chance to do outside placements to gain work experience and also work in many police departments. The general plan is that on satisfactory completion of the Cadet programme and meeting other required criteria, Cadets will be in a favourable position to join the regular police when they attain the age of 18 years. At the time of writing there has not been any announcement that Police Scotland will continue with the employment of Cadets though the legislation giving the Chief Constable the power to do so (Police Service of Scotland (Police Cadets) Regulations 2013) has been updated for the new national police service. Though, it is anticipated increasing the number of Police Cadets would greatly assist policing arrangements during the forthcoming Commonwealth Games in Glasgow in 2014.

Conclusion

In his address to new recruits, the new Chief Constable of Police Scotland told them in no uncertain terms that any officer who displays sexism, bigotry or racism will be dismissed from the service. The clear message from Scottish Policing to new recruits is that all people should be treated as if they were their own family, and that includes criminals. This unambiguous statement is telling potential police officers that if you disagree with this comment, the Police Service of Scotland is not for you.

There have been instances in recent years when, as a result of high numbers of vacancies for police officer jobs, some Scottish police forces have suspended the traditional 'home visits' by the police to the homes of potential police recruits. These visits are a means of evaluating the home environment of candidates and an opportunity to meet parents and family members, which has always been viewed as an important stage in the recruitment of a police officer. Police recruitment in Scotland will be undergoing change in the future as the new Police Scotland settles in and many are of the belief that 'home visits' should remain as a key check on the profile of all candidates for the police service. Particularly when police professional standards and the integrity of police officers are under intense scrutiny from politicians, media and the public as never before.

Regular freedom of information requests in Scotland have shown that more than 145 police officers have been reported to prosecutors for alleged corruption in the past five years – but only six have been convicted. Officers have been investigated over serious criminal allegations which include gangland links, blackmail, bribery, serious assault, leaking confidential information, perverting the course of justice, and lying in statements. These statistics do not include the previous Strathclyde Police Force which was the largest in Scotland as they deemed the cost and effort of obtaining the figures would be too high. However, the Strathclyde force did reveal in 2012 that 27 organised crime gangs were actively trying to infiltrate the force by grooming and planting recruits in the ranks and that in 2010 the force had investigated 369 criminal complaints against serving police officers. Of this figure, 218 were accused of passing information about police investigations, suspects and informants – three of those were sacked (*Daily Record* 2012a). The previous Northern Constabulary with a force complement of 715 officers had 45 accused of 102 corruption charges and Tayside had 33 officers reported to the prosecutor for corrupt practices in 2012. Central Scotland had 36 officers suspected of corrupt practices but none of them were taken to court, but six were dealt with internally by the force and two of those faced misconduct hearings, the rest received 'advice'. Grampian had 11 cases and Lothian and Borders eight with two officers convicted and sent to prison. Police officers face a high number of complaints against them on a regular basis as this goes with the job but the above allegations are of a criminal corrupt nature, and the public expect these matters to be thoroughly investigated. Police in Scotland have a reputation for treating this category of complaint very seriously and conducting methodical enquiries accordingly. The public should therefore be relieved that the number of proven cases is low but nevertheless is still a concern.

The new role of the Police Investigations and Review Commissioner (PIRC) in Scotland with additional powers to independently investigate alleged unlawful activity by police officers is discussed in Chapter 8 and shows the level of importance given to maintaining police standards by politicians and the public. There are other issues surrounding police officers with unlawful pasts, for example, there have been police officers with convictions for offences that have led to concerns of credibility in court as there is now full disclosure of officer witness' backgrounds if asked. This has also meant few officers are now suspended when suspected of an offence and remain in post during investigation. What this shows is the importance of maintaining a credible police recruitment, training and vetting system in twenty-first-century Scotland.

4

HOW DO POLICE OFFICERS POLICE SCOTLAND?

Introduction

In addition to professional training, a police officer is issued with a uniform, baton, CS spray, handcuffs, maybe a taser, and possesses a mixture of common sense and legal force and a fair degree of discretion. All these are essential for the safety of the officer and the public and to compensate for the fact that there are not enough police to enforce all laws. The police also have an increasing number of duties in addition to the traditional role in crime prevention and detection and still retain their statutory duties within the criminal justice system executing warrants and carrying out bail checks. Public order duties still take up a lot of police time and range from policing sporting and entertainment events to controlling public demonstrations and marches. On top of this, politicians and the public expect a significant investment in community policing and planned reactive and proactive initiatives and operations, such as stop and search strategies to combat knife crime, tackling the market in illegal drugs and combating the nation's continuous battle against violence. For a small country, Scotland also has its high-level responsibilities when it comes to security issues and these include North Sea Oil offshore duties; Grangemouth Refinery and major incident contingencies; Cairnryan Port with its terrorist checks; public protection duties in Royal Deeside and the capital city of Edinburgh, and, of course, the Holyrood Parliament.

Now with the new Police Scotland there are expectations that the police will continue to carry out these tasks more efficiently and effectively, with increased access to the nation's police resources still enabling officers to do what they are best at and specialists in – patrolling the streets. But this is easier said than done in these austere times with pressures on the public purse and a Scottish national budget that is being cut by 8 per cent over the period 2011–2015. Even the street dogs are barking that the public sector is facing challenging times ahead. The primary role for policing and community safety may fall to the police but, as we will see in Chapter 6, other agencies have similar roles and objectives in tandem with the police service and in many instances have little involvement with police officers. New technology has an ever increasing role in the growing landscape of public security. The substantial investment in private security and CCTV technology are but two examples.

New techniques and strategies to combat crime and disorder in communities have an important part to play in modern policing. In recent years the importance of gathering sound reliable intelligence on the criminal world has proved invaluable not only in the fight against crime and terrorism but in the everyday nuisances and anti-social behaviour problems that are a blight on local communities. Scottish policing has pioneered the notion of 'partnership working', believing the maintenance of community safety is everyone's responsibility, and over the years the Scottish police officer has facilitated community groups, private enterprises, voluntary agencies, local authority and government departments, and the general public, coming together with similar goals and objectives to improve the quality of life in their area.

Previous chapters have introduced the police recruit, who he or she is and where they come from. A general definition of policing has also been discussed and some comments on Scottish police history and tradition made. The benefit of fully understanding the political and constitutional setting of the new Police Scotland has also been discussed alongside the significant issue of police investment in training. It should now be apparent that the training of police officers is at two levels. First, in the formal setting of the classroom whether at the police college or a local facility and, second, teaching 'on the job' which begins the moment an officer commences street patrol. With a probationary recruit it will be with a tutor constable assigned to him for a period of time, and if a trainee detective it will be alongside an experienced detective officer. Similar arrangements are made for all roles in the police, whether specialist or otherwise. For example, a traffic officer will undergo lengthy training at the Scottish Police College and this will be followed up with road patrol duties accompanied by an experienced partner. Other specialist training can be at the SPC or other training centres around the UK, such as dog handlers and mounted section personnel.

This chapter moves on from the history, tradition, recruitment and initial training of the Scottish police officer, to the next stage and looks at how the police actually police Scotland in the twenty-first century. Space and time constraints prevent a comprehensive examination of what goes on in every area of policing and a selection of the more specialist areas of policing is dealt with in Chapter 5. The present chapter is a mix of things as modern policing itself is 'a blend of activities' all geared towards a common objective of improving the security and safety of communities. Understanding the mix helps us appreciate what policing is and the role of the police officer – it is analogous to a jigsaw puzzle as once the pieces are put together, we can see the big picture.

Standard Operating Procedures

In the police organisation, Standard Operating Procedures (SOPs) provide specific guidance to police officers and support staff on how to deal with a range of matters, particularly those which directly involve members of the public. SOPs make sure there is a consistency of response and service delivery across a wide range of police-related incidents. Compliance within the procedures will ensure that public expectations are met when dealing with an incident. While compliance is not mandated, any officer varying his or her response to an incident where a SOP is in place should be prepared to justify the variation in any subsequent review of actions. Where any doubt exists, statutory and regulatory direction will always take precedence. SOPs may be cited in any judicial or disciplinary procedure to either support a police officer's actions or identify non-compliance, whether considered negligent, legitimate or otherwise. The previous eight Scottish Police Forces had their own individual SOPs that in the main were very similar, to reflect generic police responsibilities and the Scottish legal system, but as one would expect there were local differences. Police Scotland will introduce a national set of SOPs based on the previous guidance and procedures but as the single police force settles into its role, it is expected that new procedures and guidelines will be brought in to reflect the national police framework.

Technology and bureaucracy

The introduction of technology and mechanisation into the police service unwittingly shaped the police service that we have today (MacGregor 2007: 56). Particularly in the economically trying times of the interwar years of the 1920s and 1930s when the police found themselves in the position of how to police a growing population with limited resources and little hope of an increase in their budgets which has quite similar to the austere environment of present-day Scotland. The increasing use of the telephone, motor car and radio communication during this period changed the way the police service carried out its work and also set in motion the demise of the iconic police box. The subsequent growth in police control rooms and mobile patrols and emergency response systems forced the police to divert resources from the traditional foot patrol and created an alienation from the public which has been well documented over the years within the context of the arguments for community policing as against reactive policing. Nowadays police officers have instant access to crime data and criminal history while on patrol, which was unheard of in the past. A detective can be at the scene of a murder with an unidentified body and if the victim is on the criminal information database, an immediate check can be made of descriptive information, tattoos, marks and scars, and even fingerprints and photograph. If the person is identified, then further checks can be made of criminal background, habits, drugs, weapons, aliases and associates, and any available intelligence, all without leaving the location. Having access to such information in the field is invaluable to the police officer in the early stages of an investigation or inquiry and has only been possible in recent times.

Technology in the Scottish police is not without its problems though, as some IT systems are somewhat antiquated and as a result of the previous arrangement of having eight police forces, each with its own local policy on information technology, there is a lack of compatibility with some systems. This has improved in recent years due to the previous ACPOS developing a centralised IT strategy for the Scottish police service but there is still some way to go, and hopefully the new single police service will facilitate uniformity in the use of technology by the police across Scotland. As in many large organisations, bureaucracy is a problem in the police and causes a great deal of duplication and triplication of input, for example, crime management requires crime report input, crime intelligence information, and a lot more information into different systems. In the past you could have a quick look at a hard copy crime report to see what had been happening in recent days, now there are screeds of information on computer systems with lots of officers running off hard copies which creates its own bureaucracy. In the past it was relatively quick to arrest and process an accused for a minor crime – normally within half an hour but today with all the new procedural demands of the technological era (crime report, intelligence input, court report, etc.), you could be looking at over an hour. The system tends to hinder an officer's return to patrol duties. Also the processing of the case management system is geared to doing more of the court prosecution work when preparing a case for court. Politicians and police management are continually searching for new ways to improve police efficiency and increase the time officers are on the street patrolling. A recent example in the Scottish police is the electronic notebook destined to be in use throughout Scotland. Traditionally, police officers would write information in their notebooks when on the street and transfer the data onto a hard copy police report or nowadays input the information onto a computer back at the police station. Now with the aid of the electronic notebook, officers can input the data electronically on the one occasion while on the beat, cancelling the need to repeat the input back at the police station. Police Scotland is optimistic that the road to a more efficient police service comes in the innovative use of new technology. Further comment on the impact of technology on the work of the police will be made in other chapters.

Communication and police interaction

Since the onset of the twenty-first century information technology has revolutionised how citizens can communicate and interface with each other both nationally and internationally. Communication is instantaneous around the world using the internet, mobile phone, social media and video. As a consequence, a nation's culture and everyday living are going through major changes. Members of the public can now chat to police officers on non-emergency topics via text-based and video-based systems and exchange information – all in real time. Communities are increasingly going online and through necessity so are the police in order to maintain a close relationship with them. However, this should not be seen as an alternative to emergency contact or replacing counter services or telephone contact, as the essence of community policing still remains one of face-to-face contact with the public.

However, the police service has not escaped the social media revolution and officers' use of Twitter and Facebook is a rapidly expanding method of communication with local communities. Police officers are regularly using social media to inform colleagues and the public of arrests being made in real time. There is a danger here of imparting information while a 'live' investigation is ongoing, so care has to be taken during pre-judicial times. These risks appear to be worth taking and guidance has been issued at the senior management level to ensure the safe use of social media. Of course, the downside to the increased use of social media by the wider society is that the Scottish police service has been inundated with reports of harassment and obscene and abusive messages on social networking sites such as Twitter and Facebook in recent years. This has resulted in another growth workload for the police. Freedom of information requests reveal a rise in complaints from an estimated 158 in 2008 to 1297 in 2012 an increase in 87 per cent, with the largest increase in the previous Northern Constabulary area with 700 reports in 2012 compared to 130 in 2008, an increase of 538 per cent, and the lowest increase in Dumfries and Galloway with none reported in 2008 and 14 in 2012 (*Daily Record* 2012b). Offences involved grooming, stalking, racially aggravated conduct, fraud and threats. This is indicative of the evolving nature of modern crime that will increasingly confront Police Scotland in the future.

Rural policing

In an archive footage of a documentary depicting the life of the country policemen in 1947, it is clear that for the rural officer the police station is his home and he relied heavily on his wife to assist him on a daily basis. For example, taking messages and dealing with the public when he was not in the station, and also the feeding and general welfare of prisoners, especially females. In the 1940s and 1950s, the rural police officer in Scotland had a different day at work from the urban officer; his day could range from going to the local school to check the brakes on children's bicycles, to taking a report of stolen hens from a local farmer and checking isolated cottages where old folk live alone. There is a lot of small detail and 'a lot of talking and listening and passing the time of day with people who know what is going on in the area and who will tell you' (Scottish Home Department 1947). The country police officer has a variety of tasks unique to their setting, as they have to work closely with farmers to help keep down the level of pests and disease that impact on the environment and livestock, for example, foot-and-mouth disease, anthrax and the 'Colorado beetle', and overseeing sheep dipping.

Rural policing in the modern era has changed somewhat with the rural population increasing, particularly those over 65 years of age (discussed later), even the Highland capital of Inverness is deemed the fastest growing city in Europe.

One commentator who has studied policing in the rural environment found that the 'controversy over the role of the police in contemporary Britain is primarily a debate over urban policing' (Mawby 2009: 39) and that traditionally crime is generally lower in the rural setting, though in recent years the workload of the rural police officer has been increasing in line with the rise in population. As a consequence of the geography, police resources are controlled via call centres with a greater reliance on patrol cars. There are also fewer police stations opened to the public on a 24-hour basis. An important change in the present day is more stability for the rural police officer who can expect less upheaval to family life than was the case in the past when officers were regularly posted to another station at short notice, particularly in the northern police forces which cover the Scottish islands. More sympathetic management and improved resource planning have led to having a stable family life that means officers can own their own home and not have to reside in police-owned accommodation. Unlike policing in the larger cities, local rural police are part of the community they live and work in and are recognised as members of the community rather than a police officer.

Undoubtedly, crime is higher in the urban areas, and rural regions are safer places to live but that does not mean that crime is not a problem in rural areas. Recent years have witnessed the rise of cannabis farms, drugs, violence and alcohol-related crime, and people living in these rural areas still experience car crime, housebreakings and domestic violence. As mentioned above, the police have always had closer relationships with communities in rural districts as they are dealing with people they know on a daily basis on and off duty, unlike in urban towns and cities, and this traditional relationship has many positive spin-offs for law enforcement when public assistance is required. The use of police discretion is key to the success of this two-way relationship, as officers will adopt a more conciliatory or mediating role rather than strict enforcement of the law – 'in the more remote areas, there is almost an expectation that petty offenders will not end up in court' (Anderson 1999: 53).

The concern that some rural police officers have is that with the introduction of a national police service and nationwide strategies and policies, the risk of the spread of target-led policing, much in evidence in urban towns and cities, could have an adverse effect on local discretionary policing, as policy is normally dictated from the centre. Now with a rising population in many rural areas partially fuelled by an influx of migrants, changes in the rural environment could be inevitable, with signs of urbanisation in some parts already evident. It is likely these changes will lead, through necessity, to the primacy of central policing policy over traditional police discretion in the rural regions and is indicative of the inevitable future change to policing in the non-urban areas of Scotland.

Police intervention

Police are involved in offering young people with the high risk of becoming career criminals the option of diversions and opportunities to do other things with their lives and help direct them from a life of crime. Many of these initiatives are in partnership with charities, social work, government funding, voluntary groups, local government, private sector, and a variety of other agencies and groups. Supporting vulnerable young people in this high risk category and giving them a worthwhile role to perform, whether it be a job or getting involved in sport, has been shown to motivate and divert them to transform their life. There is nothing new in this as it has been happening for decades in Scotland and is part of policing policy and well integrated into modern policing. It first began in the 1970s with the introduction of the Community Involvement Branch which specialised in this type of work with youth clubs and school liaison officers.

Now modern police techniques involve tracking offenders and categorising them in order of risk and from that baseline, interventions are planned that will hinder and/or eradicate criminal careers. Police and academics even discuss how to identify potential criminals before they are born by analysing the parents' lifestyles, social backgrounds and living environments. The Scottish Violence Reduction Unit (VRU) has been pioneering these strategies since 2005 and has received widespread international acclaim for its preventative work with gang members and its development work in treating the problem of violence as a 'disease' (discussed later) which can infect and spread and lead to death and disability (Violence Reduction Unit 2012). Regardless of the success factor of some of these intervention strategies, it is still a police intrusion into community life and should be considered alongside other surveillance methods being introduced, such as CCTV, DNA databases, and community intelligence. Modern policing continues on the road of increased 'community surveillance' without a proper debate on the issue ever having taken place.

The corroboration rule

The Carloway Review has recommended a change in the need for corroboration in the Scottish legal system which is supported by the Scottish Government. Removal of the need for corroboration could have a major impact on the way police officers go about their daily work, as traditionally, the police in Scotland mainly patrol in pairs for a number of reasons. First, for safety reasons, particularly if they work in the busy urban areas, and, second, under existing Scots law there is a requirement for corroboration of evidence in police cases. Hence, police officers act as witnesses to and for each other, especially in court procedures. The need for this corroboration is now being questioned as being out of step with other countries and has no place in the modern legal system (Scottish Government 2011b). The idea of removing the need for corroboration has already been rejected by High Court Judges and other legal minds who believe the present system continues to work well and is a major safeguard against miscarriages of justice. This view is supported by the Scottish Police Federation and the Superintendents Association, who are of the belief that the requirement for all key evidence to be backed by two sources is crucial to protecting police officers, witnesses and suspects in all cases. The overall view from law enforcement professionals in Scotland is that the

Scottish legal system has few miscarriages of justice and this is mainly due to the present system which insists on corroboration.

Community policing

Never a day goes by in Scotland without a police officer on patrol interfacing with members of the public or an officer attending a meeting with community groups or voluntary or public sector partners. This is the essence of community policing – the flagship of Scottish policing which combines the traditional form of police patrol with other community-linked components that are just as important. Officers are chosen to work within an identifiable community area for a period of around three years, getting to know the members and vice versa. Many modern police officers will have spent some time as a community police constable during their service or, if not, then as a Sergeant supervising a community police team. The community officer has ubiquitous duties that include regular community meetings; community forums and Neighbourhood Watch; problem-solving schemes in the community; crime and community intelligence gathering; involvement with youth groups; restorative justice representation; crime investigation; involvement with businesses; liaison with elected members and council officials; close relationships with schools; mediator and negotiator in the community; and regular contact with local authority departments.

These tasks primarily articulate the relationship between the police and the public and position the police in Scotland with an explicit role in community safety and security. It would be accurate to say that members of the public now understand community policing and what it is trying to achieve more so than in the 1980s and 1990s when it was a constant struggle to sell the concept to the wider community and even to some politicians. Most modern police innovations still have a home in community policing, for example, problem-oriented policing, broken window theory, intelligence-led policing, and third-party policing. This constant experimentation and development of policing at the local level ensure the continuing expansion of the community policing definition (Scheider et al. 2009: 701–12). Scottish policing has a unique reputation for developing the wider definition of community policing since it was introduced in Scotland in the 1950s. Examples of this are evident throughout this text and involve working with a variety of partners in the public, private and voluntary sectors. On occasions the community police officer will not be specifically involved but the services of other parts of the police organisation may be called on, for example, sex offenders or domestic violence units. In other instances the police may not be present at all and other partners such as social work, housing or education take the lead in the interests of community safety.

Politicians and police are increasingly looking to citizens to play a greater part in crime prevention and community safety. However, there has been limited success in getting an increased number of community members to be more 'hands-on' in community safety initiatives. This is partly the result of the culture of dependency, engendered over the decades by local authorities delivering comprehensive services and the public thinking that all they have to do is report the problem and local government will fix it (IPPR 2010: 15). In reality, citizens are rarely asked to participate in local security initiatives and in any event this would necessitate some training and utilising the existing skills of citizens to assist in community projects. This idea of co-production in community safety matters is to many the next level of community policing, when the community identifies problems and crafts solutions, or the authorities allow sections of the community to manage its own needs (Grabosky 2009: 96). Such an achievement should be a main objective of community policing though in many instances the solutions may not require the presence of the police. The ultimate form of community policing has little need for the police officer, as the community and its partners would be in a position to deal with many of the issues themselves. And on occasions it would work better without the police presence as the police do not always share the communities' views on safety issues. This is a viable goal in the twenty-first century as there is a risk in continuing to allow police officers to take on new community policing roles of 'social worker, educator and urban planner' as it means training the police to do other people's work (Gowri 2003: 608). There are examples of this happening at present with police officers being posted to schools and hospitals throughout Scotland. The risk is that this fuels the dependency culture and makes it difficult to withdraw the officers in the future. It also means that the police training under the auspices of community policing must also provide more than just the core knowledge to do the job; it must also include an awareness and understanding of the fundamental role of the police officer in the community and how it interfaces with other disciplines in the private and public sectors. This reminds us that the Scottish police officer never stops training and learning.

Police in schools

It is estimated that around 60 police officers patrol the corridors and playgrounds in Scottish schools, costing in the region of £2 million per year from contributions from the police, local authorities and community planning budgets. Commonly known as 'campus cops', the rationale behind their introduction is to prevent crime and offer a deterrent to weapon and drug possession in schools. For example, it is estimated there are on average ten violent attacks per day in schools. Based on freedom of information requests, figures reveal that between 2007 and 2012, 484 weapons were seized on school premises in Scotland (*Daily Mail* 2012: 12).

There is no doubt campus officers make a positive contribution to a school but there are concerns at having police officers in schools on a full-time basis away from frontline duties and of the intrusive nature of the role. An official study of campus cops in Scottish schools found there to be a reduction in criminal activity and a decrease in pupils being excluded or suspended in those schools with campus cops (IPSOS 2010). Preferred skills of a campus cop are not dissimilar to those of the community police officer and include the ability to work unsupervised in an educational environment; being a good communicator and negotiator; being friendly and approachable; being authoritative and honest; possessing sound police experience; interested in proactive policing and inter-agency work; and having a good knowledge of the local area and local issues.

Their presence within a school also helps to reduce truancy by liaising with the Education Welfare Officer, going on home visits and attending exclusion meetings when a pupil returns to school. Opposition to police officers in schools has in the past come from the teaching profession's trade union, as it viewed the campus cop as a form of surveillance in schools that changed the teacher's role into that of a police informant. The subject of whether police officers should be permanently in schools to begin with is one needing to be addressed in the twenty-first century. As was always the case in the previous century, 'police officers find themselves fulfilling a role that other agencies and parents should be doing' (Donnelly 2013: 96). Should this and other similar 'social welfare' roles be carried out by professional police officers or by other agents from within the education and social service spheres or indeed the private sector? This is an issue that has never properly been addressed by the police and politicians in Scotland in the past 50 years. Many have seen the need to hive off non-police duties best carried out by other agencies such as the civilianisation of technological posts, and administrative projects and prisoner custody and escorting duties – but little else has been achieved. In the meantime new initiatives with police and schools are being progressed like the one in Laurencekirk in Aberdeenshire where an integrated school academy and police office is being built with the objective of improving community liaison and services between the public, the police and schoolchildren.

Partnerships

Since the 1980s the police no longer have had a monopoly on policing and regularly share community safety responsibilities with private companies, partnership agencies, voluntary and community groups, outsourcing and direct payment for services. Additional collaborators have been introduced, and a change in the role of the police within community safety has resulted. It is now accepted that the responsibility for crime prevention lies with the individual community member and the transfer of the primary responsibility for crime prevention from the police to a corporate model of accountability involves partnership with local authorities and communities. This has resulted in Community Safety Partnerships (CSP) in each of the 32 local authorities in Scotland that pursue community safety, problem-solving and crime prevention initiatives in their own areas. Partner membership normally comprises of police, fire service, elected representatives, other agencies, community members and the voluntary sector, and they work alongside a higher body in the form of the local Community Planning Partnerships (CPPs). Together the partnership ensures people and communities are involved in decisions made about the public services which affect them most, such as local policing. In addition, there has to be a commitment from all public organisations to work together in a coordinated fashion to provide improved public services. Effective community planning should introduce transparency and improve decision-making at the local level, and form a link with national priorities and policies. Local policing in twenty-first-century Scotland has now evolved into partnership policing with a statutory base. It has taken many decades to get to this stage and most partners now have a legal obligation to contribute to community safety in their own areas.

Partnership working can also be introduced as a mechanism for improving other practices in the police organisation, as has been evident in recent years with the pursuit of best practice and cost savings. One example is police management's continuous search to reduce the time police officers spend in court which can be disruptive not only to the police organisation but costly too in the form of high overtime costs. This has resulted in enlisting the help of the Procurator Fiscal to cite officers for court duty whenever possible on their working days rather than on days off or during periods of annual leave. On other occasions officers are required to change their shift to keep costs down. This level of partnership 20 or 30 years ago would have been unheard of as both organisations viewed themselves as separate entities and kept their own internal problems to themselves, inevitably to the detriment of all concerned. One modern-day example of a successful policing partnership is the Community Improvement Partnership (CIP) in the City of Glasgow which is a joint venture between Scotland's largest social landlord, the Glasgow Housing Association (GHA), the police and the fire service. The CIP project exemplifies what can be achieved by good partnership working and deserves further explanation.

The Community Improvement Partnership

The main objective of the CIP is to tackle anti-social behaviour in the GHA communities and to keep tenants safe in their homes. The initiative involves the secondment of 15 police officers and a fire officer over a three-year period to work alongside GHA staff. Together the team combat issues that have a negative impact on communities such as late-night parties, potential fire risks, disorder and drug dealing. Initial research shows that of those tenants experiencing anti-social behaviour, 60 per cent report the matter to the GHA but only 30 per cent inform the police. So information sharing was not happening in the most effective way. The CIP has made some progress in overcoming these issues with the team working together with a clear shared vision, and having full access to all information for analysis and the identification of problem areas in the communities. The project has been running for over two years and is now being fully rolled out across the city. Results after an initial 18-month pilot reveal:

- 6671 stop and searches by police;
- seizure of 3435g of drugs valued at £17,000;
- seizure of 716 litres of alcohol;
- 127 warrants executed;
- 438 anti-social behaviour penalty notices issued;

- 795 joint visits carried out with GHA staff;
- 450 home fire safety visits made to vulnerable tenants.

(GHA 2012)

The seconded police officers are in addition to those already working in the area and are subject to a signed agreement by the Chief Constable and the Chairman of the GHA. Feedback from residents has been favourable and the GHA is delighted with the progress and improvement made to date:

> By sharing our skills, experience and knowledge – and by working closely together in partnership – we can respond quicker and more effectively to issues ranging from low level anti-social behaviour and noisy parties to serious crime, like drug dealing and violence, as well as fire prevention and identifying and helping vulnerable tenants.
>
> *(ibid.)*

The CIP initiative with its clear vision and objectives is just one of many successful partnerships across Scotland which have developed since the 1970s and shows that the Scottish police continue to be a catalyst for innovative ways of improving community safety.

Ethnic minorities

It has been said that, as a result of the challenges facing the modern police in relation to race issues, coupled with the regular diversity training received by police officers, an atmosphere of fear exists among some of the police who perhaps can lack a natural approach, or even avoid contact with minority ethnic people. However, at present, there is an increasing maturity of approach by the police, complemented by recruiting from a pool of younger people who possess a deeper awareness of diversity issues through their education. As a result, reflection over the past 30 years or so reveals a Scottish police organisation with an enhanced awareness of equal opportunity issues and shows significant progress in changing individual police behaviour and attitudes to ethnic minorities.

A recurring recommendation both in authoritative reports and community consultation has been for the police in Scotland to be better trained in terms of racial awareness and equality. Scottish policing has wholeheartedly embraced this need for training and has incorporated racial awareness and equality training into a broader equal opportunities approach. This has led to learning outcomes for staff to identify their beliefs and behaviours in relation to diversity issues and explains the ethos behind the drive to promote and support equality and diversity, and recognise the need for personal change, where required, in support of policy and strategy. Additional training for supervisors is also designed to provide an understanding of the leadership role and associated responsibilities with regard to diversity. The Scottish police have a proud record when it comes to dealing with ethnic minorities and this is reflected in the wider community who are 'proud of their mixed culture and ethnic diversity and have a history of welcoming people with different backgrounds and nationalities' (Burnett and Harrigan 2010: 287).

Older people

Similar to other nations in the western world, Scotland is experiencing a rapidly ageing population as a result of constant low birth rates and higher life expectancy. As the country moves towards an older population, there are signs of some emerging difficulties in addition to the obvious welfare and health issues. In 2011, 7500 persons over the age of 65 years were charged with a crime, an increase of 25 per cent on the 2010 figure. Crimes involved drugs, weapons, shoplifting, fraud and housebreaking. There is no retirement age for criminals who live as long as law-abiding citizens. With rising inflation and difficult economic times, more elderly individuals are committing opportunistic crimes. A continuance of this trend will bring its own problems for the police, particularly in the custody suite and detention centres that will have to adapt procedures and arrangements to cope with elderly prisoners and all the difficulties that brings.

Young people

Attitudes in Scotland toward children and young people have changed greatly since the 1960s and the introduction of the renowned Children's Panel and the office of Reporter have played a major part in bringing about this change. The idea is for the police to divert young offenders to the Children's Reporter away from the formal criminal justice system and coordinate service provision around the child's or young person's needs. Based on the success of this concept of diversion and improved partnership working, every effort is now made to reduce the number of referrals to the Children's Reporter and deal with, for example, anti-social behaviour in particular quickly at source. This can involve cautioning, restorative practices and mediation. The important factor is for the child or young person to take responsibility for their own actions, while at the same time acknowledging that most are vulnerable or in need of assistance and guidance at this early stage in their life. There is a common thread through most current police thinking in Scotland that a proactive approach and early intervention with children and young people have a better chance of diverting them away from further involvement in the offending behaviour. All police business areas are like-minded and have adopted intervention strategies to combat drugs, violence, knife-crime and alcohol abuse. It is now widely accepted that when it comes to children and young people, a shared and co-ordinated approach to intervention on the basis of the individual's needs is the way forward.

How a nation treats its young people is significant and tells you a lot about its society and policing system. The Scottish police service has always been at the centre of the nation's innovative approach to juvenile offenders and has had a significant influence over other partners in the criminal justice and welfare systems.

For any approach to be a success, there has to be what is now termed as 'early and effective intervention' (EEI) which involves the sharing of information on a child's or young person's offending behaviour between partners. A committed partnership working and the sharing of information lead to a better chance of successful intervention and a shared understanding of the effect the offending behaviour has on the rest of the community. The Scottish police policy on the issue of interventions focuses on:

- relating directly to the needs and behaviour of the child or young person;
- taking account of the impact on others and encouraging children and young people to make reparation and restoration where appropriate;
- supporting parental and child responsibility;
- being appropriate, proportionate, timely and fair.

(ACPOS 2011)

This 'flexible approach' is a logical progression to the earlier groundbreaking work of the Children's Panel and can be applied in the case of most offences and crimes. The important thing to remember is that the intervention has to be applied at the 'lowest appropriate point on the scale of offending' (ibid.).

Violence

Another example of innovative partnership action at the local level is Scotland's response to violent crime. It has been apparent for some time that any action against violence in the community requires coordination across a broad spectrum of social services, public, third sector and private, which focus their collective expertise, energy and resources on the single problem of violence (Carnohan and McCluskey 2010). The Scottish police have utilised the 'public health model' to combat the problem of violence which treats the problem as a disease that can infect and spread and ultimately lead to death and disability. This systematic approach takes account of not only the complexity of the problem, but the intricacy of the public service landscape. The model sets out to change attitudes and shift resources towards prevention as the cornerstone of violence reduction at the local level, while maintaining improvements in enforcement. The strategy should be delivered by a wide range of agencies including hospital staff, social work, local authority workers, police auxiliaries and many more actors in the frontline.

Violent crime is at a 30-year low in Scotland and reflects the efforts of all partners with an interest in community safety and the many innovative approaches being developed to reduce crime. One example of success has been the fall in reported knife cases over the festive period 2012–2013 (189) which saw a fall of 28 per cent from the same period for 2011–2012 (264) (COPFS 2013). One major partner in the fight against violent crime is the Crown Office, which believes a major factor in this fall in knife crime has been a zero tolerance approach ahead of the festive period, when a clear warning was issued that any offenders would be put before the sheriff and jury court and face a maximum of four years in prison. This proactive tactic, coupled with the stop and search techniques of the police over the period, resulted in a significant drop in knife crime and in all probability saved lives.

Assaults on police

Freedom of information returns estimate that in the three year period 2010–2012 there were more than 2720 police working days lost in Scotland as a result of attacks on police officers (*The Herald* 2012). Evidence from the previous Strathclyde Police Force, which employed 50 per cent of Scotland's police officers, show that annually the following estimated working days were lost: 551 days (2010), 437 (2011), and 339 (2012). This equates to a cost of £263,000 to the force. These figures highlight the level of violence police officers in Scotland face on a daily basis. For instance, attacks on Scottish police officers resulting in injuries have risen from 100 in the period 2010–2011 to around 570 in 2011–2012, with officers receiving facial injuries, such as fractures, dislocations and concussions. A breakdown of the attacks reveals the main victims were 500 constables and 13 Special Constables, 44 sergeants and 10 inspectors (Scottish Police Federation 2012b).

An assault on a police officer is an offence currently punishable by fines, imprisonment, a community payback order or a compensation order. Between 1 January 2010 and 28 February 2012, there were 4890 convictions on charges of assaulting a police officer (Scottish Government 2012c). The level of concern of the public and politicians to the rise in the number of police assaults is such that the Scottish Government has announced its intention to make criminals who assault the police in the line of duty pay for their crimes. Under the new plans the proceeds of restitution orders could be donated to charities to help injured police officers get back to work. The new orders would not replace the existing arrangements for compensation direct to victims.

Command and control

We are assured that local control rooms will still be retained and local knowledge will not be lost with the arrival of Police Scotland. New roving units will be on hand across Scotland to attend to major enquiries, serious road accidents and firearm incidents – to be discussed further in Chapter 5. There is nothing more informative to an understanding of police workloads than to examine the number of incidents the police have to deal with in the course of a year. Table 4.1 clearly shows the amount of demand-led work the police in Scotland have dealt with in the past five years. The comforting revelation is that although the figures are high, they reveal a continuous reduction over a five-year period from 2,354,101 (2007–2008) to 1,998,003 (2011–2012) a fall of 15 per cent and a drop of 5.2 per cent in the last year. There are many reasons for this positive trend which includes societal changes, a fall in crime, changes in recording procedures, better policing, improved

TABLE 4.1 Number of incidents in Scotland, 2007–2012

Force	*2007–2008*	*2008–2009*	*2009–2010*	*2010–2011*	*2011–2012*	*Rate per 10,000 population, 2011–2012*
Central	119,390	112,016	107,776	107,779	103,413	3,495
Dumfries & Galloway	85,555	79,827	76,998	74,173	69,329	4,682
Fife	158,846	146,864	138,518	137,917	134,524	3,662
Grampian	157,397	160,754	156,891	148,935	147,761	2,661
Lothian & Borders	371,670	363,801	353,104	339,399	327,520	3,404
Northern	142,017	133,608	132,635	128,644	127,481	4,379
Strathclyde	1,155,970	1,135,802	1,084,383	987,355	919,897	4,126
Tayside	163,256	159,417	180,808	183,537	168,078	4,143
Scotland	2,354,101	2,292,089	2,231,113	2,107,739	1,998,003	3,802

Source: Scottish Policing Performance Framework (SPPF) (2012: 83).

prosecution services, increased private security, contributions from public sector agencies, and so on. The key observation to make from falling incident levels is that it releases more police resources to attend to other important matters. This could turn out to be of strategic significance for Police Scotland if the trend continues as Scottish policing is now in a position to take advantage of demand change and manage its resources more efficiently on a national stage.

There is no standard definition of an 'incident' across Scotland and as a result there is a variation in their recording and grading. However, agreement has been reached by Police Scotland that the National Standards of Incident Reporting (NSIR) will be adopted by the new national force to ensure the consistency of incident recording. In the future, Police Scotland will migrate to a common command and control application which should mean greater consistency of recording and grading in the single police service.

One of the benefits of moving to a national police service has been the introduction of a non-emergency telephone number 101 that offers the public a new way to contact the police for advice and to report a crime that does not require an emergency response. The message from the police is when it is not an emergency, the number to call is 101 anywhere in Scotland to speak to a police officer. Regular use of this number should reduce pressure on the 999 emergency system and facilitate the prioritisation of the most urgent calls for assistance from members of the public. A call to the 101 number connects callers to their local service centre which determines their location and connects them to a call handler for their local area. The whole idea is to ensure callers are dealt with by staff with

TABLE 4.2 Number of non-emergency telephone calls in Scotland, 2007–2012

Force	*2007–2008*	*2008–2009*	*2009–2010*	*2010–2011*	*2011–2012*	*Rate per 10,000 population, 2011–2012*
Central	318,177	297,134	286,594	282,110	269,281	9,100
Dumfries & Galloway	183,097	176,142	167,932	157,532	151,244	10,215
Fife	431,524	390,842	322,765	313,889	292,617	7,965
Grampian	437,118	372,340	355,053	352,019	360,283	6,488
Lothian & Borders	772,070	727,660	705,633	656,731	644,349	6,698
Northern	451,282	446,216	445,335	389,291	396,069	13,605
Strathclyde	1,676,340	1,568,513	1,485,864	1,369,983	1,098,145	4,926
Tayside	363,425	322,069	267,974	254,441	246,108	6,066
Scotland	4,633,033	4,300,916	4,037,150	3,775,996	3,458,096	6,581

Source: Scottish Policing Performance Framework (SPPF) (2012: 83).

local knowledge who can give advice and assistance that reflects the needs of their communities. Table 4.2 shows there were just under 3.46 million non-emergency telephone calls made in Scotland in 2011–2012, 8 per cent fewer than in 2010–11 and the fourth consecutive annual decrease similar to the decreasing trend in the level of incidents.

Crime investigation

Control and communication between local and national crime investigations will be crucial in the new national police set-up and the key link is the Divisional Detective Superintendent. This post is there to assist in the management of crime investigation at the local divisional level and be in support of the 14 Local Divisional Commanders, and take charge in any serious or high profile criminal investigation or, when appropriate, a major incident investigation. In many ways this is what happened previously, but now with an active national police framework, this role has become even more essential to effective crime investigations in Scotland. The Detective Superintendent will also be the contact point for assistance from the new central Specialist Crime Division (SCD) of Police Scotland to be discussed in Chapter 5. The line management for Detective Superintendents lie with the SCD, so it is imperative there is a good working relationship between the Detective Superintendents and the Local Divisional Commanders since they are not in essence a divisional resource, unlike divisional criminal investigation personnel who are directly under the command of local divisional management.

Terrorism

According to the UK Security Minister in a speech in 2012, the UK emergency services are not prepared for a major terrorist attack on the streets of Britain (RUSI 2012). This includes a fast-moving attack by an individual or a group of gunman such as the attacks in Mumbai (2008), Oslo (2011) and Toulouse (2012). The responsibility of police and other security agencies is to ensure there are plans and strategies in place and that police and emergency services are well trained and regularly exercise together to guarantee an effective response to major incidents, which include chemical, biological, radiological or nuclear devices. Great strides have been made in the field of joint training which has greatly improved as the emergency services learn lessons from the past major incidents in the UK and further afield. Central government regularly funds national exercises involving all emergency service partners from around the country and encourages the sharing of ideas and experiences. But as we have witnessed in the past decades, terrorist threats continue to exist and combating the associated dangers and risks involve substantial resource investment from the police and security services.

Terrorism has taken on other dimensions such as the realisation that British citizens are overseas supporting and fighting alongside extremists in war zones in a number of countries. As a consequence, the possibility exists that, on their return, their experiences gained at the battlefront could be utilised on the streets of the UK. Police forces, particularly those with responsibilities for large urban and city areas, have had to adapt their priorities in light of these new terrorist threats, with an emphasis on the benefits of the traditional police patrol. This outcome has been described as the 'internationalisation of municipal policing' (Nussbaum 2007: 214). This new municipal focus has not only led to 'community policing' being given a growing prominence in any anti-terrorist intelligence gathering strategy but also an important role in combating organised crime through crime and community intelligence. A senior counter-terrorism officer in the UK made it clear that the police and security services have to make all efforts to 'get inside the heads of potential violent extremists' within the community and believes the 'key to unlocking fundamentalism was in communities' (Quick 2009: 10).

Although national security matters are the primary responsibility of the UK Government and not devolved to the Scottish Government, the Scottish police and its many partners have a significant role to play in the prevention of terrorism and the safety of the public. The Scottish police are fully supportive of the role that community policing and communities can play in combating terrorism, especially after the events of New York 9/11, London 7/7, and the Glasgow (2007) and Madrid (2004) bombings, which led to an upsurge in counter-terrorism initiatives and introduced a new challenge to national security across the European Union. All the parties involved in twenty-first-century community policing have a role to play in the global response to terrorism and, by association, organised crime. Through awareness and intelligence gathering, all these partners can assist the identification of possible threats to security within their own sphere, and in many instances are much better placed to gather community intelligence than the police and security agencies. The police have to achieve a balance between tough prevention and protection tactics and a strategy that safeguards communities without alienating them. So the gathering of information and community intelligence through the medium of community policing is the preferred option of the police in Scotland. In the context of terrorism, there is more likelihood of communities with trustful relationships with the police being more willing to pass on information of terrorist threats among their members. The Scottish police have shown a sound awareness of this fact over the years and instead of moving away from community policing, their preferred direction of travel is continued investment in this form of policing.

The new Police Scotland will combine counter-terrorism and the investigation of serious organised crime rather than have separate departments for these issues. Under the new single force, all the skills, technical equipment and professional knowledge will be focused on both these specialised areas of police work as the proficiencies, abilities and training of the detective officers are similar. Counter-terrorism does not carry a large workload in Scotland, compared to the threat from serious organised crime. The underlying principle is that this approach will ensure all investigators will be regularly involved in all aspects of investigatory work, including the interviewing of suspects and court work. So when anti-terrorist investigations are required, all staff will be honed and ready for action.

Conclusion

When police officers retire, they are normally head-hunted by employers in both the private and public sectors. This would be expected with their high knowledge of the criminal law; skilful driving; IT training; proven report writing abilities; good fitness level; proven ability to interface with ordinary members of the public; aptitude for dealing with aggressive, violent and awkward situations; having first-aid skills; understanding approach when dealing with ethnic minorities; dealing appropriately with people during a crisis; comfortable in partnership working with teachers, social work and the fire service; experience in committees and meetings; confident public speaker; considerate in the welfare of prisoners; understanding of evidence and court procedures; ability to give crime prevention advice; experienced in self-defence training; and much more. This all comes about at the end of a comprehensive career when the average police officer has spent many decades performing as a professional law enforcement officer, after being given the appropriate training and gaining a high level of experience and expertise. Although this chapter is only a short introduction to the varied duties carried out by Scottish police officers in what is a dynamic environment, it does reflect the skills that the Scottish police officer acquires during his or her career when they police Scotland.

5

HOW DO SPECIALIST UNITS POLICE SCOTLAND?

Introduction

In the case *Fisher v Oldham* (1930), comment was made by the court that all police officers are specialists. But in reality, and as a result of the increasing complexities of crime, the police officer cannot specialise in all the skills essential to modern-day policing. Indeed, many of the requisite specialist services have to be sought from outside the police organisation, such as criminologists, psychologists, biologists, pathologists, or psychiatrists. And through necessity the police employ within their organisation police staff ranging from lawyers and human resource managers to forensic accountants and computer experts. But the idea of specialists in policing can be traced back to an earlier period in its 180-year history and with a Scottish connection.

Sir Arthur Conan Doyle, the creator of the fictional detective, Sherlock Holmes, was born in Leith in the north of Edinburgh on 22 May 1859. The world-renowned author regularly recounted that his old professor and mentor at Edinburgh University Medical School, Joseph Bell, remarked to students that all successful medical diagnosis is the result of 'the precise and intelligent recognition and appreciation of minor differences', which Conan Doyle later interpreted to be the basis of all good detective work and sought to develop towards an 'exact science' (Lycett 2007: 110). Conan Doyle's Scottish education, together with his medical background and his love of the fictional detectives in the writings of Edgar Allan Poe, Charles Dickens, Wilkie Collins, and particularly the memoirs of Eugene Vidocq, the head of the Paris Sûreté, convinced him that the idea of a highly trained 'professional' leading a criminal investigation was the path to follow.

In his lifetime Conan Doyle also witnessed a number of scientific advancements that influenced the development of his famous detective's character and the methods used in crime deduction. Fingerprinting and photographing of criminals was just being introduced at the time and the keeping of accurate and comprehensive criminal records along with *modus operandi* and intelligence information was in its infancy. As a result, the use of these methods appeared at intervals in the Sherlock Holmes stories. These and many more scientific breakthroughs set in motion the emergence of the professional police officer and the ultimate appearance of a separate specialist investigation branch of the police – the detective. Conan Doyle lived at a time when criminals such as the body snatchers and the Edinburgh serial killers Burke and Hare,[1] reputed to have murdered 17 victims, were still fresh in the memory of the Scottish people. And interestingly it was the pioneering work in forensic science at Edinburgh University which brought the infamous duo to justice. Thirty years later Conan Doyle was being taught medicine in the same department, probably by academics who had some links to the earlier investigation of this notorious murder case.

It is not surprising that this period in the nineteenth century offered a fertile environment for the young imaginative mind of Conan Doyle. Conan Doyle's genius was to merge the real science with the fictional narrative and to give us the authentic chronicle of the specialist detective. Sherlock Holmes may have been based at 221B Baker Street in London but the real origin of the 'specialist investigator' lay with Conan Doyle's Scottish upbringing and education. On the other hand, it could be argued that what is loosely described as Scotland's first full-time 'detective officer' dates back to 1819 in Glasgow, when he was given the responsibility for the upkeep of criminal records (Gordon 1980: 24) – 40 years before the birth of Conan Doyle.

On a more up-to-date note, the creation of a single police service in Scotland is being seen as an opportunity to increase the ready access to specialist police services to a larger section of the community and in particular to focus on those remote rural areas of Scotland where such services have been limited or non-existent in the past. For example, at the time of writing, there are 135 police dogs in the Scottish police service with breeds such as German shepherds, Belgian shepherds, Labradors and spaniels. The dogs are used in drug searches, mountain rescue and many other police operations. The new single police service offers an opportunity for the police to reorganise its canine resources to ensure a more equitable coverage of trained general purpose dogs, and the more specialist explosives and drugs dogs across Scotland. Similar expansion and improving the availability of police specialist resources through a national structure can also be conducted in other areas such as a police mounted section, aviation, river patrol, crime investigation and analysis. Prior to the introduction of a national police service, forces had to request mutual aid from each other, now this will not be necessary with a single police service as all services come under a single command with resources at key locations to facilitate easy deployment. Centralisation may bring about efficiencies and savings but it also opens the door to a more strategic, smarter and effective way of managing resources to ensure better services for Scottish communities. One example is air support as the Strathclyde Police Air Support unit becomes a nationwide resource on 1 April 2013, making available to the whole of Scotland the vast amount of onboard specialist equipment including powerful searchlight, public address system, daylight and infra-red imaging camera and digital recorder. The Eurocopter helicopter can be airborne in 4 minutes and travels at a maximum speed of 138 miles per hour and can downlink and transmit real-time images from the aircraft camera to area control rooms. With a flying endurance of around 90 minutes the aircraft can refuel at a number of locations around the country and is a shared resource for Police Scotland. Normal operating hours of the unit are 08.00–22.30 hours but it is also available on an on-call basis.

This chapter describes a wide range of specialist services in the modern Scottish police service, some of which are as a result of the introduction of Police Scotland, and others which exist already will be more effective due to the presence of Police Scotland.

Specialist policing

In the HM Inspectorate Constabulary for England and Wales report, *Taking Time for Crime* (HMIC 2012), it is revealed that police spend around 20 per cent of their time on crime but if one includes police involvement when there is a risk of crime, the figure rises to 80 per cent (ibid.). There is no reason to believe this is not the case in Scotland. New demands on policing have resulted in the creation of police specialists to cope with the complexities of the new tasks and growth crimes such as domestic and child abuse, sex offender management, computer-related crime, sectarianism, etc. These specialist roles are normally 'off street' though still involved with crime investigation and prevention. So in modern policing there are many officers involved indirectly with crime who are not necessarily out on the streets being seen by the public. This growth in specialist posts is necessary as tailored training is required to do the job properly and to satisfy credibility and evidential purposes in the criminal justice and court system. In the mid-1980s when the Female and Child Units were established in parts of Scotland as a response to the rise in child abuse, the units were normally staffed by policewomen who in many instances were still on their probation – untrained for such a specialist and demanding role. Other examples of growth crimes with officers having to cope with little or no specialist training can range from serious sexual crimes to computer crimes to human trafficking. In the 1980s, the police were unprepared for many of these new responsibilities and adapted slowly. Interestingly, the 2012 HMIC's report identifies a lack of clarity about the police 'mission' in England and Wales, with some forces having different mission statements which even varied internally across departments: 'No longer can the police operate as they have in a predominately reactive way that chases increasing demand for services' (ibid.). This comment has particular relevance in these times of austerity and fiscal restraint. Hence the growth of specialist posts as it is more cost-effective than to train everyone to be multi-skilled. In present-day Scotland things have changed considerably as specialist courses are run at the regional levels and at the Scottish Police College, Box 5.1 lists a varied selection of high standard courses.

BOX 5.1 SELECTION OF POLICE TRAINING COURSES AT THE SCOTTISH POLICE COLLEGE, 2011– 2012

Advanced Wildlife & Environmental Crime Investigation
ASIST (Applied Suicide Intervention Skills) Training
Collision Investigation
Convoy Commander
Counter-Terrorism
Court Room Skills for Police Staff
Court Skills for Forensic Expert Witnesses
Designing Safer Communities
Door Step Crime
Dyslexia in the Workplace
Geographic Information Systems for Police Managers and Analysts
Honour-Based Violence
Interviewing Child Witnesses
Introduction to Disability
Introduction to Personal/Professional Development Planning
Investigating Domestic Abuse and Stalking Behaviours
Kidnap and Hostage
NPIA Senior Investigating Officers Seminar – Investigating Child Death
Offender Management
Operational Policing in a European and International Context
Palm Identification Course
Police Search Advisors
Policing 'Beyond the Playground' (Development of the Role of Campus/School-Based Officer)
Problem Solving
Psychoactive Substance Event
Scotland and Violence
Scottish Policing in a European and International Context
The Scottish Criminal Justice System and Fingerprint Legislation
Victims of Sexual Crime
Witness Protection

Source: Scottish Police College Prospectus (2012).

The CID were born out of the need for the police to become specialists in crime detection and the gathering of crime intelligence, and during the inter-war years, few police forces had any large or effective detective departments. Some of the smaller forces had none at all and, in truth, only Scotland Yard and some of the larger city forces, such as Glasgow, had any substantial numbers of detectives, and forensic science beyond fingerprinting and poisoning was unknown and unused:

'detectives were blatantly ignored during the 1920s by some forces' (Laybourn and Taylor 2011: 103–4). But in some forces investigatory skills were being developed and eventually the specialist detective was created. The same can be said for the birth of road policing during the same period. Initially, with the introduction of mass motoring, the police adopted an educational and discretionary approach and took up traffic control only when required. But as roads became busier and more dangerous, they had to go into enforcement mode and take a hard line. This brought them into conflict with the upper and middle classes who were the only ones who could afford motor vehicles and the 'upper classes (potentially at least) found themselves criminalised on an unprecedented scale' and 'an increasing number of working-class police constables found themselves regulating the lives of their social superiors' (ibid.: 182–3). Policemen found themselves in danger from speeding vehicles and regularly verbally and physically abused by drivers as they tried to enforce the law. Eventually road traffic legislation was introduced which gave the police the powers to take a firmer line and the specialist traffic officer was born.

Now nearly 100 years later in the road patrol and crime management divisions of the Scottish Police College there are a number of specialist courses taught by highly professional tutors with national reputations. These courses are open to specialist officers working within these specialist departments across Scotland. Many courses are taught, and the following is only a selection:

Crime Management

- Detective Training
- Counter-Terrorism
- Community Safety
- Covert Specialist Training
- Intelligence and Analytical Training.

Road Patrol

- Pursuit Management
- Security Escort Driving
- Road Collision Investigation
- Traffic Management.

One of the most difficult and much-sought-after of the specialist courses is covert surveillance or undercover officer training. On graduating from this course, officers have the opportunity to work in a number of specialist units and develop a high level of experience and skill. However, this particular course highlights the need for constant review and update of courses as in 2012 long-term covert officers from the Metropolitan Police came under a great deal of criticism from the media, politicians and victims for alleged abuse of their position as undercover police officers. These officers had infiltrated protest groups over a 40-year period and were allegedly involved in a number of questionable practices, ranging from adopting the identities of dead children to having distressing long-term relationships with political activists before faking their own disappearances. It now appears that a large number of female victims are suing the Metropolitan Police for damages. This of course in no way suggests that any training or course content was at fault but it does highlight the need for constant review and update of specialist training. What follows in this chapter are examples of specialist policing created and developed out of necessity in this increasingly complex world.

National policing

The reason for the introduction of a National Coordinator of Terrorist Investigation was based on experience gained during the terrorist attacks carried out by the Provincial Irish Republican Army (PIRA) on the UK mainland. It was found to be the wrong approach to have individual police forces investigate PIRA attacks independently, as the reality is that the whole nation becomes the investigator's domain in such circumstances. An example of this is recounted by the ex-Metropolitan Police Commissioner Lord Ian Blair in his 2010 book, when he talks about the terrorist attack on Glasgow Airport on 30 June 2007. According to Lord Blair, after initial discussion between the UK Prime Minister and the Scottish First Minister on whether the Scots had jurisdiction over the incident, the Prime Minister made his views clear that 'policing might be devolved to the Scottish Parliament but counter-terrorism was not. The security of the whole country was at stake. This was UK Government territory, Salmond [the First Minister] seemed unsure but Brown [the Prime Minister] was certain' (Blair 2010: 210). Scotland Yard took over the investigation. The arrival of a single police service in Scotland can only strengthen the coordination and working practices of those police and security units with the responsibility to combat terrorism and serious organised crime in the wider UK.

The National Crime Agency

The UK National Crime Agency (NCA) was created by the Crime and Courts Act 2012 and will be fully operational by the end of 2013. The NCA has a national remit to tackle organised crime, strengthen the UK borders, fight fraud and cybercrime, and protect children and young people. These responsibilities build upon the earlier work of the Serious Organised Crime Agency, the Child Exploitation and Online Protection Centre, and incorporate some of the functions of the National Policing Improvement Agency, all of which have now been disbanded. It is estimated that organised crime costs the UK between £20 and £40 billion a year and it is recognised that many crime organisations work across borders and have no boundaries when it comes to crime type and geography. There are four distinct Commands within the NCA: organised crime, border policing, economic crime, and child exploitation and online protection. The agency also includes the national cyber-crime unit that will work closely with the recently launched European Cybercrime Centre (EC3), which is cross-border by nature, and will examine attacks targeting e-banking and critical infrastructure, and crimes such as child sexual exploitation. The hope is that the NCA will offer a single national intelligence picture on organised crime and have the authority to coordinate and task the national response while working with other law enforcement partners, such as Police Scotland. The appointment in 2013 of the previous Director of the Scottish Crime and Drug Enforcement Agency to the post of Director of the Organised Crime Command of the NCA should facilitate close liaison between Police Scotland and the NCA.

The Specialist Crime Division

The previous Scottish Crime and Drug Enforcement Agency (SCDEA) was established to tackle the growing threat from serious and organised crime in Scotland at the beginning of the new century. It was formed as a Non-Departmental Public Body, where the board governance structure reflected the tripartite stakeholders of the police through chief constables, the local government through police board conveners, and the communities through lay board members. Responsible to government ministers, the SCDEA's primary role was covert targeting of Organised Crime Groups engaged in national and international drug trafficking, importation and money laundering. In addition, the SCDEA provided support to the eight Scottish Police Forces in respect of witness liaison, abduction and extortion, e-crime, covert operations and technical support. The SCDEA ceased to exist on 1 April 2013 with the introduction of Police Scotland and its responsibilities have been taken over by the new Specialist Crime Division (SCD) of the single police force. The SCD is now responsible for all aspects of crime in Scotland except those generally seen as 'local' investigation work, and includes the services hitherto carried out by the SCDEA, and specifically embraces one of its main responsibilities to combat the trafficking of illegal drugs.

Scotland has one of the most serious drug problems in Europe, the economic and social costs of problem drug use is estimated at £2.6 billion, with around 59,600 problem drug users (SPPF 2012). In addition, tens of thousands of children are affected by the drug misuse of one or more parents. The enforcement of drug legislation and reducing the supply of illegal drugs have always been an essential feature of police strategy in Scotland and although the police and other frontline workers have had some level of success, there remain major challenges ahead. For example, although drug seizures in Scotland have increased steadily year by year, enforcement efforts have had little impact on the availability, purity and price of illicit drugs. A commonly held view is that police action merely slows down the growth and expansion of the drugs market only temporarily. A previous Scottish Chief Constable, Kevin Mathieson openly admitted that:

> Over the last 10 to 20 years, if what we were doing had been successful, there would be fewer drug abusers, drugs would be harder to obtain . . . instead, we

have more drugs deaths and overdoses, more people are becoming addicted, drugs are freely available and they are cheaper than alcohol.

(Evening Telegraph, *12 May 2008)*

The Scottish police have adopted disruptive tactics against the illegal drugs market, seeking to cause as much damage as possible but even they would agree that although there have been many high profile successes, the market soon recovers and the cycle of supply and demand continues.

The hope is that, with a national police service, the Scottish police and its partners in the criminal justice sector will be in a better position to adopt a more cohesive approach that builds on the good record of stripping assets and cash from those involved in organised crime and drugs across Scotland. Cars, houses, cash and business premises have all been seized by using the Proceeds of Crime Act (POCA) 2002. Criminals are becoming more adept at hiding their clandestine assets and have access to the best legal and accounting advice from unscrupulous professionals. Ever since the SCDEA was introduced, it has been hindered by a lack of resources as it relied heavily on the eight Scottish police forces seconding the necessary skilled resources to allow it do to the job. Personality clashes between a number of Chief Constables and the SCDEA management did not help either and the situation regularly featured in the media and in official political circles. Now that the national SCD has taken over and has access to a high level of expertise in tackling the illegal drug trade from around the country, there should be no barriers to their use, and total focus on the problems at hand whether illegal drugs or other high-level crime challenges. It is presumed that the SCD will take the policy lead on tackling the organised drugs trade and divisional teams will deal with local drug dealers. In addition, there will be less ambiguity in the lines of communication with law enforcement agencies in the UK and further afield, as Police Scotland now speaks with one national voice and is in a much stronger position than was previously the case with the SCDEA.

The SCD provides national uniformity and equality of specialised services to the local level in the disciplines of major crime, such as murder and rape; organised crime, human trafficking; counter-terrorism, intelligence, covert policing and public protection. A Deputy Chief Constable heads up the SCD and there are two Assistant Chief Constables, one covers Major Crime and Public Protection, and the other oversees Serious Organised Crime and Counter-Terrorism. There is also a single Ports (Borders) Unit encompassing all of the airports and sea ports across Scotland. The SCD has a staff of around 1800 detective officers and has three investigating teams in the east, west and north of Scotland. Lesser crimes will be investigated by crime investigators at the local divisional level. Major investigations will be led by specialist teams brought in from the SCD, regardless of the location of the incident in Scotland. The SCD has also established a National Intelligence Bureau (NIB) that incorporates the previous Scottish Intelligence Database (SID). The SCD is another example of the developing ethos of the new Police Scotland which focuses national expertise on any police problem regardless of its site and delivers the service locally.

Organised crime

One characteristic of Scottish policing is its constant drive to look for solutions to its many challenges and this is no less apparent with the innovative policing approach adopted to combat the ubiquitous organised crime in Scotland. Proposals put forward by the Scottish police in 2012 aim to prevent organised criminal gangs from owning taxi businesses, security businesses and licensed pubs. Preventing this type of organised crime has always been hampered by the constant presence of intimidation and threats to potential witnesses whose identity would be known to the accused or suspect. As a consequence, there has to be a great reliance on the gathering and use of intelligence in order to thwart any attempt by criminals to obtain licences for purportedly legitimate businesses. If the Scottish policing plans are approved by the politicians, then a special judge with the title of Intelligence Commissioner would review police intelligence reports in a closed court and would be empowered to impose sanctions on individuals suspected of clandestine, malevolent or criminal behaviour, and curtail their business activities according. However, the police proposal is not without its critics, who have described the proposed plan as an infringement of civil liberties, as it involves having a significant impact on an individual's daily life and freedom, based on intelligence reports rather than evidence tested in a normal court of law. There are obvious arguments on both sides. The police, out of frustration, are stretching the letter of the law in order to modernise and update policing methods in an area of criminality renowned for legal dangers and difficulties. The more liberal view sees such a proposal as the thin edge of the wedge and is concerned as to where it could lead next. Whatever the final outcome may be, the exercise does reveal the Scottish police exhibiting a willingness to be imaginative and inventive when pursuing the criminal on behalf of the Scottish citizen, which is evident throughout this text.

Another potential controversial move by Police Scotland is the ongoing talks between Scottish and Italian police on the feasibility of anti-mafia laws being introduced into Scotland. Scottish police officers have already visited Rome and had discussions with the anti-mafia teams and believe the measures would be beneficial and complement existing police strategies in Scotland. In Italy, special certificates are issued to law-abiding firms in a strategy designed to push organised crime out of public sector contracts, which has been a growing concern in Scotland in recent years. Such measures would involve taxi and private hire vehicles, security firms, building construction, and property management and development. There are potential dangers with the model as many people under investigation have not been convicted of a crime and their business could be adversely affected and contracts lost. This could give rise to claims against the police and criminal justice agencies on the basis of infringements of human rights. Again this is another example of the direction of travel in Scotland where the police are not afraid to try new schemes in their constant search for new methods and techniques to tackle organised crime, wherever it may be.

Prostitution

At the present time, prostitution is regulated differently in parts of Scotland. On the west coast in Glasgow, the police and local authority have adopted a zero-tolerance approach but in the capital city of Edinburgh on the east coast a more tolerant and safety approach exists. Buying sex from street prostitutes or kerb-crawling was made illegal in Scotland in 2006, so the clients of street prostitutes can now be arrested. This criminalisation policy is closely adhered to in Glasgow. In contrast, in the City of Edinburgh the local council has a policy of granting licences to sauna parlours wishing to operate in their area. The belief is that prostitution is allowed on these premises and the authorities, including the police, turn a blind eye. Each area has specialist officers who maintain a close liaison with prostitutes and support groups and build up relationships that ultimately add to the safety of the women involved in this dangerous occupation. The concern for some is that with the arrival of a single police service with its capacity to introduce national strategies and policies for tackling crimes and offences, one of these approaches to the policing of prostitution will be adopted over the other and implemented nationally. The question is, will it be the softer or firmer approach?

Sectarianism

Sectarianism has been described as 'Scotland's shame' and is outlawed in Scotland and courts can even impose additional penalties on everyday crimes if they are shown to be aggravated by sectarian hatred. Sectarianism and religious bigotry go back over a century and find their roots in Catholic Irish immigrants coming to Scotland. And in the City of Glasgow what was initially football rivalry between two football clubs, Celtic and Rangers, commonly known as the Old Firm, became over time a focus for sectarian behaviour between Catholic Celtic and Protestant Rangers football supporters. Throughout the twentieth century this state of affairs has resulted in regular serious disorder and acts of religious bigotry when these football teams meet. Problems still exist in the new century with around 800 arrests for mainly football-related sectarian behaviour in the West of Scotland area alone between 2008 and 2010. The use of the internet has made matters worse as fans on both sides can use it to vilify each other and on many occasions breach the criminal law online. In Scotland as a whole for the period 2011–2012, there were 876 religiously aggravated offences, an increase of one quarter from the previous year, and less than one-third of the offences were football-related. These figures remind us that bigotry and sectarianism remain a live issue in Scottish society and continue to challenge the police. There is additional comment in the next section on domestic violence and how the Old Firm football matches have an impact on the number of domestic violence incidents whenever the two teams meet.

The Scottish Parliament introduced the Offensive Behaviour at Football and Threatening Communications (Scotland) Act 2012 as a response to the concerns from the majority of Scottish people wishing to see more positive action to be taken against sectarianism and offensive behaviour. This was highlighted in government studies which revealed:

- 89 per cent of Scots agree that sectarianism is offensive.
- 89 per cent of Scots agree that sectarianism is unacceptable in Scottish football.
- 85 per cent of Scots agree that sectarianism should be a criminal offence.
- 91 per cent of Scots agree that stronger action needs to be taken to tackle sectarianism and offensive behaviour associated with football in Scotland.

(Scottish Government 2011c)

The Act was enacted on 1 March 2012 and criminalises behaviour which is threatening, hateful or otherwise offensive at a regulated football match, including offensive singing or chanting. It is also an offence to engage in the communication of threats of serious violence and threats intended to incite religious hatred, whether by the post or on the internet. The intention is that the Act will only criminalise behaviour likely to lead to public disorder which expresses or incites hatred, is threatening or is otherwise offensive to a reasonable person. There are two new offences under the Act, Offensive Behaviour at a Regulated Football Match and Threatening Communications. The Act also covers the behaviour of players and managers and can be applied on the journey to a regulated football match. Offences under the Act are not intended to stop peaceful preaching, restrict freedom of speech or criminalise jokes and satire about religion or non-religious beliefs.

However, since the implementation of the Act, there has been criticism from opposition politicians and pressure groups that the Act may be doing more harm than good and they call for it to be reviewed. Lawyers have raised concerns that football supporters' human rights have been diminished by the new police powers, with fans being placed under surveillance and regularly stopped and questioned by the police. The Scottish Government has promised to review the legislation which was hurriedly passed through Parliament in 2011. As always in these instances, the police service is left to implement the legislation and do its best to interpret what Parliament wished to achieve with the new law.

Domestic violence

The Scottish police have a long history in pioneering initiatives to tackle domestic violence and are the European leaders in this field. They take the stance that, as with other embedded societal crimes like sex offences and child abuse, it is everyone's problem and not just the responsibility of the police and their partners. Ironically, this approach in Scottish law enforcement has encouraged more reporting of domestic violence since victims' expectations are that proper investigation and preventative action will result. There was a rise of 9 per cent in domestic violence crime from 54,752 incidents in 2010–2011 to 59,690 in 2011–2012 (SPPF 2012). This is the highest number of domestic abuse incidents reported to the police in the past five years. The Scottish police view this hidden domestic crime as a cultural and attitudinal problem that in past decades may have been tolerated by society but is totally unacceptable in the twenty-first century.

In 2012, Rangers Football Club was relegated to the Third Division after the club went into administration so there has been a full football season when the Old Firm teams have not played each other. Interestingly, this has been reflected in the marked decline in the number of domestic violence instances as it has been shown that domestic violence in Scotland experiences a surge whenever the Old Firm play each other. The police are delighted to have some respite from these football fixtures as they used to meet four or more times each year and were a constant drain on police resources. Police figures show that on a typical Old Firm weekend there would be an average of 107 incidents of domestic violence compared to the normal 67 instances. On one Old Firm weekend in 2011, the number was 142.

The 2014 Commonwealth Games

The 2014 Commonwealth Games will be held in Scotland and will attract 6500 athletes from 70 nations. Over a quarter of the total budget will be spent on security and Police Scotland has full responsibility for ensuring all the security arrangements are in place. This includes the contracting of private security to deliver 11,000 accredited personnel as part of the overall security operation. In order to support the athletes, 120,000 people will have to be accredited to work in hotels and in the athletes' village. In addition, 15,000 volunteers will be required to support the 13 sporting venues across Glasgow and Edinburgh. The costs of security and policing have tripled to £90 million from the original estimates of around £27 million. Much of the increase in costs comes in the wake of what has been learned from the London Olympics in 2012. Recommendations from the 2012 event included the need for extra physical security systems such as X-ray machines, lighting, fencing, barriers and metal detectors. Extending the use of CCTV and passive infrared detection systems (PIDS) across all venues will also be necessary. As a result, more money will be made available for private security contractors who in partnership with the police will look after venues outside the sporting stadia and the athletes' village, this includes hotels and other non-competition functions. Scottish policing has a history of hosting major sporting and international events and along with other partners has the responsibility for ensuring a safe and secure Commonwealth Games for all. There is a cost factor, and in these times of economic pressure on the public purse having a single police service to do such a big job will facilitate a more efficient use of resources. Suggestion have been made that increasing the number of Special Constable and Police Cadets would greatly assist policing the event. To mark the priority given to the planning for the event, a Deputy Chief Constable has been put in charge on a full-time basis.

The International Unit

Criminals who evade justice by fleeing abroad from Scotland have always been difficult to track down and apprehend but the Scottish justice system has had a good track record of bringing many of these fugitives to justice over past decades. Now with the onset of the single police force a new dedicated Fugitives Unit will be given the role of directly focusing on these fugitives and also those high-risk offenders from other countries who have fled to Scotland to evade justice. The unit will have specialist staff with an analytical research support team and will have the capacity to quickly access crime information and intelligence from national and international agencies. Publishing images and details of offenders will be one method used by officers, similar to the FBI tactics. In the shrinking global world of law enforcement many Scottish police officers will find themselves dealing with enquiries from overseas for the first time and having ready access to the new unit will be a source of expertise and specialised knowledge. The unit will be based at the new Scottish Crime Campus in Gartcosh, North Lanarkshire and bring together the resources and expertise of officers from across Scotland as well as liaising with the National Crime Agency, Interpol and Europol, and the International Co-operation Unit at the Crown Office. Currently, Scotland has approximately 40 suspects believed to be overseas with an estimated 60 people in Scotland wanted by foreign nations (Police Oracle 2012). If fugitives from one nationality become prevalent in Scotland, there is always the option of inviting officers from that country to come to Scotland to assist in tracking them down. This is another example of how a national police service can fund specialised units to combat the increasing complexities of modern law enforcement. The new unit will also place Scotland in a stronger international position and better equipped to tackle serious and organised crime and other security threats.

Armed response cover

The existence of Police Scotland has made it possible for the first time to introduce armed response units across the whole of Scotland. This is in response to shooting incidents such as the one on the English/Scottish border in Cumbria in 2010, when a gunman killed 12 people and injured 11 more. Criticism was levelled at the delay in the local English force getting armed police officers to the rural location which allowed the gunman up to four hours to carry out the shootings. All 14 divisions of Police Scotland will now have their own firearms teams, totalling around 400 trained firearms officers throughout the country, ensuring dedicated full-time firearm officers are on patrol with the ability to respond quickly to any situation. Events, such as the shooting of 20 primary school children and six teachers in Connecticut, USA, in December 2012, bring back memories of the similar shooting in the Scottish town of Dunblane in 1996[2] and ensure the issue of gun control and the police use of firearms remain high on the political agenda.

The vast majority of police officers are against the routine arming of the police as there is still the belief that the traditional unarmed police patrol officer is worth retaining. That said, police officers and members of the public are exposed to the demands and risks of the modern day and this necessitates the adequate coverage of trained firearm officers on duty at all times.

TABLE 5.1 Number of persons (including children) killed or injured in road accidents/collisions in Scotland, 2007–2012

Force	*2007–2008*	*2008–2009*	*2009–2010*	*2010–2011*	*2011–2012*
Central	880	867	795	704	726
Dumfries & Galloway	631	522	518	461	420
Fife	785	694	764	712	562
Grampian	1,412	1,699	1,613	1,511	1,328
Lothian & Borders	3,277	3,197	2,959	2,910	2,824
Northern	997	1,023	993	798	810
Strathclyde	6,844	5,900	5,836	5,311	5,302
Tayside	1,217	1,102	1,141	926	974
Scotland	16,043	15,004	14,619	13,333	12,946

Source: Scottish Policing Performance Framework (SPPF) (2012: 37).

National roads policing

Police Scotland will take advantage of the removal of force boundaries to increase police flexibility and visibility throughout the Scottish road network by introducing a Trunk Roads Patrol Group to patrol motorway and major roads from bases across Scotland. This will be in addition to divisional roads policing officers under the direction of local commanders. This twin-track approach of national and local will ensure 24-hour coverage and a high traffic enforcement profile on major routes and motorways. Table 5.1 shows the number of deaths and injuries on the roads in Scotland.

Although the figures reveal a downward trend in road accidents over the period of five years, of these numbers there were 167 deaths on Scottish roads in 2011–2012. There is little opposition to the fact that road patrol work in the police service is a specialist role and requires highly trained police officers dedicated to this specific discipline. In the past decade, there have been great improvements in this area of community safety but, as we have seen, statistics remain at unacceptable levels. Road safety has always been a shared responsibility with local authorities and the police but it is now accepted that road safety goes much further than improved training and education of road users, it now has a close relationship with other disciplines, such as youth, education, environment, energy, employment, public health, research, technology, justice and insurance. Shared responsibility and partnership with all these agencies are essential to ensure further progress in this important field of community safety.

Offshore oilfields

For over 40 years the police in the north-east of Scotland have maintained good relations with the energy industry and have up to 60 Energy and Protective Security

Unit (EPSU) officers trained to energy industry standards, able to go offshore to respond to any incident in the North Sea oilfields. This is important as many of the incidents that occur are not initially in the control of the police. For instance, each offshore installation manager (OIM) receives training and necessary guidelines on what to do when an incident occurs and can gather evidence and take photographs and preserve a scene until the police can get offshore. This is a growing area of expertise and one which the new Police Scotland can develop.

Further north in the Shetland Islands, the new Highland and Islands Division of Police Scotland has a similar responsibility for the Sullum Voe Oil Terminal which handles the production of oil and liquefied gas from oilfields in the North Sea and the East Shetland Basin. It is not a refinery and stores oil before it is transported by tanker. This remote location of Scotland serves as a reminder that terrorists can strike anywhere at any time as during the Terminal's opening ceremony by the Queen on 9 May 1981 a bomb blast went off in the power station not far from where the Queen stood. Fortunately it was a minor blast and no one was injured but a boiler was damaged. The attack was accredited to the Irish Republican Army and this incident still remains the only IRA attack on Scottish soil. To add to the present-day responsibilities of the Shetland police, a new Laggan and Tormore Gas Plant to the east of Sullum Voe is presently under construction and will be operational by 2014. The processing plant will treat the gas produced from the Laggan and Tormore fields along 143km-long flowlines. These are some of the most remote locations in Scotland and vulnerable to both terrorist attack and most types of major incidents. Police Scotland with its access to additional resources across the nation is in a better position to offer expert support and assistance if the worst ever happens in these remote locations.

The National Sexual Crimes Unit

A partnership involving the Crown Office, the Procurator Fiscal and Police Scotland has set up a dedicated National Sexual Crimes Unit (NSCU) with specially trained officers working with victim support groups. Rape and other sexually related crimes are notoriously difficult to prosecute due to the lack of corroboration, as the victim is normally the only witness and in many instances there is limited forensic evidence. To ensure all victims of these crimes have access to the same expertise and investigatory skills, this national unit will make its resources and expertise available across the country. This initiative highlights the movement towards closer partnerships between police and criminal justice agencies and how it enables law enforcement to tackle the insurmountable difficulties of the past. A case in point relates to the Scottish Government proposal for changes to the corroboration rule in Scotland discussed earlier in Chapter 4. Research undertaken by the Crown Office for Lord Carloway's Review into criminal law and practice found that of 141 cases reported to the NSCU during the last six months of 2010 which were placed on petition and no proceedings taken, Fiscals considered that 95 (67 per cent) would have proceeded to trial, had there been no need for corroboration (Scottish Government 2011b).

The Crown Office suggests only 25 per cent of reported rape cases come to court which is distressing for the victims as it also means many guilty individuals are escaping justice. However, the removal of the corroboration rule will not be a guarantee of an improvement in the conviction rate for rape and other sexual crimes as all partners in the criminal justice system have a duty to continually improve their responses to these serious crimes. Chapter 4 has discussed this issue and revealed some of the concerns that the police service has with its removal. At the time of writing the Scottish Government is seeking the abolition of the corroboration rule in criminal cases and shares the view with victims' organisations that its continued requirement represents a barrier to justice.

Sex offender monitoring

Police Scotland will set up a dedicated offender monitoring unit in each of its 14 police Divisions across Scotland in order to increase surveillance of the high risk offenders. In particular, police resources are being increased to focus on the monitoring of sex offenders and the application of the Sexual Offences Prevention Order (SOPO) issued by the courts. The police have the responsibility to monitor the requirements within the SOPOs and this could involve resource-intensive covert work. In the past, some police forces were criticised for failing to keep track of offenders who frequently change addresses. There have also been incidences when the police have been blamed for failing to prevent offenders committing new crimes, where a more robust monitoring system would have identified a high risk of a person re-offending. Sex offenders in Scotland are managed through the Multi-Agency Public Protection Arrangements (MAPPA) which brings together police, social workers and other relevant partners. Offenders are grouped by the likelihood of them re-offending from low to medium, high and very high. Those in the high to very high groups are likely to be targeted by Police Scotland.

The National Human Trafficking Unit

There are many new challenges facing Police Scotland and one that has been receiving much media attention is that of human trafficking. In its first annual report the Inter-Departmental Ministerial Group on Human Trafficking (IDMG) revealed there were 946 potential victims of human trafficking in the UK in 2011, 712 adults and 234 children, an increase on the 2010 figures of 33 per cent (HM Government 2012: 8). Of that figure, 93 were in Scotland. Many of the individuals are forced into a life of crime, particularly children, and the Child Exploitation and Online Protection Centre (CEOP) estimates there are approximately 300 child trafficking victims in the UK per year. Organised criminals from countries such as Romania, Slovakia, Vietnam, Nigeria and China pose the greatest threat, with victims being used for sex, labour and domestic slavery.

It is exceptionally difficult to secure a court conviction for these crimes due to the uncertainty of the witnesses' immigration status and the fact that they could face deportation back to their homeland. In common with most sex crimes, there is a fear and dishonour in coming forward due to the taboo of sex trafficking and this all adds to the difficulties faced by the police in any investigation. An inquiry into human trafficking in 2011 conducted by the Equality and Human Rights Commission (Scotland) raised a number of questions into the policing of this type of crime. The questions posed by the Commission were along the lines of have the police sufficient resources to cope with the problem? Are the police adequately aware of the nature of human trafficking? Are the police properly trained to combat this type of crime? Do they understand the issues involved? Do they look on it as an immigration issue rather than a crime?

The Scottish police would be the first to admit that this is a challenging area of police work, especially when it is difficult to quantify the scale of the problem. With the expansion of the European Union and the removal of borders, there are significant numbers of people coming to Scotland from abroad and this exacerbates the problem. But the police have not ignored the issue and did launch an operation during 2006, 2007 and 2008, targeting street sexual exploitation which resulted in 81 premises being visited and 27 persons arrested and the recovery of 45 female adult victims. At least 17 persons were convicted of immigration and prostitute offences as a result of the operation. Just like terrorism, human trafficking is another new dimension to law enforcement in Scotland and one the police will have to train and prepare for in the future. In response to the challenge, Police Scotland has set up a dedicated National Human Trafficking Unit (NHTU) to coordinate the police response to human trafficking and prostitution. The NHTU is the product of the merger of the Scottish Intelligence Coordination Unit and the Strathclyde Vice and Trafficking Unit. The new Unit will provide more focus and cohesion to combating human trafficking in Scotland with each of the 14 local police divisions identifying a 'champion' with a deputy. These individuals will act as a link between the division and the central Unit. The NHTU will not investigate cases of human trafficking as this will be carried out by divisional resources or the Organised Crime and Counter Terrorism Unit. The NHTU will be based in Glasgow.

CCTV

CCTV has been accepted by the public and politicians in Scotland as a critical tool in many aspects of community safety and has an integral role to play in local policing throughout Scotland. That said, there is still a long way to go in the development of an acceptable national CCTV model. Recent studies show the potential benefits of CCTV and give some indication as to what has to be done to progress CCTV in Scotland. Although the majority of CCTV cameras are owned and operated by local authorities, the police are normally involved with their use in crime prevention and increasingly in crime detection and the prosecution of offenders. The proliferation of CCTV cameras has led to their daily use by the police in all aspects of community safety and police resource deployment regularly leading to arrest and court appearances. It is in this area of CCTV analysis and preparation of evidence for court that the police are developing expertise, especially in the investigation of serious crime. One normally finds that any murder investigation requiring the search of CCTV footage uses officers who have gained the necessary skills and experience over a period of time and can be looked on as experts in this field of work when giving evidence in court. This is one of many new growth areas in modern policing that has necessitated the introduction of dedicated courses in CCTV use for both police and civilian staff.

Now that Scotland has a national police service, a national CCTV strategy could be developed in order to get the best return from the high cost of investment in the systems. Recommendations have already been made for the introduction of mandatory national accredited training and a licence requirement to include all public-space operators as well as the private sector (Scottish Government 2009: 19–22). This is a growing specialist role in law enforcement that is necessary for effective community safety and one for the specialist police officer and police staff to be involved in.

Migrant surveillance

With the end of the Cold War and the expansion of the EU there are now hundreds of millions of people who have the right to travel freely around the 27 member states of the EU. Add to this the heightened awareness of terrorism, illegal migration, refugees, asylum seekers and organised crime, and the EU has a major task in maintaining security within its borders. This situation poses differing degrees of problems for each member state depending on their geographic position and the length of their border. The monitoring of the movement of people is crucial not only to the security of each individual nation but is essential to the safety and well-being of the EU as a whole. Problems have occurred in other countries as they do not have the necessary monitoring systems in place to deal with 'hate crime', unlike Scotland. Victims, for example, are not encouraged in some member states to report racial crimes and, to make matters worse, official records of such crimes are not kept.

Even when immigration is legal, difficulties can still arise as witnessed in Belfast, Northern Ireland, in the summer of 2009 when hundreds of Romani people had to flee from their homes due to racist attacks and intimidation from a minority in the local population. Ironically, many of the Romani migrants who liked the Irish people and enjoyed their jobs, were in flight from similar repression in other EU states (*Sunday Herald* 2009: 25). In such circumstances immigrants come into conflict with police and other public sector employees at the local level which brings new challenges for ethnic minority–police relations, in the form of language and cultural differences. Legal and illegal migrants and asylum seekers are a growing workload for all public agencies, none more so than the police who have to learn new skills and policing methods to deal with these minority groups. This is another specialism to add to the long list of policing skills but one that is second nature to the Scottish police officer who has a sound track record in multicultural relations. This function is not solely the domain of the police but requires effective partnership working with other agencies such as the Immigration authorities and the UK Border Agency.

Conclusion

An American study of comparing job variation between police constables and infantry soldiers revealed the complexity and the degree with which each job entails working with data, people and other things, which in their own professions are viewed as specialist functions. The study found that the activities of the traditional police officer were identified as more complex than those of the soldier, 'supporting the argument that the police officer's role is more cognitively demanding' (Campbell and Campbell 2010: 341). And when soldiers take on a police role, as in peacekeeping, the job becomes more involved for them with higher performance demands as the rules of engagement in wartime are replaced by more complex ones based on peacekeeping and 'automatic decisions and instinctive reactions based on combat training give way to considered judgements and measured reactions based on cultural understandings' (ibid.: 342). In contrast, police officers taking on a military role experience less complexity and cognitive demands, and traditional police discretion and use of force defer to simpler regular armed patrols and intimidation. This study supports the view that the traditional 'man on the beat' community police officer is a highly trained and skilful specialist, whose roles other professional non-police enforcement agencies would find difficult to perform without the requisite training and experience. This is a point often forgotten when discussing the merits of the beat officer as opposed to other specialist police departments such as those highlighted in this chapter, which in fairness are at a higher level of expertise than everyday policing as a result of their additional training and experience.

Specialisation has been part of the police service since the beginning of the twentieth century and the arrival of criminal forensics and will continue to have a significant presence for the foreseeable future. Never a year goes by but the police service is in need of new skills and abilities usually consolidated into specialist units and departments, as witnessed in this chapter. This can present the organisation with the well-publicised problems associated with control, coordination, communication and integration, which are more relevant to Scottish policing in the present day with its new national police service. The creation of Police Scotland creates the potential for increased specialisation, strategic and smarter policing with a higher visible police presence and more intelligent use of limited resources and allows for better targeting of problem areas. The work of the key specialist unit, the Serious Crime Division, exemplifies how Police Scotland will deliver its services – it is nationally managed but locally delivered across the nation to keep the Scottish people safe from harm by ensuring they have access to all types of police services, regardless of location.

Notes

1 In the period 1827–1828, William Burke and William Hare were notorious for murdering victims and selling the cadavers on to the medical profession in Edinburgh for the purpose of teaching medical students. Both were eventually arrested and Hare was granted immunity from prosecution for testifying against Burke. Burke was found guilty and hanged on 28 January 1829.

2 The Dunblane Primary School shooting massacre occurred in the Scottish town of Dunblane on 13 March 1996. The gunman, 43-year-old Thomas Hamilton, entered the school with four handguns, shooting and killing 16 children and one adult before committing suicide.

6

HOW DO NON-POLICE OFFICERS POLICE SCOTLAND?

Introduction

Modern policing is not solely about the delivery of law enforcement services, as it has become more involved in the provision of wider community safety and security within communities. This has opened the way for the provision of policing through a plurality of formal and informal and public and private means delivered externally by non-police officers. Additionally, employing police support staff internally to perform much-needed specialist roles or to release police officers to focus on the specific duties for which they are trained, recognises that the police service, in many respects, is no different from any other large work organisations in requiring specialist management and administrative support in order to operate efficiently (Donnelly and Scott 2010: 30–1). This process is described as the 'civilianisation' of police posts.

This chapter offers some insight into the valuable contribution made by non-police officers and organisations to law enforcement, crime prevention and the wider community safety. Comment is also included on the ongoing changes to policing in England and Wales that puts into context what is happening in Scotland. For example, the present Scottish Government is not reducing the numbers of police officers and is ideologically opposed to expanding the use of the private sector in policing. They see policing as a 'public good' that should be fully in the hands of the public sector. A contrary view is held by many south of the border.

Civilianisation

The advent of civilianisation in the police has created the opportunity for police staff actively to contribute to policing and to play an integral and important role in the twenty-first-century model of community safety. Indeed, the high standards of policing at the local level would not be possible, if it were not for the significant

TABLE 6.1 Scottish police officers and support staff numbers (FTE), 2008–2012

Date	*Police officers*	*(%)*	*Support staff*	*(%)*	*Total*
2008–2009	17,168	73	6482	27	23,650
2009–2010	17,503	73	6551	27	24,054
2010–2011	17,328	74	6123	26	23,451
2011–2012	17,499	75	5709	25	23,208

Source: Scottish Government (2012d).

number of support staff employed in the police service. For the police service to take advantage of new techniques and technology, it has to employ staff with the necessary skills and abilities. The extent of civilianisation in the Scottish police is now considerable, with non-police officers constituting approximately one-third of the police workforce. But as can be seen from Table 6.1, the earlier trend of increasing numbers of support staff is now in reverse and as we will discuss later in the chapter indications are that this downward trend will continue while police numbers remain fairly static.

Releasing police officers from non-police operational roles and replacing them with civilian support staff began in earnest in the 1980s in Scotland. In some instances, these new posts are key support roles on the operational side of policing and introduce new skills in crime prevention and crime reduction, and are managed and administered directly or indirectly at the local level. In the past, the roles of police staff were largely determined by the individual Scottish police forces and this has led to a variable mix in their use in police support jobs. Police staff mainly occupy corporate (27 per cent) and administrative and support roles (61 per cent) and just over 10 per cent are in operational roles (12 per cent), though this can be more in some areas of the country (Stewart Research 2009: 3). Box 6.1 lists the roles carried out by support staff under each heading.

BOX 6.1 POLICE STAFF ROLES AS REPORTED BY SCOTTISH POLICE FORCES IN 2008

Corporate

Accounts, Payroll and Pensions
Architects
Audit
Business Development and Support
Customer Services, Enquiries, Facilities
Contact and Service Centre
Education, Learning and Training

Estates and Building
Finance
Human Resources and Personnel
Information Services
Media, Press and Marketing
Occupational Health/Health and Safety
Printing and Mail
Performance/Improvement and Business Change
Solicitors and Paralegals
Research and Policy
Resource Management and Planning

Administrative
Administrative Staff
Alarms and Security
Animal Handlers
CCTV and Camera Staff
Cleaning, Catering, Maintenance and Ancillary
Clerical and Secretarial
Community Liaison and Support
Criminal Records, Police National Computer and Disclosure
Command Centre, Controllers and Control Room Staff
Graphics and Designers
Information Technology
Dispatchers
Communications Technicians
Intelligence
Licensing Staff
Lost and Found/Stores
Productions
Traffic Management and Road Safety
Transport, Vehicle and Fleet Management

Operational
Custody and Detention
Financial Investigators
Neighbourhood Wardens
Process Servers (citations)
Scenes of Crime Officers
Traffic Wardens
Vehicle Examiners
Wildlife Crime Officers

Source: Stewart Research (2009)

Across the civilian workforce in 2009 less than 1 per cent held senior management positions and 3 per cent occupied middle-management roles with a 'deployment gap' at the senior level in the specialist areas of human resources and finance, and only four forces out of a total of eight had a senior position in IT. The distribution and make-up of these positions may change with the arrival of Police Scotland and a new national organisational network. The situation is reflected in past experience which shows police staff occupying a low status position in the organisation with limited opportunity for advancement and poor career prospects compared to their colleagues in uniform. Change has not been easy for the reformers as many obstacles exist that prevent the advancement of civilianisation in the organisation. Some of the barriers to progress are legal, fiscal, cultural, police opposition, contractual issues, police restrictive duties, and set-up costs.

In the first 10 years of the Scottish Parliament, the number of police support staff members rose by 70 per cent while police numbers rose only 8 per cent and, according to the Scottish Police Federation, if police numbers had risen at the police staff rate, the figure would now be at 25,000 as opposed to the present-day average of 17,450. So it is not surprising that the introduction of civilian staff into the police service has for decades been opposed by many rank and file police officers who see it as a threat to their numbers in the law and enforcement organisation. The official rank and file representative body, the Scottish Police Federation, who support the valuable role delivered by police civilian staff, do not accept that 'as a blanket position a job which does not require police powers is almost best undertaken by a member of support staff' (SPF 2012a: 4).

In Europe, the process of civilianisation is progressing at a much slower pace. For example, in France, politicians expect that wherever possible police and gendarmes should be replaced by administrative civilian staff and static guards, personal protection, escorts and judicial transfers should be outsourced or the cost of police services charged whenever possible. This particular approach to the replacement of police officers in specific duties began in the 1990s in both the national police corps of technical and scientific support and civilian staff for administrative and back office duties. It is expected that by 2018 the number of gendarmes in the corps of technical and scientific support will be 6000 compared to 4500 in 2008, and the number of civilians will grow to 6000 compared to 2000 in 2008 (Donnelly 2013: 87). At the present time civilians represent 10 per cent of the total police numbers in France. This percentage figure remains much lower than other European countries, for example, the figure in Scotland is around 33 per cent and in Belgium 20 per cent. In the Republic of Ireland there were 2093 full-time equivalent police support staff in the Garda in December 2008, a rise of 24 per cent from the previous year (Garda Siochana 2009: 6). This figure equates to a civilian complement of approximately 14 per cent of the total strength of the Garda, which is still far behind the average of 33 per cent in other UK police forces. No other European country has civilianised police posts to the extent of the UK and many European police forces, particularly those with militant trade unions, vigorously oppose the civilianisation of police posts.

In the health services, nurses and other non-physicians carry out medical duties previously performed by doctors, in order to release doctors to do more of the specialised medical work they have been trained to do. Similar initiatives have been introduced in the teaching profession with teaching assistants and auxiliaries reducing the workload of teachers. Comparable schemes are possible within law enforcement for, as we will see throughout this book, highly trained police officers will be in great demand for other specialist duties in the future. The same can be said for highly trained support officers, particularly in the field of new technology and computer systems, who will be eagerly sought after just as much as their police colleagues for similar reasons, for example, as highly qualified intelligence analysts.

It is worth highlighting that police officers in the UK are appointed by the Crown and cannot be made redundant, but can be compulsory retired after they have reached their full pensionable service which is normally 30 or 35 years, depending on when they joined the service. On the other hand, civilian support staff do not enjoy this protection and can be subject to compulsory redundancy as in other employment sectors. A trend is now emerging in England and Wales as a result of economic pressures on municipal budgets to replace regular police officers in specific posts with police civilian staff. To a lesser extent this is happening in a number of EU countries.

Auxiliaries

In recent decades the responsibility for community safety has fallen to a wider range of community members, whether they are individual citizens, public groups, private or voluntary sector agencies. The loss of social control agents such as caretakers, park wardens, bus conductors, rural and neighbourhood policemen, has left a vacuum in community control and safety, which since the beginning of the twenty-first century has been filled by the introduction of civilian auxiliaries who go by many titles: community warden, city warden, community officer, neighbourhood warden, environmental enforcement warden, and more. Wardens assist the police and reassure the public with an increased visible presence of a uniform authority on the streets.

Community wardens

Community wardens are a mechanism that offers a consistency of interface between partnership agencies and the public, giving community members more control over community safety issues in their area. A regular warden patrol system constantly interacting with the community is more representative than a community meeting or local agencies making decisions on their own. The Scottish Government has provided some level of finance to local authorities to enable the introduction of community wardens since 2003. While they are not a replacement for the police and do not have police powers, they are, according to Her Majesty's Chief Inspector of Constabulary in Scotland, an extra resource which provides a 'reassuring presence to local people, promoting community safety and community development' (HMICS 2006: 25).

Warden schemes are generally designed to combat anti-social behaviour, reduce the fear of crime, prevent crime and improve the environment. As there was a degree of flexibility in the design and organisation of the community wardens, local authorities produced their own versions based on local needs. As a consequence, a variety of models now exist across Scotland that primarily deal with crime prevention or environmental improvement or embrace both. It is generally accepted that a combination of both functions is an effectual way of engaging anti-social behaviour. An analysis of the original aims and objectives of the Warden Schemes recognised a mix of intended outcomes, and the main themes are listed in Box 6.2.

Wardens are a flexible resource and can turn their hands to most municipal preventative and minor enforcement duties. Initiatives have included the targeting of noise nuisance, dog fouling, litter enforcement and anti-social behaviour patrols. Wardens also work on joint initiatives with partners such as the police, tackling disorder and street drinking. They can offer 24-hour patrols and on occasions have taken over security checks on council premises from private firms and regularly patrol on foot, bikes and in clearly marked vehicles.

Now that specific financial support for community wardens has been subsumed into mainstream local government funding, concerns are that in these austere times with budget cutbacks, local authorities may re-direct funds to other priorities.

BOX 6.2 AIMS OF COMMUNITY WARDEN SCHEMES IN SCOTLAND

Reduce fear of crime and increase public confidence
Improve environmental quality
Reduce anti-social behaviour
Reduce crime and increase crime prevention
Reduce youth crime
Increase community safety
Deter vandalism
Improve quality of life
Improve communication between partners and community
Reduce fire-raising
Contribute to best value
Encourage community engagement
Improve housing
Increase use of mediation
Reduce litter and fly-tipping
Reduce the number of void properties
Support victims of crime and anti-social behaviour

Source: Scottish Executive (2007).

Community wardens in the European Union

The move away from the traditional police officer has been described as 'new uniforms' when talking in the context of the role of wardens in community safety in Belgium where 'new uniforms carry out surveillance and regulation in public spaces' (Smeets 2008: 179). Agents are hired by the local authority to prevent street disorder and crime through routine patrol and surveillance of parks, schools, car parks, town and community halls, public and commercial buildings, feeding back information and intelligence to local authorities and eventually the police. These agents have no police powers or powers of restraint but do carry out patrol duties. This widening of general police functions and the transference of tasks have been stealthily progressing across most European countries with varying momentum for the past 20 years or so. In Belgium in particular, there is a new order or manner of considering governance of security and Sweets asks if we should consider whether the objective of 'new uniforms' is not to fight crime but to reduce the social vulnerability of an area or neighbourhood, with, for example, social bonding and good citizenship. However, this style of police patrol is hindered at times due to a level of mistrust in communities policing themselves and the fear of bias, unfair treatment and vigilantism, which dates back in history in most European countries to a time of autocratic rule and communities informing and reporting on each other. Unlike the police, auxiliary support is less dependent on coercion and requires communities to agree to this form of community safety (ibid.: 187).

A growing trend by local authorities in the European Union relates to the use of by-laws and enforcement measures to target anti-social behaviour. Local authorities have the power to introduce local police auxiliary patrols with the special purpose of acting as local patrols together with the regular police. In some instances, this includes working in tandem with private sector security firms employed by businesses to protect their premises. Though the private security guards may not possess any additional enforcement powers, they refer to the right of citizen's arrest and interpret it as a general right of intervention. Cooperation between the police and profit-oriented security firms is becoming a regular feature and on occasions is increasingly happening on a contractual basis, both operationally and on a day-to-day basis.

England and Wales

According to the former Metropolitan Police Commissioner, Lord Blair, the public like seeing the police on the streets and as part of a strategy to increase the numbers of uniformed officers on patrol, he championed the introduction of 'community support officers' (CSOs) and 'police community support officers' (PCSOs) with limited enforcement powers (Blair 2010). Lord Blair believed the reality is that many police officers do not like patrolling, despite the fact that the beat officer is hailed to be the most important individual in policing, and many look to join specialists units during their careers such as traffic and crime investigation. Whereas CSOs/PCSOs enjoy patrolling and in many instances the public find them more approachable than their police colleagues. This may be due to the fact that the modern police officer is laden down with all sorts of frightening equipment, from a large baton to CS spray and stab-proof vests, which the ordinary citizen may find off-putting.

One of the surprising features surrounding the introduction of the CSOs/ PCSOs in England and Wales was the extraordinary explosion of interest in the new posts from individuals from minority backgrounds. At the time the Metropolitan Police struggled to get 5 per cent of its staff from minorities, in spite of the fact that 30–40 per cent of people who were economically active in London came from these communities. Within weeks of the new posts being advertised, applications from minority groups for CSOs/PCSOs numbered 30–35 per cent. A lot of the minority citizens were 'coming to have a look at us and they liked what they saw' and in a short space of time many applied for a post as regular police officers. Within a few years the Metropolitan Police moved from 5 per cent to 20 per cent of minority officers and the 'face of London policing began to change' (Blair 2010). There could be valuable lessons to be learned from this strategy for the Scottish police who still face the persistent challenge of recruiting sufficient numbers of ethnic minorities into their ranks. According to Blair, refusal of the Police Federation to accept community support officers into the Association and leave them with the unions was a serious strategic mistake.

Private security firms

The bad press directed at the failures of the private security industry such as the G4S London 2012 Olympics débâcle in 2012, when the G4S security firm misjudged the size and complexity of the security task they were being asked to deliver, has not helped the case for further involvement of the private sector in policing and community safety. Closer to home in Scotland, the same private security firm G4S was fined £350,000 for thousands of late deliveries of prisoners to Scottish courts, amounting to 21,735 occasions since they took over responsibility for the escorting of prisoners in January 2012. However, this amounts to a drop of around 40 per cent from the previous private operator, Reliance, and, according to G4S, it now equates to only one in 990 deliveries, resulting in a delay at court. Sadly, a few negative stories can overshadow the many good examples of public–private collaboration and the valuable contribution it makes to improved community safety and crime reduction. For example, information technology and support systems; crowd safety at sporting events; delivering new technology to reduce bureaucracy and intelligence gathering and analysis; developing new software systems to tackle modern complex crime and fraud; and improved online communication and interface with police and the public. The introduction of these initiatives has reduced police officer involvement in non-operational tasks and returned many officers to patrolling the streets of Scotland.

The growth of the private security services industry is exceptional and in the European Union alone it is estimated to have a turnover of 35 billion Euros per year with up to 50,000 private companies with 1.8 million employees (Vejnovic *et al.* 2010: 389). While private security services are 'for-profit' agencies, their clients can come from the private and commercial world and the public and municipal sectors. This means that employees from private security companies can be found working in a business enterprise, government institution, local authority department, voluntary and charitable schemes, and other quasi-public establishments. The role of private security in the modern society is more than just an approach to crime prevention and policing of private venues; it can be described as 'governmental efforts to "responsibilize" non-state organizations in working towards crime control as a shared goal' (Wakefield 2005: 542). In other words, the expanding role of the private security sector subjects the public to constant surveillance in both the public and private spheres, and in so doing offers an additional level of crime prevention and community safety to the public.

It has always been difficult to estimate the size of the private security industry due to lack of reliable information. However, it is widely believed that the number of private security personnel exceeds the number of regular police in most European Union countries. The total number of police officers for 2009 for the European Union was estimated at 1,671,000 and the figure for private security guards a year later in 2010 was around 1,662,000 (Donnelly 2013: 90). About 50 per cent of the 27 EU countries had a higher number of private security guards than police

Sharing services

At the time of writing, hundreds of police and support staff posts in England and Wales are due to be lost as police forces agree to sharing services in the future. Warwickshire and West Mercia will see a merging of support services and reorganisation of policing assisted in some respects by private sector support. Warwickshire is set to lose 235 police officers by 2015 with West Mercia due to lose around 170. In addition, as a result of the merging of services, 650 police staff jobs are to be lost by 2016. Both forces have to save £30.3 million and the proposed changes will result in two joint Assistant Chief Constables responsible for policing in both areas, with two directors being appointed to deal with support functions. Policing will also be divided into seven geographical areas, each with a chief superintendent, neighbourhood policing team, response teams, local investigation and harm reduction. As can be seen, there are similarities in this micro-model to that of the new model of national policing in Scotland where services are now shared across the nation. One wonders if it is only a matter of time before there is consideration given to the official merging of police forces in England and Wales.

Police support staff in Scotland

On 1 April 2013, all police staff in Scotland transferred to the new single police force and became employees of the Scottish Police Authority (SPA). Contingent on the business area in which the staff work, they will either be under the direction and control of the Chief Constable or the management of the SPA Chief Executive. The transfer process followed the normal European guidelines which means that terms and conditions of employment are safeguarded and remain the same. Ongoing discussions relating to HR policies may see changes after negotiation and agreement.

The SPA have pledged that there will be no compulsory redundancies among police support staff, as it is anticipated that any redundancies will be through the non-replacement of people who have left as a result of retirement and voluntary exit schemes. The hope is to achieve an estimated savings of around £40 million a year. A national redundancy scheme to facilitate the reduction of police staff numbers in the new single police force is estimated to cost £60 million and has in principle the backing of Scottish ministers and the SPA. The rationale behind the plan is to cancel out any duplication of posts and to help maintain the present number of police officers across the nation, and is based on around 1400 police staff being cut. As support staff leave the service, a balance will also be maintained to ensure Police Scotland retains the right skills and expertise to continue to support the Scottish police. The SPA has introduced a number of HR policies to assist support staff during the transition period of the new Police Scotland. These include guidance on voluntary redundancy, early retirement and national redeployment schemes. A programme entitled 'Skills for transition' is available to all support staff in Police Scotland during the transition period to the single police force. This involves a set of modules that update staff in the skills required for career change, for example, transferable skills, CVs, application forms, and input on interview skills. Other modules are aimed at supervisors to ensure they are prepared for dealing with the impact of change and how to respond appropriately to their staff. This is the first national training programme of its kind in Scottish policing.

Corruption

As would be expected, Police Scotland will be negotiating new terms and conditions for police staff in the next year or so and included in the discussions will be the sensitive issue of 'anti-corruption' measures and vetting for police staff. The topic of anti-corruption methods specifically designed for police officers in the Scottish police service has been touched on in Chapters 3 and 8 but the concerns that criminal gangs are just as likely to target and corrupt police staff is very much an active issue. Attempts by the previous Strathclyde Police Force to introduce a scheme to compel police staff to declare gifts, pertinent business interests and second jobs, failed after opposition by the staff union UNISON, on the basis that their members have the right to a private life protected by the European Human Rights Convention. Unison are also of the opinion that the existing criminal and misconduct procedures are sufficient to deal with any breaches of the rule of law. Those police staff members who are presently in sensitive roles dealing with confidential information are security vetted and all police staff undergo a security check when they are first employed. The belief is that these checks would pick up on anything untoward in the private life of individual employees, which is not entirely accurate, as we see in other chapters of this book, it is not uncommon for police officers to be involved in corrupt practices and they go through a higher vetting check than their civilian colleagues. Police staff are key players in modern-day policing and many have similar access to criminal information systems as police officers and, as such, are as much a target for criminals as police officers. The police and the SPA along with trade union representatives will, one would imagine, be treating this matter with the urgency it deserves.

Emergency 999 calls

One of the many examples of the good work carried out by support staff is the duties they perform in police control rooms and manning emergency telephones. The number of 999 telephone calls answered within 10 seconds is looked on as a measure of quality of service delivered by the police in emergency situations. In 2007–2008, the figure was 91 per cent in Scotland and since 2009–2010 the figure has risen to 95 per cent and been maintained at this level for the past three years. As the number of 999 calls in 2011–2012 for the whole of Scotland was around 624,601 (SPPF 2012: 20), this is no mean achievement for the operators of the police emergency telephone service – a significant number of whom are police staff. Police support staff do similar high standard work throughout Scotland in updating crime information and performing administrative tasks in the delivery of citations, running warrants units, and analysing intelligence information and maintaining databases.

Non-police agencies

Many of us would not accept sworn police officers manning CCTV surveillance cameras on a full-time basis but are content for privately or publicly funded employees to do so within a framework of local community safety. It is also acceptable for retired police officers and police staff to be re-employed in the private and public domains where good use is made of their expertise in local initiatives and enforcement. These are normally growth posts new to the world outside the police organisation, for example, ex-detectives becoming investigatory or surveillance officers, and ex-civilian intelligence analysts using their skills at the local authority level, all within a community safety framework.

We no longer think about local policing as solely a function to be carried out by a sworn police officer as it is now widely accepted that many others can and do carry out similar roles on a regular basis, for example, retired fire-fighters, military officers, security service personnel, audit investigators, inland revenue inspectors, legal officers, and many more are re-employed by local and central government and private organisations to carry out many enforcement and investigating tasks. In addition, there are hundreds of national and local organisations and agencies with widespread enforcement responsibilities that can submit reports for consideration of criminal proceedings direct to the Scottish Prosecution Service with no police involvement. These non-police professionals regularly deal with local Procurator Fiscals on a wide range of issues, many of which impact on community safety at the local level. A small selection of agencies involved are the Scottish Fire Service, the Atomic Energy Authority, the Benefit Fraud Inspectorate, the Benefits Agency, Customs & Excise, the Data Protection Commissioner, Marine Safety, the Medicines Control Agency, the Ministry of Defence, TV Licensing, the Vehicle Inspectorate, the Forestry Commission, Health & Safety, Hydro Electric, the Inland Revenue, and many more. Within limitations, these non-police organisations have a crime prevention and enforcement role which the general public is often unaware of and which is hidden from general view.

Wildlife crime

One example of active non-police agency work is the arrangements for dealing with wildlife crime in Scotland, which were given prominence in 2008 when the HMICS and the Inspectorate of Prosecution published a full review of this type of crime across the nation (HMICS 2008). Later, in 2011, the Scottish Parliament debated the issue at length and in the following year the Wildlife and Natural Environment (Scotland) Act 2012 was published. A number of recommendations in the Act related to the work of the Partnership for Action Against Wildlife Crime (PAW) Scotland, whose membership encompasses a wide range of bodies with an interest in combating wildlife crime and includes conservation, land management, shooting and law enforcement. The point being made here is that although there is a role for the police in this important work, many of the partners have no links to law enforcement as such, but still play a crucial part in prevention and enforcement of the legislation. For example, the Executive of PAW Scotland is chaired by the Scottish Minister for the Environment and Climate Change and its members come from the police, Scottish Land and Estates, RSPB, Wild Life Management, a sheriff, a journalist, Scottish Natural Heritage, Scottish Wildlife Trust, and the Game and Wildlife Conservation Trust. PAW Scotland also has a number of working groups and sub-committees who regularly meet to discuss matters relating to tackling wildlife crime and report back to the Executive. The PAW Scotland organisation engages with all stakeholders and highlights the importance of knowledge sharing and partnership working in the fight against wildlife crime and is a continuous reminder that wildlife crime is unacceptable and has no place in modern-day Scotland. One example of progress is the introduction of Vicarious Liability in the Wildlife and Natural Environment (Scotland) Act 2012, which is designed to deal with landowners and managers who turn a blind eye to employees committing offences against wild birds on their land. There are initial signs that the new wildlife legislation is having a positive impact on the numbers of birds being poisoned in Scotland. This is just one of many examples of successful prevention and enforcement strategies carried out by non-police agencies that could be built upon in the future. The important point to remember in all this is that a police presence is not always necessary.

Oversight

Policing has broadened over the decades and in addition to sworn police officers, it is made up of police cadets, Special Constabulary, force support staff, neighbourhood and community wardens, police auxiliaries, and quasi-public and private security officers. Policing no longer has a monopoly within the law and order community. There are now many providers coming onto the market who are seriously challenging the traditional working practices of the police. Within this complex mix of community security and safety politicians and society in general have to articulate what it is they require from this new expanded system of policing and in particular what standards of service are expected of all the players. The modern police service works under increasingly robust scrutiny and governance rules and independent investigation, which is discussed later in Chapter 8. What is not so obvious is the existence of appropriate methods and mechanisms of scrutiny and oversight for the private and public non-police agencies to ensure accountability, compliance and performance levels.

The full implications of inappropriate and inadequate systems of governance and accountability in this new world of multi-policing have not yet been identified nor is the mindset 'to devise and implement institutions and mechanisms of governance and accountability that would be more suitable for this new policing environment' (Stenning 2009: 31). Taking a broader view there is a blurring of boundaries between the police and regulatory agencies, private security, the intelligence and security community and the military, and this new emerging landscape of policing and security could have 'profound implications for human rights, privacy and civic society' (Hoogenboom 2010: 6–7).

Finally, if the non-police components of the community safety model continue to extend into communities as are shown in this text, then how do the public measure the success of the services given and how are standards maintained and improved? For instance, how do we measure the contribution of the ever expanding private and voluntary sectors to community safety as separate from the police input? If plural policing and partnerships are being acclaimed as the way forward in twenty-first-century community safety and security, then new forms of measuring their impact on community crime and safety levels need to be introduced. The advent of a new single police service that speaks with one voice throughout the nation should be of assistance in the search for new improved performance measurement and governance systems.

Police Scotland

With the creation of the new Police Scotland, around 17,400 police officers and 6,000 support staff transferred over. The speculation is that many thousands of non-police staff will leave the service as a result of the mergers. A Scottish Government guarantee of no compulsory redundancies has been accepted by Police Scotland and the Scottish Police Authority. Promises have been made that efforts to reduce the support staff numbers will be through voluntary redundancies and natural wastage. This will be a tall order indeed especially with the large numbers of staff involved and the main drive for the reform to save money. After much debate it has now been accepted that the Chief Constable has control over the majority of police support staff rather than the SPA.

Five of the previous force areas, Dumfries and Galloway, Fife Constabulary, Central Scotland police, Tayside Police and Northern Constabulary, become divisions of the new Police Scotland after 1 April 2013. The new Scottish Police Authority has replaced the regional police boards which took their representation from local councillors and in so doing have raised some concerns over the scrutiny and oversight of the police being taken away from locally elected members and transferred to the SPA. The response from the SPA is that they will be in a better position to scrutinise Police Scotland and test the Chief Constable's decision-making. These issues are further discussed in Chapters 8 and 9.

It is estimated that by 1 April 2013, 1,000 support staff jobs will have been lost as a result of the police reforms. In fairness to the police and SPA officials, they do not have control of their destiny in this matter as it is the politicians who are creating the situation by introducing a policy to maintain 1000 additional police officers. And for the time being the Chief Constable has to maintain the number of officers. This claim is one the Scottish Government would deny, suggesting it is for the Chief Constable to decide how to deploy police resources. But with reducing budgets, the police are running out of ideas and are left with only one viable option – to reduce the number of support staff, which has started already.

Investigative Support Officers

As an indication of how modern policing is changing, in 2012, over 20 retired detective officers were recruited by the previous Strathclyde Police Force to support the reinvestigation of a number of unsolved murders. This came about as a direct result of changes to the 'double jeopardy legislation'. The Double Jeopardy (Scotland) Act 2011 amended the law in Scotland to allow suspects previously acquitted for a crime to be retried in particular circumstances. The former detectives are initially employed for six months to assist the investigation of cold cases dating back 30 years or so and are given the title 'investigative support officer' and work in support of the Serious Crime Review Team. The officers are recruited through an agency that interviews and selects applicants within a given criteria. The recruitment of retired officers was necessary as there is an exceptionally high workload of cold cases at the present time.

Privately funded police

According to Freedom of Information requests, the number of Scottish police officers hired by private companies has doubled in recent years to around 40 full-time posts which equates to over 8000 hours and brings in approximately £1 million to the police coffers. These figures relate to just four of the previous police forces in Scotland – Strathclyde, Lothian and Borders, Fife and Central Scotland – and the venues include shopping centres, bus groups, prisons, and housing associations. Not everyone is in agreement with the initiative as many are of the belief that the police should not be a private service for hire and voice concerns of the risk that a two-tier system of policing could result in those who pay the money getting a better service. One specific example is a police officer patrolling Loch Lomond for a fee of £35,000 per annum.

Investigative assistants

In recent years there have been a number of projects running in Scotland and England involving the use of civilians as crime investigators. In Scotland the Priority Crime Unit (PCU) was set up by the previous Central Scotland Police on 1 April 2008 and employs a number of civilian 'investigative assistants', primarily to take statements and to interview witnesses. The feedback has shown that with fewer civilian staff and police officers, these teams can cost-effectively investigate an increased number of crimes in less time (Home Office 2008; Scott and Sproat 2010). The PCU is a mix of investigative assistants and police officers with the remit to investigate volume crime. The PCU has been able to better manage workloads by matching policing tasks and responsibilities to the skills and powers of officers and staff. Those tasks which require police powers, such as apprehending and interviewing suspects and providing reports for the Procurator Fiscal, are dealt with by the police. Those duties which can be carried out by police staff trained as investigative assistants, such as interviewing victims and witnesses, carrying out door-to-door enquiries and scanning CCTV footage, are performed by the non-police officers section of the PCU. Scott and Sproat's evaluation has shown the PCU has been very successful in delivering a better quality of investigation and reducing the life cycle of lower-level crimes; in providing a very good quality of service, especially to victims of crime, which has been met by widespread acceptance and appreciation by the public; and which has released significant amounts of time for frontline officers. The success of this pilot should encourage similar initiatives in other parts of the police as there are a number of police roles that professional civilian staff could take over from police officers, such as case management preparation and minor investigative work. There is also the potential of rolling the PCU out across the new single police force.

Third party policing

A new world of 'third party policing' is emerging which describes police efforts to persuade or influence third parties such as landlords, parents, local government regulators, public housing agencies, property owners, health and building inspectors, schools, railway authorities, public utilities, and business managers to take on some responsibility for preventing crime or reducing anti-social behaviour (Mazerolle and Ransley 2005; Wood and Shearing 2007). The use of 'third party policing' is similar to that used in civil regulation. For example, in order to ensure business corporations are not involved in fraudulent practices against their clients, government regulators place civil and criminal constraints on accountants and lawyers. And in the world of athletics, sporting organisations are encouraged to self-police themselves in relation to 'drug taking'. Even banks and building societies have introduced measures to combat money laundering and organised crime and in the light of the present world economic crisis, we will be seeing more stringent controls in the financial sector. This form of regulation is pervasive in society, so it is of no surprise that such approaches are being introduced for crime control.

A similar thing is happening in Scotland in the fight against drugs, prostitution, domestic violence, anti-social behaviour and street crime. Partners are being enlisted to help police in these areas, such as property owners, parents, bar owners, government agencies, local authority workers, insurance companies, business owners, private security, transport, railways and many more who are willing to partner up with the police to take on some kind of crime prevention or crime reduction role. Practical examples include education authorities who prosecute parents for their children's non-attendance at school; licensed bar owners who help reduce drunkenness on the street; property owners and landlords maintaining the physical condition of their properties and screening potential tenants; agencies being given additional responsibility for environmental health and safety.

Such moves seek to control the behaviour and alter the routines of those parties that the police believe might have influence over a crime problem. For example, police in Scotland draw on partners such as government agencies, statutory authorities, pubs, nightclubs and shops to help with alcohol, tobacco and knife control and local disorder. Government also expects the licensed trade to pay for some of the policing of disorder in the vicinity of their premises, similar to football clubs who now pay for hundreds of stewards to police football matches. It is increasingly apparent that all parties in the community and not just the police have a role to play in maintaining community safety, especially if they indirectly contribute to the problem.

Police surgeons

Forensic and medical services are crucial to policing and maintaining an effective criminal justice system in Scotland and are delivered by qualified doctors who examine victims of crime and accused persons who are held in police custody. Payments for the service are made directly from the police budget. Many police surgeons are self-employed doctors in general practice who work for the police on a part-time call-out basis in addition to their daytime job. The workload of the police surgeons has escalated as society struggles to cope with drug and alcohol abuse, the overall rise in sexually related crimes, demands for DNA testing and the police use of CS spray, all of which require the attendance of police surgeons, regardless of the time of day. There is also a need for their attendance on many occasions when police officers are assaulted on duty; when police are called to sudden and suspicious deaths; to examine accused persons, victims of crime, drunk and drugged drivers; persons in police custody complaining of being ill or having drug withdrawal symptoms; and to take blood and other forensic samples in the course of criminal investigations.

The problem facing Police Scotland is that due to spiralling costs, the estimated bill for this service over the past three years is more than £13 million, with the highest earning police surgeon receiving over £200,000 and many more being paid over £100,000 in the past year. The new national police service is under pressure to reduce these costs as they face massive reductions in their budget. In particular, politicians and the public are now questioning the fairness and appropriateness of individuals getting six figure sums for being on call when they have highly paid jobs in addition. There is also the impractical situation of doctors in general practice working excessive hours and having their own patients to look after. Remuneration for police surgeons is set by a national committee which includes senior police officers, councillors and members of the British Medical Association. Under general guidelines they can be paid a retainer of up to £10,000 a year and can claim £80.00 for a first call-out between 7 p.m. and 8 a.m. and each subsequent examination attracts £52.00. Claims can also be made for issuing written reports and business mileage.

Police surgeons are not employees of the police and provide a service normally external to the National Health Service. Any review of this medical service will be a sensitive issue as it is vital requirement for policing, prosecution and courts service, and other branches of the criminal justice system. The issue of the sustainability of police surgeon payments comes at a time when Police Scotland is having to lay off large numbers of police civilian staff and other parts of the National Health Service are under pressure to reduce budgets and become more efficient. Some police forces currently use NHS doctors so that is an area worth investigating as is the use of hospital staff and other medical professionals. Again it is an example of non-police professionals playing a vital part in frontline policing but one that has to be fully understood and respected by the police officer who works in partnership with them.

Conclusion

Community wardens and other auxiliaries operate in Scotland and are supplemented with other local prevention and security initiatives that bring together relevant municipal bodies and the private sector. Even those agencies not normally associated with responsibilities for criminal issues, such as health, housing, education and youth work, find themselves interfacing with auxiliaries as well as local police. Included in this are street-workers and motivated local citizens, such as street pastors. A good example of this is the work done in Scottish hospitals to combat violence and domestic abuse. It is becoming increasingly difficult to fund auxiliary support in the present economic climate but what is accepted and evidenced by research is the positive contribution they make to community safety and reassurance.

When discussing the reduction in support staff numbers in the Scottish police, Atkinson came up with the interesting concept of de-civilianisation in Scottish policing which he defines as 'the process whereby a decreasing number of roles, functions and responsibilities in the police service come to be undertaken by un-sworn "civilian" police staff' (Atkinson 2011). This is of course the unforeseen consequence of a Scottish Government policy decision to maintain an additional 1000 police officers at the expense of losing substantial numbers of support staff rather than an intentional strategy of 'de-civilianisation'. In fact you would be hard pressed to find many citizens or politicians in the modern world who would support the idea of fully trained sworn police officers doing back office work that civilians normally did in the past.

The Police Federation carried out research in 2010 into the changing make-up of the police workforce in England and Wales and presented some stark findings that are relevant to Scotland. When discussing the changes in the workforce mix, the research concluded that as police posts are handed over to police staff, the remaining roles will be those that require police powers. It is said that these posts will have a higher probability of public confrontation that 'could have major implications for the relationship between the police and wider community' (Meade 2010: 3). The logic of the argument is that in order to ensure a robust and healthy community policing system, police officers need to interface with the public in non-confrontational everyday situations as well, in order to achieve the correct balance that society expects.

The reality in twenty-first-century Scotland with the continuing pressures on the public purse is that politicians of whatever persuasion and senior police leaders are duty bound to look at better ways of delivering the best value in policing, such as increased strategic partnership and collaboration with the private sector. Most senior police officers in Scotland are comfortable with a limited increase in outsourcing some police tasks to the private sector, though they may have to argue their case with the present Scottish Government. Future challenges facing the police will require investment in high-level technical support and collaboration with the private sector as they have the necessary skilled personnel and expertise.

Sustaining the high numbers of police officers will be increasingly difficult in these austere times unless additional funding is forthcoming or further savings are made in other parts of the police organisation. Police Scotland with its central control of resources is in a much better position to tackle these issues than it would have been if it had remained as eight separate units.

7

HOW DO WE DEVELOP AND PROMOTE POLICE OFFICERS?

Introduction

The police service in Scotland has come through a period in recent years when there has been a sufficiency of funding and resources. This is now changing as a result of economic constraints and a level of uncertainty exists as to the impact on future police funding. This is against the backdrop of increasing public demands and higher expectations of performance and outputs. Now more than ever before the police service is in need of highly motivated officers and staff who work towards a clear vision of where the organisation wants to be. Managing and developing the police workforce is crucial to achieving these goals particularly in challenging and testing times, as is maintaining officers' and staff morale. Earlier chapters highlighted initial training in the police and some of the courses available at the Scottish Police College. This chapter gives a brief insight into the background of the changing approach to the management and development of human resources in the Scottish police and offers some comment on the present-day police promotion system.

Police management

As far back as 1986, it was identified that among the public and those agencies that dealt with the police there was a lack of knowledge and awareness of the 'nature of police organisation and police work and of the problems involved in managing them' (Bradley *et al.* 1986: 7). This lack of knowledge and understanding could also have been levelled at a large number of police management ranks themselves, unless you were fortunate enough to be one of the chosen few who worked in police headquarter jobs and had privileged insight into the workings of the police. There was a view that 'knowledge was power' and no effort was made to share information on the internal workings of the police organisation. Middle-ranking police officers had little knowledge of how the tripartite system of policing worked on a daily basis or the machinations of police finance and the interface with local police authorities. In the words of one senior chief police officer in the 1990s, 'If divisional commanders know as much as we do, it will lead to a whole bunch of mini-fiefdoms – so the less they know, the better!' This was also the position with local elected councillors who were limited in their knowledge of the police organisation and tended to follow the guidance given by the Chief Constable – whom most councillors were in awe of! One story is told that in the 1990s a senior police officer returned to headquarters after attending a meeting on the progress of an important IT project and was incensed that one of the local councillors who was a member of the Police Authority had the 'audacity' to quiz him on how the project was progressing, and how the money was being spent and whether there were any problems! The councillor's statutory responsibility to oversee how public money is spent seemed to be forgotten. On another occasion during a high-level meeting with police and outside consultants, convened for the purpose of discussing the findings of a Police Authority-commissioned research project into the performance of the local police force, it became apparent that some of the findings were highly critical of the police organisation. It was at this point that senior police officers made it quite clear that if this report was published, they would ensure that the consultant firm would find it difficult to get another public sector contract. It was not as if the survey results were untrue or inaccurate but simply that the information was critical of the police organisation.

A principal concern of a Police Authority was always police finance, the workings of which were known to only a chosen few both inside and outside the police. Can we remember any time in the past hundred years when the Chief Constable's budget was thrown out or drastically amended? Or when complaints against senior police were rigorously pursued by a Police Board? Until Etherson's study in 2010, there had never been any meaningful research into the effectiveness of Police Boards and local Police Authorities in Scotland. The prevailing view was that until very recently Police Boards and Police Authorities had passively accepted the demands of their chief constables. This brings us to the position of the top man in policing – the Chief Constable.

The Chief Constable takes a lot on his/her shoulders and has sole overall responsibility for the efficient administration and management of police operations. Until recent times a Chief Constable could virtually do what he/she liked within their own force, formulating policies, allocating resources and the like and has always been supported by the doctrine of constabulary operational independence which dictated that neither central nor local politicians should be allowed to interfere in police operational decision-making. However, current thinking is that no public official, including a Chief Constable, can be said to be 'independent' and the phrase 'operational responsibility' rather than 'operational independence' is a more apt term to be used in modern democratic policing (Vaughan 2006: 18). Built into the tradition and culture is the assumption that Chief Constables will behave like Plato's philosopher-kings – policing being in the hands of those who, by virtue of their skills, abilities and talents, will be able to police their communities in good, impartial and intelligent ways.

To acquire these guardians of the peace, the formal process wants the candidates to come from the ranks so that they move through from constable to sergeant to inspector to chief inspector to Superintendent to Chief Superintendent to Assistant Chief Constable, then usually to Deputy Chief Constable. This ensured, it was thought, that chiefs would know all the jobs that the police force did. This might have made sense in the days when the police force of Coatbridge, say, was about 12 officers but it is not possible for a Chief Constable nowadays to know all the jobs that a police force does. How many chiefs can pilot a helicopter, train a dog, interrogate computers, or run a murder enquiry?

Times have certainly changed, a 'snapshot' of British society and its police at the time of the Royal Commission in 1962 shows a people who looked on 'drugs' as something you purchased with a prescription; 'prostitution' as a topic for the Victorian era; 'homosexuality and lesbianism' pertained to the court of Oscar Wilde; and child abuse did not exist to any degree of concern. The early 1960s was a time when in a court of law if a senior detective gave evidence that an event was factual, then that was so, and the court and jury never doubted it. It was a time when it was believed large-scale public disorder could only be dealt with by the use of 'baton', 'horse' and 'dog', with little strategic thought needed for planning or implementation of police tactics. This we know now not to be the case.

Crime intelligence consisted of a 'minority' of interested police officers forwarding on crime information, gleaned during their duty time, to be disseminated among their colleagues for the benefit of all. It was a time of low police pay and morale and unacceptable quasi-corrupt practices. It was also a time when the relationships between uniform officers and their CID contemporaries were poor and had been so for some time. Even as far back as the 1929 Royal Commission on Police Powers and Procedures, committee members commented that there was a tendency for the detective branch to 'regard itself as a thing above and apart, to which the restrictions and limitations placed upon the ordinary police do not, or should not, apply' (Home Office 1929: 40). In the 1960s a trawl for educational qualifications throughout the rank-and-file of the police service of the time would reveal the odd 'O', 'H' or 'A' level and if it was a good day, you may catch a glimpse of an elusive university degree, which normally meant that its holder was for the higher ranks, whether on merit or otherwise. The use of civilian personnel was limited to the three 'Ts': tea-making, typing and telephones. And female police officers were not allowed on patrol, being mainly confined to dealing with crimes involving women or children. This was the era when the ranks of the British police suffered from the 'demob' profile and relied heavily on officers with previous military experience keeping the organisation functioning properly. As with the business and industry sectors of the time, the police service also exhibited a glaring lack of skills and academic disciplines which needed to be addressed, particularly in the fields of technology, legal, administration, personnel and management.

On the other hand, a comparative examination of British society and policing 50 years on reveals marked changes. Illicit use of drugs has become a way of life for many citizens, resulting in heavy financial costs to the criminal justice system and the health service. Not to mention the human misery associated with drug use and addiction that cannot be measured in monetary terms. The creation of new offences during the 50-year period also added to police workloads. Growth crimes included computer crime, a wide variety of sexual crimes, anti-terrorist legislation and an extensive array of minor offences. Police workloads have spiralled over the period – there may be three times as many police officers now as in the 1950s but there are ten times as many crimes. The management and administration of police investigations have also been transformed from the *ad hoc*, piecemeal, and 'gut feeling' approach of detectives, to a more professional and systematic investigatory discipline that makes great use of new technology and forensic advances.

New police management

By the 1970s, the government's income policy was hitting the police harder than most and by 1976 the Police Federation claimed the average pay of a constable had fallen to 82 per cent of average earnings in industry. Morale had dramatically fallen and officers were leaving the service in large numbers. There were consistently high levels of manpower wastage, particularly in relation to well-trained and experienced officers, which was a primary concern of the police and the government of the day, resulting in the establishment of a Committee of Inquiry under the chairmanship of Lord Edmund Davis in 1978. The Committee was tasked to review the work of the police service, taking into account responsibilities and workloads, threats to public order, and restrictions on officers' private lives, and to make recommendations on police conditions and appropriate levels of remuneration.

The Committee accepted that the pattern of gradual slippage in the pay league was not confined to the Police Service. However, it was considered an important task to try to assess why the existing pay and conditions of service machinery had been unable to maintain a fair position for the police over the years. The Inquiry reported back in 1978 and recommended that pay scales for federated and superintending ranks should be updated in subsequent years in accordance with changes in the index of average earnings (Home Office 1978). Similar recommendations were made in relation to Chief Officers. All the recommendations were subsequently implemented by the end of the decade. As a result of implementing the Edmund Davis recommendations, good quality recruits began to flood into the police service across the nation that placed the police organisation in a favourable position for change.

Since the early 1980s, there had been major reform in other parts of the public sector, with the injection of business management principles into its organisation and management – now it was time for similar change in the police. Traditional models of public administration had been replaced by new management techniques and processes and re-titled 'new public management'. By the mid-1990s this new model of managing the public sector was introduced into the police and encompassed many philosophies, approaches and doctrines – new managerialism, market-led initiatives, entrepreneurialism and efficiency and effectiveness. A heavy emphasis on management style and less on policy and bureaucracy became dominant, with the expansion of many forms of performance measurement techniques. From these management concepts and ideas have emerged some of the techniques we still use in the police today: inputs against outputs; value for money; decentralisation and flexible management; setting of targets; objectives and goals; and performance-related pay. New public management (or new police management) had arrived with a bang into the core of policing.

It would be inaccurate to portray the police service of the time as being totally isolated from internal reform, to such an extent that all change had to be imposed externally. Comment was made on this very fact:

> There is no doubt contemporary police managers are now far more inclined to be sympathetic towards the new managerialism than their predecessors. They are likely to have been fully immersed in the philosophies of NPM [new public management] through their professional training programmes.
>
> *(Savage and Leishman, 1996: 250)*

Such views can be validated by the appearance of dedicated management training courses, at police training establishments throughout the nation during the 1990s with 'strategic management' related topics in the syllabi. However, it also became apparent there was a need for significant investment in the development of police officers and staff at all levels of the service if the new management practices were to be a success. This has continued to be the case to the present day, hence the considerable investment made by the Scottish police in human resource management policies.

The Personal Development Review

In line with most modern organisations, the Scottish police service has introduced personnel policies that enable all staff to play a role in their own career development. The national Personal Development Review (PDR) in the Scottish police is one example which allows all police officers and staff to play an active part in their own performance and development. It is a joint review of an individual's past performance and future development and covers both police officers and police support staff. In strategic terms, it is also linked to the organisation's performance as the individual's achievements and objectives must be inter-linked to the targets and goals of the wider police service for them to be relevant and meaningful. The PDR process records, analyses and discusses a person's work record and successes over a yearly period and highlights any development needs and future career plans and potential. The system is held electronically and as it is 'live', it allows for continuous update and review throughout the year. A vital part of the process is the gathering of evidence in support of the analysis of performance. So for the PDR to work effectively there has to be good communication between all parties involved – from the individual member to supervisors and management.

The PDR system developed by the Scottish police reflects similar approaches to personal development found in other private and public organisations. The PDR replaced the out-dated appraisal system for police officers introduced in the mid-1970s which never attained full credibility from rank-and-file members and did not cover police support staff.

Promotion

In the past, police officers could only be considered for a promoted post in the Scottish Police service if they had achieved a pass in a group of statutory examinations known as the Police (Scotland) Promotion Examinations. Unfortunately, by the turn of the twenty-first century the exam system was coming into some disrepute and by 2004 one in four officers due to sit the annual police promotion exams in Scotland failed to turn up, which equated to 300 out of a total of 1200 candidates. This was consistent with the previous four years and reflected an inherent problem in the police organisation for many decades when it came to police officers genuinely wishing to sit the exams and doing the necessary preparation. There were many reasons for the poor turnout – difficulties at home; officers being pressurised to sit the exams by their line managers when they did not wish to; and those few individuals who just wanted a day off work and were not interested in exams. In addition to the costs and time wastage when candidates fail to appear, there was also the concern about officers' exam marks with a significant number scoring less than 10 per cent. This led to one Federation spokesman remarking 'If they are scoring poorly in the exams, how are they performing when they are out on the beat serving the public and what confidence can their colleagues have in them?' (*Police Review* 2004: 8). At the time, the cost factor was a sensitive issue as individual police forces covered the financial outlay for the exams that included the costs of those who opted out. This led to suggestions that officers should pay a fee themselves and be reimbursed when they sit the exam. The Police Federation was not too keen on the idea of a fee unless it was a minimum amount. So it became obvious to all and sundry in the Scottish Police that the time had come for a close scrutiny of the traditional police promotion exam system.

Confidence in the ability of the police exams to prepare officers for promotion had decreased over the years to such an extent that they were replaced by the Diploma in Police Service Leadership and Management (DPSLM). The Diploma introduces a new selection system on the basis of management and leadership potential and organisational and operational knowledge. The Diploma commenced in April 2007, and by the end of the first year had around 700 students studying towards the award.

The qualification tests the students in the important areas of Leadership and Management and Policing in Scotland and the course material is delivered electronically to facilitate distance learning. The core modules of the Diploma are:

- Developing Skills for Personal Effectiveness
- Contemporary Policing
- The Criminal Justice System in Scotland
- Professional Knowledge in Policing
- Professional Ethics
- Decision Making
- Organisational Management
- People Management
- Leadership.

The programme takes 18 months to complete and involves around 8 hours of study per week. Since the introduction of the Diploma, there have been 3690 students registered and 1653 have successfully completed the course. Currently there are 923 officers doing the Diploma at some stage or other. The attrition rate in Scotland was initially high, at one point peaking at over 60 per cent but focused efforts to bring this down have been successful and the present annual attrition rate is 18.5 per cent. Officers do not pay for the Diploma at the present time as it is funded out of the central training budget with some students being supported in their local areas.

The Diploma is a prerequisite for promotion to Sergeant in Scotland as once officers have achieved the DPSLM, they are deemed to be eligible for promotion. That said, officers who have only passed the old-style police exams are still being promoted. The DPSLM offers a standardised level of competence across a nationally agreed range of skills and experience, demonstrated through the successful completion of the course. Only on the successful completion of the course can a candidate apply for promotion to Sergeant. Prior to the introduction of the new single police force, officers qualified for promotion still had to pass their own local in-force promotion process which varied depending on each force. This normally began with the submission of an application form which sought evidence in relation to the various PDR competence areas that are considered to be appropriate to the role applied for by the officer. Beyond this there would be a number of job simulation exercises to go through, culminating with some form of interview in most cases. The PDR was used as an indicator of the candidate's readiness for promotion by one force but not so in the remaining force areas. Promotions up to the rank of Chief Inspector will continue to be honoured by Police Scotland on a needs basis – Constable to Sergeant; Sergeant to Inspector; and Inspector to Chief Inspector. However, there is a moratorium on promotions from Chief Inspector to Superintendent and Superintendent to Chief Superintendent. A new promotion process for these ranks is presently being developed and will be implemented in the future by the national police service. There will be much discussion on the issue of what promotion system should be introduced for the new Police Scotland as there has been a lack of uniformity in the process to date.

For comparison purposes it is worth looking at the system in England and Wales, which differs from that in Scotland, and where the future of the existing promotion process is uncertain as their new College of Policing launched a review in 2012 into whether the current system is fit for purpose. At the present time there are around 9000 constables and sergeants qualified for promotion to the next rank with little likelihood of that happening for the majority in the next few years due to budgetary cutbacks and reduction in the number of promoted posts. In England and Wales in December 2012, out of a total of 1561 constables who took part in the Sergeants' promotion assessment centre, 1272 (81 per cent) were successful. Many believe it pointless for officers to enter into the promotion system if the chances of promotion are minimal. So there appears to be growing support for the prevailing view in modern policing to plan for the continuous development for all officers throughout their career which may now span 40 years, whereas in the past it was 30 years, with less emphasis on the end product being specifically for promotion. There are many senior police officers in England and Wales who are attracted to the Scottish DPSLM system of development and favour a move in that direction.

The Accelerated Careers Development Programme

All police officers with the requisite skills and qualifications can seek promotion and advance through the ranks if successful. Ever since the 1960s the police service has offered another accelerated pathway to promotion for those persons who display the necessary qualities for rapid advancement to the senior levels. The accelerated promotion scheme has gone under different titles over the past 50 years and ranged from a one-year full-course at the Scottish Police College, to distance learning and on-the-job management training with short visits to the college for additional tuition. The present scheme is the Accelerated Careers Development Programme (ACDP) which is structured around preparing the police officer for senior command posts in the police service. The programme is open to probationary officers, constables and sergeants with the necessary skills and abilities and who possess the commitment, desire and ambition to progress in the service.

The ACDP is linked to the Senior Careers Development Programme (SCDP) which supports police superintendent ranks and equivalent police staff grades in their career ambitions. In the past it was acknowledged that there was a need for developmental support for those officers in senior management posts in the Scottish police. In response, the Scottish Police College set up the Senior Careers Development Service (SCDS) in 2007 with a remit to enhance the leadership capability and capacity in the police service to meet the growing challenges at senior strategic levels. There are various developmental streams available for specific groups, such as chief officers; graduates of the Senior Command Course; candidates for the Senior Command Course; and many more. The ACDP is one such stream which offers students development opportunities tailored for their profile. For most of its existence the ACDP offered an entry path to both graduates and undergraduates from outside the service. This has changed and the ACDP for the present at least is only open to in-service eligible probationers, constables and sergeants from the Scottish police service and the British Transport Police. The three access routes are:

- Probationary Officers – with a minimum of 12 months service who have been performing satisfactorily;
- Constables – outwith their probation whether qualified for promotion or otherwise;
- Sergeants.

There is no requirement for applicants to be degree qualified and unlike in the past the ACDP is no longer open to inspector rank or external graduate entrants.

Diversity

There are equality and diversity streams also available through the SCDS which focus on 'under-represented' groups, such as the Women's Development Forum (WDF), the Gay Police Association (GPA), SemperScotland, and the Strathclyde Police Women's Association (SPWA). The SCDS has facilitated workshops, meetings, and liaison with national diversity groups. The SCDS is continually on the lookout for other minority groups and is always willing to offer support.

An HMICS study in 2007 focused on the diversity impact of promotion policies on female officers and those from black and ethnic minority communities (BME). The findings showed an under-representation for female officers at the time but that has now improved in recent years. Due to a small number of BME officers eligible for promotion, it was difficult to draw any sound conclusions. There was a perception in the Scottish police that female officers were generally unlikely to apply for promotion until they had all the officially recognised requisite skills, whereas their male colleagues were likely to apply when they believed they had most of the desired skills. No evidence was found that suggested there was anything inherently discriminatory about the promotion processes (HMICS 2007). Although numbers of female officers at the highest levels in the service were low at the time, things have improved over the years but there is still some way to go (see Chapter 2). The more members of minority groups are promoted, the more role models there will be for others to aspire to, whether it be females or BEM. Unfortunately, as was discussed earlier, we are some way off from having an appropriate number of BEM officers in senior posts. The HMICS highlighted the need for the police to guard against 'discriminatory practices' and ensure there are fair and proper career development and promotion processes in place and that the benefits of external advertisement outside the resident force should be encouraged at all times.

A prerequisite to attaining chief officer rank in the UK police is successful attendance on the Strategic Command Course (SCC), and at the time of writing the criterion for police officers applying for the SCC (including Scottish officers) is to hold the rank of superintendent or chief superintendent and have their chief constable's endorsement that they are ready for promotion to chief police officer. No black or ethnic minority (BEM) officers from the UK applied to attend the SCC in 2013. The successful candidates for the course numbered 27 males and 8 females from across the UK which also included senior police staff but no BEM students. This gives rise to the concern that a lack of BEM candidates for upcoming SCCs creates the prospect of an imbalance of community representation at the chief officer level due to the lack of BEM participation. Over the years there have been extensive efforts by the police service to develop talent from diverse backgrounds across the UK but with limited success. However, there are a number of BEM officers who believe they are not ready for additional responsibility for senior command or to go on the SCC. Others believe they may not receive the necessary support or endorsement at the local level. And of course there are always those officers regardless of ethnicity who are content to remain at the superintendent and chief superintendent levels for whatever reason.

Though the police service continues to develop initiatives that encourage talented officers to realise their potential in their police career, the right balance of prospective talent has to be brought into the service initially.

Leadership

Traditionally, leadership has been regarded as a key factor in policing and differing leadership styles and types of leaders have been widely debated in the academic literature for some time. It is safe to assume that most police officers of whatever rank have received some input on leadership on their training courses and been given an opportunity to consider how a leader can lead by example. Other approaches include distinguishing between leaders and managers; understanding the importance of strong leadership, and identifying leadership styles. There is an acceptance that at the highest levels of the police organisation, leadership is crucial to establishing direction and priorities, to implementing change in policing policies, strategies and culture, and to producing effective policing performance. In addition, in most new and developing situations such as the present police reform in Scotland, there is the need for strong management at all levels and not just at the top. Some leading management scholars believe leaders and managers do similar things as they are both responsible for the same things, such as deciding what needs to be done; appointing people and developing relationships to achieve it; and ensuring people do the job.

However, an opposing argument would suggest a number of tasks leaders may have that managers do not. For example, managers are responsible for the setting of targets and objectives, resource planning, budgets, delegation, and monitoring performance, whereas we look to leaders for vision; strategy; being a good communicator with all partners; as a source of direction; effective motivation; and being a factor in the organisation's ethics and values.

A good leader is expected to be a good planner and strategist but then that is the same for a good manager. And just as it is important that an organisation has the right leadership that suits its goals and objectives – the wrong type of leader could have a negative impact on an organisation's goals. An example of this relates to one Scottish police force in the 1990s that was experiencing high levels of violent crime and use of firearms across its region. On the arrival of a new Chief Constable, the question was asked of the Assistant Chief Constables as to what they were doing about the disturbing increase in this type of crime. The ACCs explained the set-up in the force was one of devolved responsibility given to Divisional Commanders and CID and that the strategy was down to them. The new Chief Constable quickly replied that the question he had asked was 'What are *you* doing about the rise in violent crime?' In other words, where is the vision, strategy, motivation, direction, communication and the plan to attack the problem? From that day onward the force adopted a more strategic style of leadership.

This is not the place for a lecture on leadership styles though an awareness of different styles helps define an organisation's leadership and leads to a better understanding of how the organisation works. Although theoretical knowledge of appropriate leadership styles is important, actions often speak louder than words. Nothing will build and sustain credibility more than a police leader/manager leading by example. Whether you help out when things are tough, or are the first to ask the hard questions, or are willing to admit when you got it wrong. The leader sets the standard for his/her officers and staff who will be observing closely as to whether the leader also meets those standards. Though training and development of leaders/managers are crucial to an organisation's success, it should be remembered that there is no 'one-size-fits-all' model. A mix of leadership styles and management approaches reflecting an organisation's needs would appear to be the preferred option.

There is more to police leadership in the modern day than having charisma, sharing a vision and adopting a high profile, they have to lead by dictating policy and do so openly in a manner that not only shows a high regard for the safety of the community but with an empathy with officers and staff who have the 'coalface' responsibility to deliver the policy outcomes. Scottish police leaders have attempted to address this by producing meaningful pragmatic policies that can be easily understood by frontline officers and assist them in developing action plans, tactical briefings, local plans and orders, and objectives and targets. One example is the ACPOS diversity guidance issued to the police service in the form of an easy-to-read 'booklet' that covers the police response to age, disability, faith and religion, gender, gypsy travellers, lesbianism, gay, bisexual and transgender, mental health, race and asylum and hate crime (ACPOS 2008). The document recognises the need for officers and staff to have the necessary knowledge and understanding to enable them to respond to the various minority groups in society and to make decisions and take action, and enhance the quality of service offered.

The Scottish police have through the Scottish Police College for some time recognised the need to support middle to senior ranking officers in their career development as managers and leaders. This allows officers at Inspector, Chief Inspector and Superintendent rank and police support staff equivalent to select modules tailored to their individual needs and flexible enough to minimise abstractions from the workplace. The programme is also linked to the national PDR competencies, national occupational standards and integrated competency frameworks to ensure it is based on national quality standards. Some examples of existing modules are:

- Ethics, Equality and Diversity
- Financial Management
- Effective Leadership
- Business Management Principles
- Operational Command
- Police Incident Officer Training
- Firearms Tactical Commander
- Match Commander (Football).

The ongoing programme at the SPC continues to be delivered successfully with a consistently average satisfaction rating of 90 per cent. The programme also draws upon the expertise from within the police service and other public sector areas, making considerable financial savings in lecturing fees.

Vetting

Chief police officers and other individuals in specific sensitive roles require to be vetted. This is over and above the normal vetting checks all police officers have to go through during the recruitment stage. This 'high level' vetting normally involves one of two vetting checks. First, there is the National Security Vetting (NSV) which is carried out by the Foreign and Commonwealth Office or the Defence Vetting Agency. Second, is Police Personnel Vetting which is carried out by local vetting units. These arrangements are due to change in England and Wales as vetting will be handed over to the new College of Policing. Local vetting deals with recruitment vetting, management vetting and enhanced management vetting, and depends on the level of access a chief officer requires to sensitive police information. According to present guidelines the vetting should be updated every five years but could be earlier if the person's circumstances change. The NSV deals with various levels of security clearance, including counter-terrorism vetting checks. The level required for both procedures normally depends upon the nature of the officer's role and the level of restricted information he or she has access to on a regular basis, regardless of rank. Vetting is an essential safeguard to ensure those with access to sensitive information are thoroughly security checked to the correct level. Some of the checks can take months to complete and can include interviewing a subject's friends and colleagues and people they have regular contact with such as employers and partners. The end result is to formulate a pen-picture of the subject which may highlight an issue of potential concern.

Well-being

It is now an accepted fact that employee well-being in any organisation is linked to overall performance. Police work by its nature can be both dangerous and stressful and with the added pressures of meeting targets, goals and objectives, the role is becoming increasingly demanding. Measuring police officers' well-being and levels of stress is now seen as essential to improving the performance of policing (Juniper *et al.* 2010: 561). The first place to start has always been the police shift patterns which numerous surveys have shown increase fatigue and sickness, have a negative impact on family life and are a hindrance to delivering a good quality work–life balance. Police medical officers have always been staunch critics of police shift patterns and continually strive to work with police management to achieve better systems. Police regulations do not help, due to their inflexibility and regular last-minute duty changes, and the infamous court attendance which is normally outwith the control of the police exacerbates the best laid plans. The core problem is the nature of police work and the statutory responsibility for the police service to ensure the appropriate numbers of police officers are on duty at the right time, in the right place and with the correct skills, in order to protect the public and combat crime. On top of this the public expect an efficient model of community policing to be running effectively and not interrupted too much by mainstream response policing – it has never been easy.

Freedom of information requests across the previous eight police forces have shown that police officers and support staff absences due to stress have risen by a third over the past four years with around 533 officers and staff being off work due to stress in 2011–2012 compared to 390 in 2008–2009: a 37 per cent rise. Although there are various reasons for stress in the police, the ongoing police reforms in Scotland will be a contributory factor for some. Particularly for support staff who are seeing their numbers diminish as the eight forces merge to form the new single police service. In 2012, a survey was carried out by the trade union UNISON Scotland which suggested that over 1000 support staff posts had already gone, with at least 53 per cent of the jobs being covered by police officers (UNISON Scotland 2012). UNISON Scotland has been calling on the Scottish Government to commit to a more balanced police service and claims if the present situation continues with vast reductions in support staff being replaced by untrained police officers, then it is a retrograde step back to the 1970s and all that has been gained in the previous decades will be lost. Valuable expertise will disappear from the police service and will be difficult to regain as staff will have left.

On the issue of well-being and welfare, there are Occupational Health and Welfare services widely available in the Scottish police service and with the nature of the job they are regularly used. All police and support staff receive specific inputs on stress in the workplace and supervisors are aware of causes and symptoms and receive counselling tuition to assist staff. The causes of stress in the police organisation are many and include long hours worked and shifts; type of role and workload/overload; relationships at work, particularly with your boss; lack of career development such as promotion prospects or move to another job; organisational structures and procedures; and home and work interface and personal demands. Though each individual has his/her own method of reducing stress, the important thing is to be aware of it and understand how to self-manage the problem when it arises. Either by removing the cause such as reducing workloads or moving jobs or changing roles; taking up physical exercise or engaging in relaxation exercise. In some instances the solution to stress at work can be part-time working to reduce hours to a more manageable level. In any event, police managers and supervisors receive training on identifying the causes of stress and possible solutions and the topic is fully covered in the DPSLM syllabus.

As an aside, the police organisation has always assisted serving and retired personnel whenever they are in need of welfare support, and this is made possible through charitable police benevolent funds administered by the Police Federation. Each local police force had its own benevolent fund but with the merger of forces in 2013 these funds have combined into the Scottish Police Benevolent Fund, which is a registered charity. This will not affect the rights of individuals continuing to seek assistance as they did in the past. The main objective of the Fund is to assist, by monetary grants, members and ex-members, and their widows and dependants who have pressing welfare needs. The Fund can also give grants and other extraordinary expenses in connection with illness, accident, death or serious emergency, and make appropriate donations to charitable organisations. This is another indication of the inherent interest exhibited by the Scottish police officer in the social welfare of others, whether within the police organisation or outside of it.

Part-time police officers

Maintaining a highly motivated police workforce in the modern world goes hand-in-hand with flexible working practices to suit the varying needs of officers and staff. The Scottish police have recognised this for some time and made available part-time and career breaks for all personnel. Part-time work has normally been associated with low-paid non-professional jobs but not so in the present day. In the police service, for example, many part-time workers are in well-paid professional positions (Hyde 2008). As can be seen from Table 7.1, the popularity of part-time working has increased in the Scottish police service by approximately 13 per cent (FTE) and 11 per cent (headcount) over the past three years.

The police service found the management of part-time working difficult in its initial years but this has gradually improved and not all part-timers are female officers and police staff. In 2012, around 6 per cent (headcount) of the total of part-time workers were males. Many male officers are attracted to this form of working with its offer of flexibility to an individual in the busy hectic life of the modern world. In some instances, part-timers are given their own status and specific job. With police pensionable age being increased, the likelihood is the number of part-timers will rise in the future as the rigours of police work take their toll. The management of part-time police officers will become an issue just as much as disabled police officers and absence management when the numbers increase

TABLE 7.1 Full-time/part-time breakdown (Scottish police officers), 2010–2012

	2010	*2011*	*2012*
Male			
Full-time	12,912	12,735	12,664
Part-time (headcount)	44	43	49
Part-time (FTE)	35.2	34.3	36.9
Female			
Full-time	3,978	4,027	4,097
Part-time (headcount)	698	750	789
Part-time (FTE)	498.7	542.7	575.3
All officers			
Full-time	16,890	16,762	16,761
Part-time (headcount)	742	793	838
Part-time (FTE)	533.9	577.0	612.3
Total headcount	17,632	17,555	17,599
Total FTE	17,423.9	17,339.0	17,373.3

Source: Scottish Government (2012e).

significantly. What has to be remembered is that if there were no flexible working arrangements in place, the likelihood is that many would leave the police service and take with them valuable skills.

Conclusion

Universities and academia in Scotland are playing an increasing role in police leadership development and the police organisation has shown a willingness to work with education establishments in preparing courses and qualifications, such as the DPSLM. This is an effective way of ensuring the necessary skills to face future challenges are kept up to date. We only have to go back to 1962 when the Royal Commission informed us that there were no graduates in the police, with 1 per cent having 'A' levels and 10 per cent with five or more GCSE equivalent qualifications (Home Office 1962). Now police managers are highly qualified and still continue their development into postgraduate studies. Continuous professional development and the pursuit of looking to be as good as you can be at your job, are the way forward in most modern organisations not just the police service.

One of the main benefits of being a police leader is that they have all undergone at least 20 years police duties dealing with the public on a daily basis. You do not forget this and most senior police officers will admit it was one of the most enjoyable periods in his/her career and an invaluable experience that has greatly assisted them in their senior command role. Police leaders in Scotland are going to have to manage uncertainty in a changing environment in difficult economic times. In the past, chief police officers would regularly interface with their local Police Authority or Police Board but due to the introduction of Police Scotland, the situation will change and in all probability the chief constable and his deputies will spend more of their time with central politicians and the SPA as they will have more to do with issues on a national scale. This leaves the Assistant Chief Constables, Chief Superintendents and Superintendents to liaise with local politicians – the logical thing to do. These new collaborations will require additional skills and changing attitudes and perspectives to be adopted by these senior and executive police officers. The ACC will deal with things the CC normally dealt with and the Superintendent and Chief Superintendent ranks will fulfil duties previously carried out by the ACCs. An expansion of the Scottish Police College's continuous professional development programme with the addition of new modules to assist with these new-found responsibilities would be the logical next step.

Merging the eight Scottish police forces has removed a significant number of chief officer posts and although it reduced the overall bureaucracy of the previous ACPOS system and greatly improved the lines of communication and accountability, it has also resulted in a slowdown of career movement at the Superintendent and Chief Superintendent levels as there are fewer posts to move on to. Add to this an increase in retirement age and the ongoing economic constraints and budget cuts and it seems there will be a log jam at this level in the future. Similar situations in other organisations have created an environment where it is difficult to retain quality people with the right skills. All that would be needed is a change in the police pension regulations so that pensions become more flexible and transferable and the police service could be faced with the threat of losing many of its talented officers. This may be hypothetical and sceptical at present but so was a single police force three or four years ago. Fortunately, the majority of Scottish police officers do not aspire to these positions.

Prior to the 1980s, promotion was a long road in the Scottish police unless you were one of the fortunate individuals who gained rapid promotion for a variety of reasons. For the vast majority of officers, selection was part of a waiting game as you had to do your apprenticeship on the beat and then move on to specialist uniform duties or gain an appointment to the CID or Traffic. In most cases it was a case of 'dead men's shoes' and wait your turn. The story goes that in the Glasgow CID, officers could work out the promotion moves years before they happened as the staff moved desks as the promotions occurred and everyone knew whose turn it was next. This method of human resource management in the police seemed to work for the organisation but pressure on the police brought change in the 1970s as there was a need for new blood and organisational reform and a feeling prevailed that the right individuals were not getting into the key managerial posts necessary to bring about innovation and change.

This chapter has shown how the Scottish police service and the Scottish police officer did change and adapt over time and how the new Police Scotland and the Scottish Police College are in a favourable position to offer high quality tuition and relevant courses to officers of all ranks to prepare them for the challenges that lie ahead.

8

WHO OVERSEES THE POLICE IN SCOTLAND?

Introduction

Police governance and accountability in Scotland have always been high on the political agenda. When considering both terms it is important to focus on who instructs the police to take a particular course of action and who gives them the means to do so. In the past, in Scotland, the position was fairly clear as it had a tripartite system of police governance with central government, the chief constable and the local police authority each having a role to play in the oversight of the police. All parties went to great lengths to ensure that the police were responsive to local needs and that neither level of politician interfered with the chief constable's 'operational independence' safe in the knowledge that the police were still accountable to the rule of law and to the courts of the land. Now that Scotland has a national police service with significant changes to their constitutional set-up and the addition of non-elected players in the form of the Scottish Police Authority, the question arises as to who oversees the Scottish police and who are they accountable to in twenty-first-century Scotland? At the same time 'new accountabilities' in the public sector have a direct impact on the police, such as Audit Scotland, Inspectorates, and the Police Investigations and Review Commissioner. The key issue now in the twenty-first century is how these changes will impact on the independence of the police and whether the developing system of police governance is adequate in the present day.

There are now more than the traditional players in policing and security, the appearance of a variety of performance audit groups, changing inspectorate roles, increased accountability to local communities and other organisations through multi-agency partnerships, community planning and safety, freedom of information, and the strengthening of the police complaints procedures, all present a formidable scrutiny machine for policing in the twenty-first century. The police organisation is well aware it needs to demonstrate fairness and transparency in its dealings with the public but the dilemma for the police is how to balance openness with the effective provision of a law enforcement service. Meeting the requirements of these 'new accountabilities' requires time, energy and resources and runs the risk of diverting attention away from the primary role of the police. As a consequence, the new Police Scotland will have to respond to the expressed needs of its communities and manage and prioritise its resources in ways that are efficient and effective. An additional challenge will be to find effective strategies for coping with the new checks and balances in the ever-changing landscape of police accountability and governance.

Accountability plays a key role in the democratic process of police governance and is simply a mechanism for citizens to receive an accurate account of how the police organisation makes decisions and utilises power delegated to them by the citizenry. In other words, the public are willing to co-operate and play their part in policing but there has to be a system of holding the police to account. An accountable system can include overseeing how police resources are used, measuring performance, being involved in setting police objectives and plans, appointing senior police personnel, ensuring equality and diversity, setting budgets, upholding human rights, and enforcing priorities and improvements in policing (Donnelly 2013: 130). On the other hand, governance of public organisations can mean government, oversight, control and direction and often embraces non-governmental bodies and agents in the private sector. It can also encompass bodies at the executive, legislative and judicial levels, agencies within civil society, police management, and the media.

This chapter gives a general overview of police oversight and governance in Scotland at a time of constitutional changes to policing and therefore does not have all the answers. The important message is that there are now many players in policing and community safety, some are at the frontline delivering the service and the others are in the oversight role. This chapter will try and identify most of these players.

Police governance

Up until 1 April 2013, the governance of policing in Scotland was a shared responsibility between central government ministers, eight local government police boards/authorities and the eight chief constables. The members of police boards in Scotland were all elected politicians chosen by their council reflecting the political balance. In a 2009 survey of police board members, 81 per cent stated they had shown an interest in joining the police board prior to their selection, the remaining 19 per cent were chosen without showing any prior interest in police board business. In addition, members of police boards also had other council responsibilities to perform and over 90 per cent of the survey respondents indicated that they were on at least three local authority committees or sub-committees as well as the police board (Etherson 2010). Police board duties carried out by members normally included finance, management, human resources and governance. Nearly three-quarters of respondents indicated they had some experience in management but only half had any experience in finance, and around 40 per cent had some experience in human resources and/or governance. The general profile of the average police board member was found to be male, at least 56 years of age and relatively new as a councillor and police board member and on average spending around two hours per week on police business. The survey uncovered little evidence that existing police board members had above-average experience or knowledge of policing. This brief insight into the experience and capability of those charged with the overseeing of policing in the past is a concern as many would have had an important role in community safety and planning and a key part to play in Best Value responsibilities within the police authority.

The previous tripartite system of police oversight of the eight Chief Constables has now ceased with the establishment of Police Scotland and the one Chief Constable now has control and direction of policing across the whole nation and is overseen by the Scottish Police Authority (SPA) with its non-elected membership appointed by Scottish ministers. The SPA has the statutory responsibility to maintain Police Scotland through its budget, human resource management and procurement. Scottish Ministers still set the overall strategic framework for policing and decide on the final police budget, and can also give some specific direction to the Chief Constable or SPA, such as the level of police numbers and priorities in fighting crime that the police should consider when developing policy, for example, sex offenders, domestic violence, and sectarianism. The previous tripartite system may not now be with us but local politicians still have their traditional statutory role as elected members of questioning the actions of the police and the non-elected SPA has a significant part to play in overseeing policing. The Chief Constable's and the Scottish ministers' key roles and responsibilities for policing still remain though modified by recent legislation. In the past, the eight Chief Constables were in charge of eight different budgets but now decision-making has been centralised with the creation of Police Scotland. This places the single Chief Constable in a more powerful position and this has been recognised by the Scottish Parliament and additional scrutiny measures have been built into the reform legislation.

The SPA has considerable powers to oversee the new Police Scotland organisation and hold the chief constable to account for the policing of Scotland, maintain the police service, and allocate financial resources. Initial disagreements as to who should have control over finance and support staff have been resolved in the interim period at least, with the intervention of the Justice Secretary, who directed the Chief Constable has the primary role in most instances. Resistance to change always accompanies major reform in any organisation and police reform is no different, especially with the emergence of an extremely powerful chief constable at the head of a national police force. Politicians and the public are already calling for closer scrutiny of the single police service, in addition to what existed before in the regional police forces and that offered by the new legislation. Initial problems between the new chief constable and the SPA as to who has the ultimate responsibility for certain human resource management and technological issues have drawn criticism from some politicians as to who is in charge of policing in Scotland, and calls have been made for more clarity in the roles of all the key players. The Justice Committee of the Scottish Parliament is so concerned with the issue that it has set up a sub-committee with cross-party representation to help oversee the introduction of the new single police service. The committee will meet four times a year. One thing for certain is that senior police officers in Scotland will have to get used to the tighter monitoring system that will emerge and accept this is part of modern democracy.

Local accountability

The introduction of local policing plans for all of the 32 local authority areas along with 353 ward-level community policing plans will reassure communities they are being listened to and ensure a heightened accountability in the new Police Scotland. New scrutiny arrangements will also accompany these changes and local councillors and community members will have hands-on roles to play in close partnership with the 14 local police commanders. Local community councils are still active at the local level and play a key part in community planning and community safety strategies and have a significant input into local policing plans. Ever since their introduction in the 1970s, community councils have given local communities a voice to express their views to the appropriate local authority and public services such as the police and housing. Policing is frequently under intense political and media pressure and it has long been recognised that successful policing cannot be achieved without the consent and cooperation of the public. Consequently, the relationship between police and local politicians is seen to be an essential feature in public consultation.

The arrival of Police Scotland with local councillors being given a lesser role in police governance should not reduce the legitimacy of local elected politicians to ask questions of their local divisional police and hold them to account. After all, the local councillor will have had an input into the development of the local policing plan with its targets and objectives and have every right to ask questions of their local police if things are not going according to plan. It follows that close contact is also maintained between police and local agencies such as housing, education, social work and a series of other local representatives. For example, ethnic groups, neighbourhood watch, crime prevention panels, voluntary organisations, victim support and many more, who are given the opportunity to voice opinions and concerns on a wide range of policing issues and in an indirect manner, hold the police to account. This local accountability network which has been working effectively for many decades will continue and will in all likelihood be strengthened and become more meaningful with the introduction of the local policing plans. It should also facilitate the dispersal of power away from the centre down to the local level although we should remember that local government exists at the whim of central government and is created by an Act of Parliament. Scottish policing has had a long history and close relationship with municipal authorities and the general public, and from that has developed a genuine concern for the public good and well-being of the community. As a direct result of this association the police have always been willing to go a step further than their primary role as crime-fighter and have repeatedly shown this to be the case in the past 40 years. So it would be highly unlikely for the new Police Scotland to change its community-centred approach to policing as a result of the recent constitutional changes. The message being delivered by the new Police Scotland is that local services will still be locally delivered and communities will have access to specialist services and equipment whenever it is needed and for some areas of Scotland this will be for the first time ever. The important point is that statutorily there will be more scrutiny and accountability at the local level than ever before.

The Police Investigations and Review Commissioner

In an article in *The Spectator* which covered the publication of the Report of the Royal Commission on the Police in 1962, specific mention of the arguments presented by the Commission opposing the taking of any power from the police to investigate themselves was described as 'quite unconvincing and unacceptable naïveté' (*The Spectator* 1962: 740). Unfortunately for the police service and the general public, this comment was shown to be correct. By the early 1990s, police corruption within the Metropolitan Police was so pervasive that it caused the then Police Commissioner Sir Paul Condon to state that 'I do have a minority of officers who are corrupt, dishonest and unethical. We believe, sadly, that they commit crimes, they neutralise evidence in important cases, and they betray police operations and techniques to criminals' (McLaglan 2003). Intriguingly, 20 years later, the Independent Police Complaints Commission (IPCC) in England and Wales refused to allow the Metropolitan Police to investigate the police shooting of a misidentified terrorist suspect in the Stockwell Underground in London on 22 July 2005, and did the investigation themselves with the full support of the public. To the credit of the Scottish police service, there has never been a suggestion that embedded police corruption has ever existed within its precincts. Nonetheless, any complacency when dealing with the potential of wrongdoing and corruption in any organisation carries an unacceptable risk, especially in the modern day with increasing financial pressures and temptations. The police service is not immune to this.

An essential mechanism to holding the police accountable is the existence of an efficient and effective police complaints system which ensures members of the public have the confidence that all complaints against a police officer, police force and other police bodies will be taken seriously and robustly investigated. Being able to analyse complaint data is also a valuable tool for managers when measuring the quality of service being provided by personnel under their command, such as letters of complaint or appreciation. To secure the trust and confidence in a police complaints system there has to be an element of independence, gone are the days when citizens accept the police investigating police.

Since 2007, Scotland has had a Police Complaints Commissioner for Scotland (PCCS) who is appointed by Scottish ministers with the main role of reviewing how police forces handle non-criminal complaints against the police, with the local prosecutor (the Procurator Fiscal) having the responsibility of directing and supervising the police in the investigation of criminal complaints involving police officers. Criminal malpractice in the activities of police officers in Scotland over the years has been minimal and the existing system of investigation has generally worked well. However, with the tide of practice elsewhere in the policing world being one of independent investigation of police complaints, there was an obvious need for reform.

As of the 1 April 2013 the Police and Fire Reform Act 2012 changed the role and remit of the existing Police Complaints Commissioner for Scotland (PCCS) and renamed the PCCS the Police Investigations and Review Commissioner (PIRC). However, in addition to the existing PCCS functions, the most important change is that for the first time in Scotland, the PIRC offers the provision of independent investigation into policing in Scotland, conducting investigations into criminal and serious misconduct allegations against the police, as well as investigating death or serious injury in police custody or following police contact, police use of firearms, complaints against senior officers and any relevant police matters where the Commissioner considers it would be in the public interest to do so. In addition to the Commissioner, there is a Director of Investigations who is a retired Detective Chief Superintendent and a Head of Investigations who previously was a regional manager for the Care Inspectorate which inspected local authorities' delivery of social work services and monitored children's agencies. In the new role, the Head of Investigations will lead a team of 20 investigators and coordinate all investigations and deputise for the Director when required. The team of investigators have a wide spectrum of investigative experience from a range of backgrounds – not just the police service. These backgrounds can include the private sector, insurance, tax revenue, health and safety, fire service, trading standards, military, and many more. The idea is to attract the best investigators with a broad experience and to develop them into an independent and efficient team. The PIRC will also call on other services as needs, for example, forensics, communications, technical, IT, and others if required, and not necessarily from within the police service.

As for the statistics of police complaints, at the time of writing, complaint allegations against the police in Scotland increased by 13 per cent in the year 1 April 2011 to 31 March 2012 a total of 7933 allegations compared to 7009 the previous year. Noting that one complaint case can contain a number of allegations, there was also a rise of 4 per cent in complaint cases which were up to 4206 from the previous year (PCCS 2012). The most common type of complaint falls into the category where it is thought officers have not carried out their duty well and amounts to 37 per cent. Incivility amounted to around 15 per cent where an officer is seen to have acted in a rude or inappropriate manner, and neglect of duty amounted to around 12 per cent and related to officers who failed to perform a duty. Although the number of complaints has increased, cases submitted to the Procurator Fiscal alleging a crime may have been committed fell from 649 to 479 a drop of 26.2 per cent. Although there are areas of rising numbers for the period, the general message from the PCCS (now PIRC) is that the overall picture for the long term is one of declining numbers of complaints made against the police in Scotland.

All too often when discussing police complaints there is a one-sided emphasis on the police with little scrutiny of the persons making the complaint. This is appropriate in most instances but as most police officers will tell you there is a small group of 'persistent' complainers who can cause major difficulties for the police organisation. So while having an independent, accessible and transparent complaints system does have its advantages, it is not to say all service users will end up satisfied. The police organisation, more than most public sector bodies, has to deal with persistent 'complainers' who are rarely satisfied and utilise a disproportionate amount of police time and effort. Research published in 2012 describes this group of complainers as 'querulous' meaning they are complainers by nature, and can demonstrate anger, aggression, and are threats to themselves and others, can be dishonest and have their own strong views of how the complaint should be dealt with, and if the result is not to their liking, then they will repeat the complaint to other agencies (SoFMH 2012). Police organisations regularly have to strive to satisfy what are usually 'unreasonable and unrealistic expectations – sometimes at the expense of the majority of service users' (ibid.). This research revealed that when dealing with complaints against the police, it is not always one-sided and police can find themselves in lengthy conflict with an individual with no end in sight.

ACPOS

Prior to the introduction of the Police Service of Scotland on 1 April 2013, the coordination and the development of the Scottish Police Service was overseen by the Association of Chief Police Officers Scotland (ACPOS). A collective group made up of eight Chief Constables, nine Deputy Chief Constables, 14 Assistant Chief Constables, and a number of senior civilian police staff. In the past, criticism had been made by the Public Audit Committee, the Justice Committee, the Auditor General for Scotland and the HMICS, of the lack of transparency and accountability of ACPOS and that the only avenue for effective accountability was through the local police authorities holding individual Chief Constables to account. This proved to be a less than satisfactory arrangement and drew criticism from Scottish ministers among others. All this is now somewhat academic as ACPOS ceased to exist on 1 April 2013 with the creation of Policing Scotland and, as mentioned earlier, a new structure for monitoring and coordination in the single police force was introduced comprising the Chief Constable, the Scottish Police Authority and Scottish ministers.

In fairness to ACPOS, it could never be accused of standing still when it came to developing police policy, and as a professional body it produced a set of modern strategic policies for the guidance of the eight Scottish forces. Policy development was categorised by nine Business Areas:

- Crime
- Criminal Justice
- Finance Management
- Information Management
- Operational Policing
- People Development and Diversity
- Performance Management
- Professional Standards
- Road Policing.

The problem was that numerous individual and specific policies were introduced under each of these Business Areas, which involved a myriad of committee and sub-committee meetings accompanied by frequent correspondence to all corners of Scotland. At its height, ACPOS had become a self-perpetuating bureaucracy which in reality had no statutory foundation. Though never challenged by local government, over time central government politicians and watchdog bodies became critical of the ACPOS position and voiced the need for reform. Reform has now taken place and the need for ACPOS is no more. It is highly unlikely that the new national police management and coordination structure will be as cumbersome and over-bureaucratic as that of the past.

As for ACPOS's equivalent counterpart in England and Wales, a similar set-up existed to that in Scotland with most of the work done by volunteers from the chief officer ranks on a national basis with no extra remuneration and in addition to their day jobs. Though this may be a cost-effective way of carrying out important strategic policy-making, it does detract from chief officers' primary role as senior managers of their local police forces, employed by local politicians on behalf of their constituents. Government funding for ACPO ceased at the end of 2012 and as ACPO is a limited company, the belief is that the present system of ACPO leadership and national coordination could continue with funding solely from chief constables, if costs were kept to a minimum. The introduction of the new College of Policing in England and Wales will assimilate ACPO's non-operational business areas. At the time of writing, ACPO is still in negotiation as to what its future role will be.

The Justice Committee

A central premise of the Scottish Parliament is its promise of a more open and transparent government. One way of achieving this has been through the creation of strong parliamentary committees. The Parliament has set up cross-party committees which are wide-ranging in their roles. There are 17 parliamentary committees that in many respects are seen as the 'driving force' of the Parliament.

Eight of the committees are mandatory – Audit, Equal Opportunities, Europe, Finance, Public Petitions, Procedures, Standards and Subordinate Legislation. The remaining nine are subject committees, which can be modified or amended at each Parliamentary session. The Justice Committee falls into this category and is one of the busiest committees in the Parliament.

Committees not only shadow the work of a particular ministerial department, they have a part to play in initiating as well as scrutinising legislation and in conducting enquiries into subjects of their own choosing. All public sector agencies have therefore come to expect an increase in parliamentary scrutiny and monitoring to ensure that satisfactory standards and levels of service are being maintained. The police service is no different as already representatives of police organisations such as the previous ACPOS, the Association of Scottish Police Superintendents and the Scottish Police Federation have been called to give evidence before the Justice Committee on a number of occasions. The political and popular importance of law and order has ensured the Justice Committee maintains a high media profile and has dealt with a number of protracted police-related inquiries, such as playing a key role in the recent police reforms in Scotland. Indeed, some issues relating to Police Scotland and the SPA have come to the notice of the Justice Committee and both parties have been summoned to answer questions from the Committee members on specific matters of police reform, so much so that a sub-committee of the Justice Committee has been created solely to monitor the implementation of the police reform measures in Scotland – another tier of police accountability.

The Crown Office and the Procurator Fiscal Service

The responsibility for the investigation of and prosecution of crime lies with the Crown Office and Procurator Fiscal Service (COPFS) with the police carrying out investigations into crime and obtaining evidence under the direction of the local Procurator Fiscal. The Fiscal retains primacy at all times. The legal position is that the Lord Advocate, as head of the Scottish Public Prosecution Service, can issue instructions to chief constables to report on alleged offences. Indeed, it is possible as a matter of law for investigation as well as prosecution decisions to be undertaken by the Crown with minimal or even no involvement on the part of the police. This is different from the situation south of the border where, until the 1980s, the police were historically also responsible for prosecution decisions. The creation of the Crown Prosecution Service in 1985 to some extent mirrors the role of the procurator fiscal system, but has no investigative role and its relationship with the police in England and Wales is less dominant than the situation in Scotland.

As a result of COPFS being the sole public prosecution authority in Scotland, the police are seen as more of an agent acting on behalf of them and being accountable to them during criminal investigations – another form of accountability. This position is further strengthened with the fact that the decision on whether to start criminal proceedings in Scotland rests purely with the Prosecutor, whether or not a person has been arrested or charged by the police. There is a long-established practice that the Crown does not have to give any reasons for their decision to prosecute in any individual case or not. There is no law in Scotland which says that a crime must be prosecuted and the public prosecutor has considerable discretion over what action to take. The Fiscal makes the key decisions: whether or not to prosecute; in which court the prosecution will take place; and what type of procedure. The position of Prosecutor in the criminal justice system is one of power and it would be fair to say it is a more dominating role than that of the police and an indirect key factor in police accountability.

HMICS

Prior to 1 April 2013, it was the responsibility of Her Majesty's Inspector of Constabulary for Scotland (HMICS) to report on the state and efficiency of policing in Scotland and this covered the eight police forces and the common police services of Forensic Services, the Scottish Police College, the Scottish Crime and Drugs Enforcement Agency and Information Services. During this period the HMICS highlighted the challenges facing policing and how they performed, and made many recommendations for improvements. The need for an independent inspection role is self-evident for a public service with a revenue budget of £952.6 million in 2011–2012, but in actual fact it only spent £928.6 million and made a saving of £24 million, with some assistance from the HMICS. Now with the arrival of Policing Scotland and the ongoing programme of police reform, the development of a new inspection model for the new single police force is a work in progress for the HMICS and others. Traditionally, HMICS is viewed as an independent body who works with the police, local government, the Scottish Government and other partners, to improve the performance of Scottish policing. Its own report in 2012 states that it 'exists to reassure the Scottish Parliament and the people of Scotland as to the effectiveness and efficiency of the police service in Scotland' (HMICS 2012). To achieve this goal there are three main areas of work:

- facilitating and monitoring the self-evaluating processes used by Scottish policing to assess their performance;
- inspecting policing on a thematic basis, making recommendations for improvements and identifying good practice;
- carrying out Best Value audits and inspections.

To date, the HMICS has contributed to the current police reform in Scotland and believes it opportunistic to simplify policing across Scotland, improve efficiency, governance and accountability, and has made it clear on a number of occasions that there should be clear separation of powers between Scottish ministers, and the new Scottish Police Authority and the new chief constable.

In an innovative move to assist the inspectorate regime in Scotland, a pool of Associate Inspectors is being assembled in 2013 to work with the HMICS and other inspectorates. These new posts will take part in a variety of inspectorate work and participate in the HMICS reviews and inspections. Associate Inspectors will be employed on the basis of their skills and expertise and offer strategic and specialist advice to senior staff on complex and unusual aspects of work. While having a background in policing and child protection would be an advantage in the new role, the ability to analyse complex information and make good judgement calls is a necessity. The introduction of the Associate Inspector posts is indicative of the significant changes taking place in the approach to public sector inspection in Scotland and to scrutiny of the police in particular.

Official audit

Review and audit of the Scottish police are part of the remit of two bodies: the Accounts Commission and Audit Scotland. The Accounts Commission is responsible for securing the audit of the 32 unitary councils and the 34 joint boards in local government. The Commission reports and makes recommendations to the Scottish ministers as well as to audited bodies. It also promotes value for money, assists audited organisations to achieve economic, efficient and effective use of their resources, and publishes performance information. Audit Scotland is a statutory body which was set up in 2000 to hold public bodies to account for the efficient and effective use of over £200 million of public funds. This is achieved by carrying out audits to ensure the highest standards of financial management and governance and by carrying out performance audits to ensure best value. All of the Audit work is reported openly on its website. The work done by these official audit bodies complements the inspection work of the HMICS and again maintains another level of scrutiny of the police service.

The Scottish Policing Performance Framework

Since 2007, the Scottish Policing Performance Framework (SPPF) has shown the Scottish public how the previous eight police forces and other national services have been performing, and has also made available a wide array of management information for police managers at all levels in support of performance improvements. The SPPF was a combination of collaborative work between ACPOS, the Scottish Police, the Scottish Government, HMICS, Audit Scotland, the Scottish Police Authorities Convener's Forum and the Scottish Police Services Authority.

Now with the arrival of Police Scotland, things have changed and all systems are national. At the time of writing, ministers are in discussion with HMIC, COSLA, Police Scotland and the SPA as to the future arrangements and presentation of policing performance data for the new single police service in Scotland. However, the SPPF remains true to one of their original objectives of producing a suite of performance indicators that mirror the wide variety of police activity across Scotland. To this end, they collate information on 37 performance indicators and eight context measures and furnish the data in their reports for the information of all partners in the Scottish police and criminal justice system. Their aim is to support managers throughout the police service and facilitate the understanding of performance and encourage improvement in the Scottish police. This, it is hoped, will lead to enhanced accountability through the easy access to performance data. The SPPF has split the indicators into four sections and high-level objectives are identified within each one highlighting the main policing activities they represent:

Service Response

- Improve public satisfaction with service delivery.
- Increase public confidence.

Public Reassurance and Community Safety

- Support the delivery of safer communities.
- Preserve and restore public order.
- Investigate crime effectively.
- Contribute to the reduction of crime.
- Contribute to increased public reassurance.

Criminal Justice and Tackling Crime

- Contribute to an effective, efficient and accessible criminal justice system.
- Assist in safeguarding national security.
- Tackle serious and organised crime.

Sound Governance and Efficiency

- Manage resources effectively and efficiently.
- Operate in a manner that is ethical, accountable and transparent.

(SPPF 2012)

The performance indicators are divided into three areas:

- Outcomes – what is achieved.
- Activities – the activity or process used.
- Inputs – the resources committed.

There is a further section on Context Measures which is used alongside the indicators to provide contextual information on the various demands placed on the police from the environment in which they operate. The model is comprehensive and has been intelligently honed over the years. However, more recognition of the contribution that is made by the private and public sectors to community safety would offer a more complete model as opposed to solely police input.

Operational independence

Modern-day chief police officers in Scotland should not be surprised to be asked to explain why they made decisions as it is part of the accountability and monitoring process of the new single police service. Why a police operation has been set up and at what cost are valid questions for representatives of the public to ask, and only impact on operational decision-making when moves are made to prevent it going ahead or to alter the plan. A chief constable may embark on expensive and resource-intensive initiatives to combat traffic-light offences, road tax dodgers, prostitution, illegal parking, etc. But what if the public wish the police to concentrate on other offences and nuisances and believe the budget should be spent on these? That certainly could put pressure on police operational decision-making and impact on a chief officer's independence but maybe that is not a bad thing in modern democratic policing. Elected members or officials acting on their behalf have a duty to ask these questions. This is not about telling the police how to carry out an operation or who to arrest, rather it is about checking how public money is being spent and examining if there are other ways of doing things for less. The police service does not have all the answers, nor do teachers, doctors and social workers in their professions. Good financial management at a time of limited public service resources must involve setting priorities and making choices and at times making different choices from those made in the past.

The sound-bite that the answer to improved community safety is always 'extra police officers on the beat' is in danger of being outdated in the twenty-first century as there is a need to look beyond the traditional causes and symptoms and search for new and better solutions to community problems. Indeed, the political decision by the Scottish Government to maintain police numbers at a specific level limits the Chief Constable's flexibility when it comes to spending on technology and police staff. This could have an operational impact as the chief constable may believe investing resources in these other areas of policing may give a better return on community safety than continually increasing police numbers. This all points to the need to look deeper into what actually improves police services to the ordinary member of the public – is it just as important to have quicker response times on the telephone with better advice and assistance than a few extra officers on the street? Maybe the police should employ more civilian police staff, community wardens and auxiliaries, or hive off some traditional duties to public sector partners or the private sector? Politicians and some police managers have lulled the public into believing that the answer to improved community security and safety is simply a matter of increasing the number of police officers on the beat, but this police philosophy is being questioned in the new century as new opportunities and methods with the potential for preventing crime and improving community safety are coming to light. What has to be remembered is that the record low levels of crime and high detection rates in Scotland have run in tandem with the expansion of civilianisation in the police, new technology and increased involvement of the private and public sectors in crime prevention and community safety, and, dare we say it, increased scrutiny of the police – it is not all down to the good work of the

Scottish police. There is no simple panacea or single answer but restricting the flexibility of decision-making of chief police officers does not help.

Freedom of Information

The Freedom of Information (Scotland) Act 2002 gives the public the right to access information held by public authorities in Scotland, which includes the police service. The total number of Freedom of Information (FOI) requests received by Scottish police forces over the previous five years gives an indication of the demand that this places on the police organisation (Table 8.1).

TABLE 8.1 Number of FOI requests, 2007–2012

Date	*Number*
2007–2008	3248
2008–2009	4511
2009–2010	5125
2010–2011	5019
2011–2012	5335

There were over 5300 FOI requests submitted to Scottish police forces in 2011–2012, a 6 per cent increase on 2010–2011 and over 2000 more than the number received in 2007–2008.

Scotland already has the most robust FOI regime in the UK and plans to introduce further legislation to bring more organisations under scrutiny in the future. As a first step, arm's-length bodies set up by local authorities to provide cultural, leisure and sports activities will be subject to FOI law. It is then the Scottish Government's intention to include other groups created by local councils under the legislation. Such a move will increase transparency and openness and make more information available in the public domain. Since the police are becoming increasingly involved with public sector groups under the umbrella of community safety initiatives, any expansion in FOI will probably have an impact on them and be seen as part of the expanding scrutiny model of policing.

Police research

We now have national organised crime policing and intelligence units, national policing plans; and increased oversight by central government, auditors and inspectorates and now in Scotland a national police service. The impact of these changes reveals a police organisation not only with higher expectations, accountabilities, target-setting and public evaluation but also one with more sanctions, interference and directions for constant improvement. Police forces are currently finding themselves with little option but to follow the signposts laid out by government policy and have to abide by the new rules of police governance and performance management that are now steeped in statute. Against this background of increasing central government control of policing, there has never been a greater need for insightful research into the modern police service. Part of such a move should be engaging police officers in regular in-house research, whether in partnership with academia or not. This would lead the organisation to regularly question why they do things and more importantly, why it is they are being asked to do things.

An important parallel development to all this for the new Police Scotland is the pressure to create policy-making at the national level that reflects the complex and dynamic nature of local communities. Such policy-making requires the availability of current information and research which, up to recently, has been drawn from government research groups, Audit Agencies, Inspectorates, government and non-government working parties, universities and sponsored research from a variety of other sources. Already some academic institutions have established units concerned with policing education and research and some research has been conducted by police officers themselves from their collaboration with professional researchers.

In Scotland, we have the Scottish Institute for Policing Research (SIPR) established in 2007 and supported by investment from the Scottish Funding Council and the Scottish Police. SIPR is an alliance between 12 Scottish universities and the Scottish police service with the objective to engage in high quality independent research and make evidence-based contributions to policing policy and practice. There is a close police involvement in the work of SIPR that is aptly described on its own website:

> Police representatives play a key role at all levels of the management structure of SIPR and there is a senior police representative on each network steering group whose role includes bringing forward proposals for research from within the police service and helping facilitate access to police personnel and data for researchers undertaking research projects. These police representatives also sit on the Executive Committee so have a role in developing the strategic research direction of SIPR.
>
> *(SIPR 2012)*

The opportunity for researchers in the new century interested in investigating the police service is endless and also encompasses the wider criminal justice system. How the police organisation makes sense of its world and interfaces with other groups has become a fascinating subject to many audiences and SIPR has played its part in this. SIPR has developed into a professional body that has done much to promote police research in Scotland and further afield and has influenced and encouraged both academics and police officers to get involved in research projects into policing. However, there is one issue that arises with SIPR and that is the high level of police involvement in the management of research into its own organisation and whether this has an impact on the topics chosen to be researched (or not to be researched) and the independence of research undertaken. Intriguingly, there was an absence of research work and comment from SIPR during the initial years of debate and discussion on the topic of police reform in Scotland and the concept of a national police service – which was a surprise to many.

Policing has existed in a dynamic social and political landscape since the turn of the twenty-first century and has witnessed novel approaches to policing policies and methods. There has never been a more lucrative period in policing for valuable research and evaluation of initiatives, strategies and policies. A police literature review examined the state of police research between 2000 and 2007 and highlighted the wide-ranging categories of police research ongoing at the present time:

Police and Society	Organizational Change	Training
Hiring and Retention	Militarization	Privatization
Media Relations	Attitudes of Police	Accountability
Occupational Stress	Minority Issues	Corruption
Police violence	Police Control	Patrol
Discrimination/Profiling	Community Police	Sexual Assault
Technology/Equipment	Investigative Tactics	Drugs/Alcohol
International/Global	Domestic Violence	Cyber-crime
Intelligence-based	Citizen Satisfaction	Measurement

(*Mazeika* et al. *2010: 522)*

Credible research is the life-blood of good policy-making, regardless of which organisation it relates to, as the data enables successful implementation of policy. Police Scotland requires nothing less, particularly in the present climate of increased reform and performance management of the policing function. New government policies have meant that monitoring, evaluation and independent and objective research are indispensable to the overseeing and development of police policy and to legitimising the statutory audit function. However, there is still a requirement for more in-depth research into how the police service actually operates, as there are increasing responsibilities being placed on the shoulders of policing which intensifies the need for specialist knowledge and skills. In recent times the police have had to cope with new methods in investigating and preventing child abuse, domestic violence, internet crime, terrorism, hate crime, anti-social behaviour and much more. Also the Europeanisation of policing and liberalisation of border controls have not only introduced new policies, practices and codes of conduct into policing, but have also established new dimensions in organised crime, human trafficking, and the problems associated with the influx of asylum-seekers and other migrants.

So any independently conducted examination, review or research into policing in any of its forms can only add to the level of police scrutiny expected by politicians and the public in a democracy. This in itself would serve as an additional method of monitoring, evaluation and oversight.

Conclusion

There are at least four ways of looking at an organisation. You can look through its annual reports, mission statements, corporate strategies, objectives and job descriptions and find out what the organisation thinks it is up to or would like others to think it is up to. You can also enquire of the organisation's participants, customers, clients, suppliers and buyers what they think the organisation is doing. Then you can try and find out what it is in fact that the organisation is doing. Then you can ask the question, is this what the organisation should be doing?

The four perspectives, sometimes labelled formal, assumed, real and evaluative, can provide great illumination in understanding organisations, especially those in the public sector, such as the police who have a high level of accountability to the public. In the ideal world, however, what the organisation says it is doing should be communicated to all the people concerned with it and what it is doing should be what it should be doing. But more often than not, in the real world, many different answers are supplied to these four questions.

What this chapter has shown is that there are a lot of players in the police scrutiny game who have the responsibility to look at the police service from a formal, assumed, real and evaluative standpoint and if you include the media in all its forms, then it is a nonsense to think that the police in Scotland are 'under'-scrutinised, as some would wish us to believe. That said, it would be safe to claim that, apart from obviously interested bodies like the police, civil liberties groups, politicians, and of course criminals, most Scottish people would not be aware of the individual powers of the various parties involved.

Accountability and performance measurement are important in any organisation but more important is having an effective system of redress for the public when the standard of service falls below an acceptable level, particularly, when it calls into question the behaviour and practices of individual members in the organisation and, worse still, when the allegations are of a criminal nature. As we have seen, mechanisms have been developed to assist the monitoring of police performance and these have been in the form of performance frameworks comprising an assortment of indicators which measure most aspects of police functions and outcomes. Performance frameworks or models are a valuable tool for the politician, auditor and members of the public, and can even highlight the correlation between funding and the ability of a police force to achieve its stated objectives. Performance models can also identify good practice and poor practice. As this chapter highlights, Scotland is awash with performance data, and all that is left is for police managers to be fully aware and capable in its use.

When the Police and Crime Commissioners (PCC) were appointed in England and Wales to oversee the local Chief Constables in 2012, comment was made in the academic world that the addition of the PCC and its Police and Crime Panel now meant there would be a 'quadripartite' governance system in place of the 'tripartite' system (Jones *et al.* 2011: 234). In 2007, research by the UK Cabinet Office revealed 68 per cent of people were attracted to the idea of having a locally elected person who would hold their police to account and a 2008 IPSOS MORI poll revealed that only 19 per cent disagreed that a politician should be directly elected to the police authority to look after the issues on crime and policing in the locality (Home Office 2010). Further research revealed only 8 per cent of the local wards had a councillor on their police authority. Opposition to elected police commissioners comes mainly from rival political parties, local councillors and chief constables, all of whom are vehemently against the proposal and worry that it could result in 'Dirty Harry-style policing' emerging with local populist policies and an influential and powerful police commissioner (*The Economist* 2010: 24). This system has not been adopted in Scotland where there are no directly elected commissioners or mayors with responsibility for the governance of the police. What we have in Scotland is a mix of statutory, non-governmental, legal, official and unofficial bodies, who in their own way oversee the police.

Prior to the creation of the Police Investigations and Review Commissioner (PIRC) serious complaints against the police in Scotland were investigated by the police from another Scottish force, now that there is only one national police service, this is not possible and the role falls to the independent body the PIRC. However, there has been some disquiet over the fact that 8 out of 11 senior investigatory posts in the PIRC have been filled by former police officers and out of the overall staff of 20, there will be 13 ex-police officers. The situation has caused questions to be asked as to the level of independence of the new PIRC with so many former police officers in their ranks. Especially at a time when Westminster politicians have called for the equivalent watchdog in England and Wales, the IPCC, to have the number of former police officers in its organisation reduced after criticism of the IPCC being too ready to accept the police version of events in a number of investigations in England. The present ratio of former police officers in the IPCC is much lower than that proposed in the PIRC. The only way to make certain of public trust and belief in the independence of the PIRC from its inception is for the staff to display through their professionalism and investigatory skills a totally unbiased approach to their work. There will always be the critics as there are always winners and losers in these situations but a willingness to be transparent and honest at all times will go a long way to dispel any fear of bias during investigations. In fairness to the setting-up of an organisation responsible for investigating complaints of such a serious and sensitive nature, most would agree to the need for a high level of investigatory skill and experience to ensure its success in the initial years. Hence the leaning towards employing those with a track record in complex investigations. Nonetheless, there is no reason why the number of former police officers cannot be reduced over time when other PIRC staff get up to speed and become more experienced and gain additional investigatory skills.

Having a watchdog body like the SPA who will not simply 'rubber stamp' police financial decisions without interrogating the rationale behind them will ultimately result in a change in the police management mind-set. It is not going to be a case that examination and assessment will always come after the event has happened. There will be occasions in emergency or specific operational matters that scrutiny can only take place at a later date. The ongoing police reform underpinned by statute has introduced a new form of police oversight in Scotland that not only calls the chief constable to account but also requires a change of approach to policing matters from other partners in the community safety regime. This has been evident from the behind-the-scenes power struggle between the SPA and Police Scotland over who should have direct control of police finance and Human Resources, and the subsequent involvement of the Justice Secretary and the Justice Committee. The Justice Committee found they were unable to resolve the issues and it was only when the Justice Secretary stepped in and took the side of the chief constable that an interim solution was found. This is an intriguing development as the SPA management believe their interpretation of who should take the lead in finance and Human Resources is correct, as set out in the reform legislation which was passed by the vast majority of the Scottish Parliament. The opposite view is taken by Police Scotland and supported by the Justice Secretary who believes that such an arrangement would establish a disproportionate level of power skewed towards the SPA and introduce an element of confusion as to who runs Police Scotland. The SPA remains unhappy with the decision and raises concerns that problems lie ahead on the road to full police reform if similar disagreements arise every time a difficult decision is made.

It will take some time for Police Scotland and the SPA to settle in to their new roles and there will be some teething problems to begin with, as one would expect. There are other issues that will need clarified over time, for example, the role of the local councillor in the new constitutional set-up. What would help is for some bodies presently on the sidelines to back off and give these parties room to learn to work together towards offering the Scottish people the best police service possible.

9 WHAT LIES AHEAD FOR THE SCOTTISH POLICE OFFICER?

Introduction

Centuries before the Treaty of Union in 1707, disparate kingdoms became established to form the Scottish nation, a sovereign state with its own Scottish distinctiveness. Even after the Union, Scotland developed in its own manner and governed itself for centuries with a Lord Advocate and Criminal Justice System based in Edinburgh, responsible for Scottish law and order and the police service. It was in the second half of the twentieth century that a growing number of Scots began to foster a feeling of Scottish identity which culminated in the Scotland Act 1998 and elections to a Scottish Parliament in May 1999 with a devolved form of government in Scotland. Fourteen years on from this date Scotland now has its first national police service to reflect the growing feeling of Scottishness in the nation. Policing in a modern democracy is expected to mirror a cross-section of the population so it is not surprising that there is now evidence of a distinctiveness in Scottish policing that singles them out from other parts of the UK. Previous chapters in this book have shown this to be the case and indications are that this trend will continue in the future.

As a small country, Scotland has always punched above its weight and regardless of the result of the Independence Referendum in 2014, there will be changes in the way Scotland is governed, either as an independent country or one with increased devolved powers. Public services such as the police will inevitably be impacted upon within a changing political and constitutional landscape. It is difficult to gaze into a crystal ball and forecast the future for Scottish Policing when it is in the current state of change and reform. For example, the Police and Fire Reform (Scotland) Act 2012 which created Police Scotland also enabled the introduction of the new Police Service of Scotland Regulations 2013 which relate to the governance and administration of the new national police service. The key objective of the updated police regulations is to facilitate a smooth transition during the police force mergers, particularly, in relation to police officers' conditions of service. Police regulations cover a police officer's private life; conditions of service and pay; Special Constabulary; cadets; conduct; performance; and promotion. Many of the regulations will remain unchanged and others will be modified to reflect future working practices in the years to come but not to the extent of the current police reforms in England and Wales. This chapter gives some insight into what may lie ahead for Scottish policing and the Scottish police officer and how the future is being influenced as much by what is happening outside of Scotland as what is occurring within its borders. As witnessed in other parts of this book, evidence suggests that the direction of travel is towards a more distinct and discrete police service in Scotland to that in the rest of the UK.

Social change

As mentioned in Chapter 1, Scotland has a history of its people continuously migrating to greener shores but in recent decades demographic data has shown a dramatic turnaround. For the first time people are coming to Scotland in large numbers and not only from Europe and further afield but from England and Wales, and indications are that this migration will continue. According to the 2011 Census, Scotland's population increased from 5,062,011 in 2001 to 5,295,000 in 2011, an increase of 4.6 per cent (Scottish Government 2012f). This is the highest population figure ever recorded in Scotland and the increase is due to a combination of more births than deaths but mainly because more people migrated to Scotland than have left. In addition, to these figures being good for the future economic growth of the nation, they will also have an impact on how the police tackle the demands from an ageing population. The number of people aged 65 years and over increased by 85,000 from the 2001 figure and now represents 17 per cent of the population in Scotland, and those aged 80 years and over was up 19 per cent to 230,000. There is also the economic downside of the number of elderly outnumbering the younger population, as for the first time, the number of 65-year-olds has exceeded the under-15-year-olds. While more people are continuing to work after retirement age and the average life expectancy in the UK is forecast to rise from the present figure of 87 years to 91 years in 2050, the question still arises as to who will pay to provide public services for the ageing population, such as health and policing? For many years the Scots have enjoyed free university tuition fees, health care, medical prescriptions and elderly bus travel, and a police service that has managed to maintain its present complement of police officers. Many see this as unsustainable and deceiving the public and believe there should be a debate on the issues now.

What may exacerbate the future challenges brought about by increased longevity is the parallel rise in problems associated with poverty. The Scottish Index of Multiple Deprivation in 2012 highlighted the fact that Scotland's poor are now more widespread across the nation rather than focused solely in the larger cities (Scottish Government 2012g). In the present austere economic climate with the fear of unemployment and looming welfare cuts, the situation will not be helped and the perennial difficulties associated with citizens facing hard financial times are likely to increase. This will include growing demands on most aspects of policing from social and community policing to low level disorder and serious crime. The Scottish police officer working within the new national policing structure should be better placed to cope with these pressures.

Present-day attitudes

The police service has on occasions been criticised by sections of the media and some politicians particularly in England and Wales, that they are overpaid and continually looking for more improvements to their conditions of service – taking more and giving less. This cannot be said in the present day with the historic changes to their conditions as per the Winsor Review in 2012. And in fairness to police officers, they have always given the police organisation and the public some of their time without payment in past years. Especially when officers were expected to turn up for duty 15 minutes earlier before their shift commenced in order to be briefed prior to going on duty without any payment. Similar requirements were made of employees in other professions that required briefings to take place but payment was always made. A modern-day example of how times are changing can be found in Europe. A German police officer calculated that it took 15 minutes of his own time each day to put on his regulation undershirt, trousers, truncheon-holding belt, handcuffs, weapon and gas canister, overshirt, tunic, boots, protective kneepads, hat and gloves. The officer also added that it took him 15 minutes at the end of each shift to reverse the procedure. The officer's claim for 45 hours overtime per year was rejected by senior police management who stated it was part of his duties as a police officer. The officer who was representing 120 other officers took the test complaint to the local administrative court and won his case. This means the officers are now entitled to an extra paid week's leave which will have a significant impact on the police budget at a time of austerity and cutbacks. The employers have the opportunity to take the matter to appeal in a higher court (*The Telegraph* 2010). There are many more similar examples across the Western world in Spain, Greece and France, to name but a few, which highlight the changing outlook of police officers in the modern day regardless of their nationality. This is brought on by the pressure on public finance that is having a negative impact on police conditions of service and living standards and forcing a change in police attitudes. We only have to look at what is happening in England and Wales at the present time to witness historic changes to traditional policing and its effect on police morale and ask, how long can this continue? Scottish policing has been protected from similar draconian measures to date due to political decisions but again the question has to be asked how long can this continue? Especially in the current austere economic environment which shows little sign of improvement and when political decisions and, more importantly, governments can easily change. Further police reform in Scotland may only be an election away. Reference is made later in this chapter to a survey of police officers and police staff that gives some insight into attitudes and feelings in the present day.

Scotland versus England

Since Scottish devolution there has been a growing divergence at a number of levels between Scotland and the rest of the UK, ranging from the political to the delivery of national and local services such as policing. The following are a number of examples but there are many more. To set the scene, the Scots have put their own stamp on how a number of key public services are delivered and financed. One example is the restoration of free higher education with the abolition of graduate endowment fees in 2007, the end result being record numbers of students studying higher education in Scotland. In contrast, England has seen enrolment in universities falling dramatically with the presence of high tuition fees for students. This highlights the two clear routes in the delivery of higher education being followed north and south of the border and in Scotland we can add free personal care for the elderly and the retention of public spending, such as health and water in public hands. Police examples of different approaches to policing between Scotland and the rest of the UK have been discussed throughout the present text but the following examples illustrate more specifically the emerging divergence in policing between Scotland and the rest of the UK.

Police pay and conditions

The future of police pay and conditions of service is uncertain and the traditional methods of negotiation are due to change. This is against a backdrop of the police not having the right to take industrial action and concerns over the need for any new negotiation system to be fair and transparent, and to include the availability of independent arbitration. The basic criteria for joining the Police Service of Scotland are basically the same as for the rest of the UK. The selection process involves a standard entrance exam, interview, fitness and medical tests, and, as one would expect, a comprehensive background check. But it now appears that in the future this equity in entry standards into the police organisation will change once the recruits have been sworn in, starting with different remuneration packages between England and Wales and Scottish officers. This will mean that from day one there is the beginning of distinctiveness between both sets of police officers which is a major change in UK policing. This is due to the UK Government pressing ahead with plans to reduce the starting salary of new recruits in England and Wales from £23,000 to £19,000 – a drop of £4000 (Winsor Review 2012). The Scottish Government, on the other hand, has made it clear that they did not commission the Winsor Review on police reform and will not impose the recommended changes such as the reduction in starting pay of police officers. There is also the likelihood that British Transport Police (BTP) officers working in Scotland will be subject to a lower starting salary similar to the police south of the border. At present, they are paid on a par with their Scottish counterparts. The fear is that if the BTP starting salary is reduced to the £19,000 level, then potential BTP recruits may apply to join Police Scotland to boost their salaries.

On a separate issue, the UK Government plans to introduce a new 'career average' police pension scheme in 2015 to replace the current final salary scheme and a new pension age of 60 years will also be introduced. This will increase members' average pension contributions to 13.7 per cent. Officers with less than 10 years to serve will have their current pensions protected, those officers younger in service will not. This has led to anger and resentment between officers, claiming it creates a two-tier system with the potential of significantly affecting morale. These changes are against the backdrop of public sector pension reform which has cross-party political support. The majority of police officers in Scotland are opposed to their future pensions being decided by the UK Government when the rest of their pay and conditions are decided by the Scottish ministers. They believe they should negotiate pensions directly with the Scottish Government.

At present the Police Negotiating Board (PNB) provides a forum in which representatives of police officers and those who manage and fund police forces can consider questions relating to police hours of duty, leave, pay and allowances, pensions, clothing and equipment. It operates on a UK basis and the Home Secretary, Scottish Ministers and the Department of Justice in Northern Ireland are required to consult it before making regulations on relevant matters. However, as a result of the recommendations of the Winsor Review of police remuneration and conditions in England and Wales, the Home Office intends to replace the UK PNB with a Police Remuneration Review Body for England and Wales. As a consequence, the Scottish Government is proposing to establish a new Police Negotiating Board for Scotland to negotiate the pay and conditions of service of police officers in the Police Service of Scotland. This is but another example of a breakaway from the traditional police organisation and administrative framework that has existed in UK policing for many years.

Another feature likely to be introduced in England and Wales is voluntary severance for officers to enable them to exit the service before their pension age. Officers would receive a compensation payment immediately they leave the service following agreement with the chief constable and still collect their pension when reaching normal pension entitlement age. At the time of writing, the Police Federation in England and Wales has planned a vote among its members on whether they want the Federation to pursue the right to take industrial action, but, as it stands at present, the Scottish police have no similar plans. Intriguingly, a yes vote for the right to strike in England and Wales would further alienate colleagues north of the border.

Drink driving

It is the contention of the Scottish Government that statistically up to 30 lives are lost each year as a result of drinking and driving and that the current drink driving limit leaves too much confusion and sends out the wrong message to motorists. The Scots have been urging the UK Government for the power to lower the limit from 80mg of alcohol per 100ml of blood to 50mg of alcohol per 100ml of blood as road safety was one of the powers retained by the UK Government following devolution. This has now been changed in 2012 and the Scottish ministers have been given the power to set both the drink-drive and speed limits and legislation is planned for 2013. Lowering the drink-drive limit would bring Scotland into line with other European countries and, as things stand at present, England and Wales will be among the only places within the European Union where the 80mg limit is still in force. Norway, Poland and Sweden have a 20mg limit and Germany, France, Greece, Italy, Spain, Portugal, Turkey, Belgium and Denmark, 50mg limit. In Malta, Estonia and the Czech Republic, the limit is zero.

If the move goes ahead in Scotland, it will have major implications for motorists and will step up pressure on the UK Government to follow suit in England and Wales. A number of issues will arise out of these changes, such as how to proceed south of the border when someone has been found guilty of driving above the new lower limit in Scotland and resides in England and Wales. The Scottish Government also wish to be given the authority to introduce the breathalysing of drivers at random and to introduce stricter drink driving rules for younger drivers. At present, the police can only stop a vehicle and breathalyse the driver when they have reasonable suspicion of a moving traffic offence or the consumption of alcohol or drugs. These additional proposals have been rejected by the Westminster Government.

Air weapons

Air weapons are not required to be licensed in Scotland or for that matter the rest of the UK but for a number of years the Scottish Government has lobbied the Westminster Government seeking the additional devolved powers to do so. It is estimated there are as many as half a million air weapons in Scotland and politicians and pressure groups have argued that in light of the number of injuries and even fatalities caused by the weapons in recent decades, there is now a need for legal control over ownership and monitoring their use in Scotland. The Scottish Parliament has now been given this power under the Scotland Act 2012 and the Scottish Government introduced proposals for consultation in 2012. The new licensing regime has still to be decided upon but in essence it will cover the type of air weapon, identify the legitimate reasons for possession, competency and safety issues, time-scale for system implementation, licence fees, offences and penalties. The proposals will affect anyone presently owning and wanting to continue to do so, anyone wishing to purchase an air weapon, and anyone wishing to bring one into Scotland for competitions or otherwise.

Regardless of which agency will be given the main role of overseeing and administering the new licensing regime, there is no doubt the Scottish police service will have a major role to play in the enforcement of the legislation. This has always been the case in the past with new legislation with a high enforcement potential and is inevitably accompanied by a significant additional workload for police officers. As a guide to the present licensing firearm set-up, there were 25,831 firearm certificates and 48,726 shotgun certificates on issue in Scotland at the end of 2011 (Scottish Government 2012h). It will be interesting to see how many apply for ownership of air weapons and how many are accepted or rejected. More importantly, as the key issue is one of community safety, it will be essential for the thousands of air weapons presently at large in the community not granted a licence, to be surrendered and taken off the streets. To put the issue of the licensing of weapons in perspective, particularly, for a nation the size of Scotland, and in the wake of the multiple shootings of schoolchildren and teachers in the USA. In the month of November 2012, in the USA two million persons applied for a licence for at least one firearm and only 2 per cent were refused after background checks.

Forensic services

The Scottish Government has made it clear on many occasions that it is not greatly attracted to privatisation in law enforcement and policing and favours retaining services within the public sector. This is certainly the case with forensic services in Scotland that can trace its beginnings to the first fingerprint and photographic department in the Glasgow City Police in 1931 (Fraser and Ludwig 2010: 381). It has always been the intention of the Scottish Government to avoid going down the same privatisation and outsourcing route as England and Wales and prefers a public forensic service accountable to the Scottish Police Authority.

Police misconduct

Moves are afoot to ensure police officers in England and Wales who are found guilty of criminal and misconduct matters are entered onto a register and prevented from continuing a career in the police service. The IPCC is also to be given the power to continue to investigate police officers who resign before misconduct or gross misconduct enquiries are completed. In addition, new standards for vetting police officers and chief police officers are to be introduced and the responsibility for implementing the change will be down to the local police force. Add to these changes the Winsor recommendations for policing and the UK Government proposals for police pension reform and we have the biggest shake-up in police conditions of service in its history and more significantly a growing divide in policing between Scotland and the rest of the UK.

Foreign recruitment

As discussed in Chapter 3, foreign recruitment of direct entrants to senior ranks in the police in England and Wales is being considered by the UK Government but there are no plans to introduce a similar policy in Scotland. The police associations south of the border vehemently oppose the initiative as they see it as individuals joining the police as superintendents and above with no police experience in the UK and believe it unworkable. If this were to happen, and the senior levels of the police in England and Wales were populated with a mix of home-grown and foreign senior police managers, one can foresee a major shift in HR policies between Scotland and the rest of the UK. As mentioned earlier in the text, security concerns would become an issue as chief police officers have a crucial part to play in counter-terrorism across the UK with links to the security services and high level intelligence. Whether Police Scotland would be comfortable in discussing its nation's security matters and sensitive information with foreign nationals with differing backgrounds is something to be tested. Indeed, it would be a matter for the Scottish Government to consider along with its security advisors including the police. At present, Scottish police officers apply for police posts in other parts of the UK, in particular those officers who have attended the Senior Command Course and who put themselves forward for chief officers' positions. Allowing foreign nationals to apply for the same posts would certainly introduce an added competitive factor.

Minimum alcohol pricing

The introduction of minimum unit pricing for alcohol is part of the Scottish Government strategy to tackle the scourge of alcohol abuse which is responsible for many alcohol-related deaths, is a continuous burden on the resources of the nation's health services and is a major contributory factor in crime. At the time of writing, the Scottish Government is pushing ahead with its plans at a time when the UK Government is not prepared to introduce a similar initiative in England and Wales. If the plan goes ahead in Scotland, then it will be illegal to sell alcohol for less than 50 pence per unit and will ultimately lead to one part of the UK (Scotland) having minimum pricing and a probable consequence of a surge in cross-border and internet shopping for alcohol. And if the Scottish Government's projections are correct, Scotland is likely to witness fewer alcohol-related deaths, a drop in hospitals admissions and a reduction in crime. The Scottish Government still faces fierce opposition to its plans from the commercial sector and will have to fight its case in the UK and European courts. Again this is another example of the potentially expanding gulf between Scotland and the rest of the UK which inevitable has an impact on the police organisation. Agreement has already been reached within Police Scotland to introduce a new National Violence and Alcohol Reduction Unit that will ensure a coordinated approach to tackling violence and alcohol-related violence across Scotland. The plan is to have a central core unit that will liaise with Local Police Commanders and coordinate and plan activities and campaigns.

Future mergers of public services

Most of Scotland's local authorities have little choice but to cut their budgets in the coming years and this means reducing staff levels by thousands across the country. The quandary facing local government is what services to prioritise and in some instances which ones to axe. Although recent police reform has relieved local government of the responsibility of querying police finance, they will still be inextricably linked to the community safety of their area and closely tied in to policing through local policing plans. So any cuts to local services will have some impact on policing and safety initiatives. Police officer numbers may be protected for the time being but this is doubtful to continue in the present financial climate and there is every likelihood numbers will fall if there is a change in government policy or a new Scottish government comes to power. Reduction in non-essential services and the closure of police offices may need to be considered as a direct result of budget cutbacks. Politicians and senior police officers would be naïve to think otherwise.

Now that the nation has merged its fire and police services, questions are being asked as to the benefits and practicalities of similar mergers in other public services and institutions. In the new century when public sector budgets are under close scrutiny, politicians are focusing on closer integration of services and cross-boundary working as a means of not only saving money, but improving the services to the public, and reducing bureaucracy and duplication. The question also arises as to why the police and fire services are going through reform and not local councils and health boards. For example, local government Councils in Scotland spend £40,000 every minute, with a total of £21 billion annual budget and, according to an official watchdog report, they do not explain clearly how this is spent. Important facts were found hidden away in lengthy council reports and details of how councils spent their budgets was of 'poor quality, unclear and incomplete' (Audit Scotland 2012). The general theme is that during this period of financial constraints councils need to maintain effective performance management systems and ensure best value for their citizens.

At the present time there are 32 local authorities and 15 health boards. With the new single police service having 14 police divisions across the nation, there appears to be obvious advantages in other public services sharing similar boundaries and populations. This very question was asked of the Scottish Justice Secretary in November 2012 to which he responded: 'The status quo is not tenable in the police and it is not going to be tenable in other forms of public life' (MacAskill 2012). Accepting that not everything can be a single service, it is apparent that the merger of police and fire services into national units may not be the last in the Scottish public sector. The inference is that at the very least there will be more shared services and partnerships and increased working with the voluntary sector. All of which will have strategic and operational implications for how Police Scotland performs its responsibilities in the future.

Portrait of the police

The Police Mutual Assurance Society (PMAS) commissioned an independent market survey of their members in the UK police service between December 2011 and January 2012. The report was published in May 2012 and a total of 4906 respondents took part from across the UK and included more than 700 civilian support staff, 2800 serving officers and 1315 retired officers (PMAS 2012). Although, the study was not specific to Scotland, over 600 respondents taking part were from there. Questions were asked relating to personal issues, career, financial, social and economic, retirement, lifestyle, health and well-being. Analysis from the study is worthy of inclusion in this text as it gives a current insight into the thoughts and feelings of police officers and police staff in the UK in the twentieth century that has a generic feel to it and therefore has a bearing on Scottish policing.

Unusual for the police service, a third of respondents worry about their financial security and a fifth are considering a new career, with one-seventh believing the feeling of insecurity has a negative impact on their performance at work. A significant 80 per cent of serving police officers believe their role is under greater pressure than at any time in their career, citing paperwork, bureaucracy, changes in public attitudes towards police and the relentless pursuit of targets, as the main reasons. Around 40 per cent of police staff are increasingly worried by the threat of redundancy and, as a result of the deteriorating economic picture, 65 per cent of all respondents have had to delay or cancel a major life plan. Around a third surveyed said low morale was affecting their health, long-term career plans, family relationships and job performance.

The single biggest priority for all serving and retired police personnel (over 40 per cent) is finding their way in retirement – life after the service. It is also the main fear of three out of 10 serving officers. In simple terms, officers' aspirations are normally one of the following – to complete their police service, receive their police pensions, embark on a new career, create their own business or fully retire. Only one in eight propose to stay in service past retirement age.

When respondents were asked to give examples of how they 'wind down' after work, the most popular was a visit to the cinema or theatre, closely followed by do-it-yourself home improvements. Table 9.1 contains the most popular ways to wind down given by respondents.

The survey may have limitations with its tightly focused parameters on everyday financial and job security concerns of police officers and police staff. Nevertheless, a not too surprising picture emerges when viewed in the context of other recent findings and research on modern policing in the UK, for example, the Winsor Review (2012). However, some of the results may not reflect the position in Scotland, for a number of reasons already discussed in this text. For example, it is accurate to state that police officers' morale in Scotland is higher than that in England and Wales due to the current UK Government reforms and changes in police conditions of service. Though it is doubtful this can be said for police staff in Scotland as they face an uncertain future with guaranteed cuts in police support

TABLE 9.1 Ways that police officers wind down

Activity	*(%)*
Cinema/theatre	35
DIY	34
Gardening	31
Participating in sport	29
World travel	27
Music/concerts	26
Following football team	25
Hiking	18
Camping	13
Following other sports	13

Source: PMAS (2012).

levels with the introduction of the new single police service and the political commitment to make considerable savings on police budgets and retain present police numbers mostly at the expense of police support staff.

The PMAS survey is an indicator in this age of austerity and gives some insight into how police officers and police staff are no different than other community members. Financial pressures are impacting on everyone and as police personnel experience similar career and family aspirations this increases individual stress across the service with the risk of having a negative impact on job performance and effectiveness. The emerging contrast in police conditions of service and pay scales between Scotland and the rest of the UK has the potential to be quite pronounced in the future as the Scottish Government has made it known they oppose most of the ongoing reform measures south of the border.

In addition, the Scottish Government's promise to maintain an extra 1000 police officers may not be sustainable in the future under current financial cuts. The Chief Constable of Police Scotland is on record in December 2012 insisting that police numbers will have to be cut in the 2014–2015 and 2015–2016 financial periods unless more money is available, he stated: 'It's not about money, it's about a political choice – the government decide the budget the police get, not the police' (*Scotland on Sunday* 2012). More than ever before which political party is in power will determine the future make-up of policing, not only in Scotland but the rest of the UK.

Advantages of a single force

The creation of Police Scotland was initially seen by many as a cost-savings device to reduce duplication and top heavy management in difficult economic times. However, what is becoming apparent as the new single force takes shape are the additional benefits that accrue from bringing about fundamental changes in how

Scotland is policed. As we have seen throughout this text the centralisation of police services opens the door to expanding existing specialist units and introducing new ones, each with high levels of expertise in key operational areas. Ultimately, these moves will improve frontline services for local communities across Scotland at a time of severe financial cutbacks and introduce a more equitable police service for all Scottish citizens. The establishment of the Scottish Police Authority should also lead to better accountability and more transparent governance and improved community relations. Increased political scrutiny of the police better than that of the past coupled with a clear statutory duty for Police Scotland to provide adequate local police services must be a good thing. And the appointment of local police commanders for each local authority area with their individual local policing plans, which set priorities, objectives, targets and other arrangements, will safeguard existing partnerships between police, politicians and communities at the local level. The establishment of the independent PIRC will ensure a more effective and publicly acceptable system of dealing with police complaints and the investigation of serious incidents and criminal offences allegedly involving police officers.

As has been seen in this text, Policing Scotland has its challenges but there are as many opportunities to improve and maintain the standard of police service offered to communities regardless of where they live in Scotland.

Scottish independence

Scottish politics have changed significantly since the advent of devolution and the issue of Scottish independence is firmly at the top of the political agenda in both Scotland and the rest of the UK. The question being asked in modern-day Scotland is whether the Union in its present form is fit for purpose in the twenty-first century against the backdrop of devolution, political change, international and European influences – and 'the shifting alliances and loyalties of the electorate' (Mcleish 2012: 204). Our date with destiny will be 2014 when the Scottish community goes to the polls with a referendum to vote for or against Scottish Independence. The battle lines have been drawn and regardless of the final referendum outcome, there will be major constitutional changes in Scotland with either independence or further devolution probably with additional financial powers for Scotland. There is a growing divide between the UK Westminster Parliament supporting the Union and a substantial number of supporters for Scottish independence in Scotland. Added to this is the growing feeling of Scottishness in the nation and the realisation that much has been done within Scotland since devolution, particularly in the realm of policing.

An independent Scotland would have its own security service to tackle international threats, for instance, terrorism, cyber-attacks and serious organised crime. Such a domestic intelligence agency would sit alongside and liaise with Police Scotland. How close a relationship there would be with the UK intelligence services and what level of access a Scottish stand-alone intelligence agency would have to UK intelligence data would be the subject of much deliberation.

Surveillance or policing

Police Scotland increasingly asks the Scottish people to report to the police anyone they suspect may have made money illegally or who have a lifestyle above their means as a result of the proceeds of crime. The main point being driven home by Police Scotland is that as a result of organised crime communities are suffering from the side-effects of drug dealing, product counterfeiting, violence and other associated crimes. As a consequence, communities have a growing responsibility to assist the police in surveilling the populace in Scotland. And as criminals have no respect for policing boundaries, the arrival of a single police service helps facilitate this panoptic approach to tackling crime.

However, there are other concerns as to where the surveillance road is taking society. All indications are that as the science of surveillance develops in the twenty-first century its definition will broaden and encapsulate other components of social society which relate more to care, welfare and control; risk reduction; crime prevention, detection, and investigation; fear reduction; state control of citizens; constant monitoring of bars, discos; nightclubs, and hotspots; traffic control and the deployment of police officers. In this context surveillance in all its forms is an increasingly important tool in the arsenal of policing. The police monitoring of websites, cameras, surveillance facilities, identity documents and migrants, not only assists in the prevention of anti-social behaviour and street crime but also plays a prominent role in combating terrorism and organised and serious crime, and enhances national security. This monitoring function will expand in the future, albeit within a tighter framework of regulations. Increasingly, modern policing is becoming more about surveilling the community than most other forms of policing. There is a risk, however, that the traditional role of the Scottish police officer depicted throughout this text will change to accommodate this increasing surveillance of Scottish communities.

Conclusion

When the Chief Constable of Police Scotland Steve House was appointed to his new role in 2012, he said he wanted to be a Chief for all of the country and not just parts of it and that he was not 'a big city' Chief. The challenge facing Police Scotland and the Scottish police officer and support staff is to deliver a police service that ensures all communities, wherever they are located, feel they are not disadvantaged in the quality of policing they receive and that they are part of the national community safety network and that their police service, whether local or national, cares for their safety.

When it comes to recent police reform in Scotland with its single police service, other nations may view the changes as an example of good practice in the development of contemporary policing and may choose to follow. It is surprising that politicians and the vast majority of senior police officers in England and Wales have ruled out a national police service or police force mergers and are prepared to continue into the future with 43 police forces with their costly and bureaucratic system of governance and control.

Unlike their colleagues in England and Wales, Police Scotland has avoided the changes to pay and conditions under the Winsor Review. The changes are so draconian that officers south of the border are demanding the right to strike and work to rule. In addition to these reforms is the expansion of privatisation which is not the case in Scotland, albeit senior police officers in Scotland would be happy to see some outsourcing to be made in those areas best suited to the private sector, such as IT, procurement and administrative services and much more. This could be something for the future as it appears it is only the current Scottish government ideology that is preventing it happening. There has been some criticism levelled at the Scottish Government by the UK Government in reply to the Scottish complaint that the financial constraint on the Scottish public purse and policing is a direct result of the Westminster Government fiscal policy. The UK response is that the Scottish Government has more flexibility than it lets on. For example, it can modify the rate at which pensions are built up each year and change arrangements for those wishing to retire early or later.

In one of the few books on police management to come out of Scottish academia the authors recount a humorous story of change in the Scottish police:

> We have heard of a newly appointed chief of police who complained to a friend that within a short time of being in office he realised he ought to get rid of half his force. Asked why he did not proceed with the purge, he confessed to not knowing which half to sack.
>
> *(Bradley* et al. *1986: 1)*

Policing has moved on apace from the 1980s and as we have witnessed in this book the Scottish police officer is more professional and better trained and prepared than ever before. Indeed, they are also better led by more strategically minded leaders with a vision of what policing should look like in the twenty-first century. This could be crucial for, as this book has shown, there is the likelihood that for the first time in British police history citizens will experience different policing and law enforcement systems dependent on where they are at that particular time in the UK. Finally, the current transformation to twenty-first-century culture, lifestyle, crime and society, leisure pursuits and employment, will undoubtedly continue to have a major impact on policing and now that the Scots have their own national police service, the nation is better positioned to tackle the known and unknown challenges that lie ahead.

Appendix A

OCCUPATIONS OF POLICE RECRUITS PRIOR TO JOINING STRATHCLYDE POLICE FORCE (OCTOBER 2008 TO OCTOBER 2010)

Job title	*Number*
Accountant	5
Accounts Assistant	8
Actor	1
Admin Assistant	47
Admission Advisor	1
Advertising Assistant	2
Advisor	2
Aircraft Dispatcher	1
Aircraft Fitter	1
Analyst	2
Analyst Programmer	2
Anti-social Behaviour Investigator	1
Apprentice Electrician	1
Architectural Technologist	1
Area Development Manager	2
Army Guardsman	1
Army Officer	2
Art worker	1
Assistant Manager	3
Auditor	1
AutoCAD Technician	1
Aviation Fire-fighter	2
Bagpipe Maker	1
Bank Manager	3

Job title	*Number*
Banker	1
Banking Advisor	10
Banking Cashier	7
Bar staff	26
Bar Supervisor	2
Benefit Assistant	2
Betting Facilitator	1
Biomedical Scientist	1
Biotech Sales Assistant	1
Booking Office Clerk	1
Bricklayer	1
Building Contractor	2
Business Administrator	5
Butcher	2
Cabin Crew	5
Call Centre Agent	16
Car Salesman	4
Carer	9
Case Worker	1
Cashier	9
Catering Assistant	7
CCTV Operator	1
Check-in Assistant	1
Chef	6
Childminder	1
CIT Operative	1
Civil Servant	22
Claims Handler	8
Cleaner	2
Clerical Assistant	22
Climbing Instructor	2
CNC Operator	1
Coachbuilder	1
Collections officer	3
Communications Operator	6
Community Animator	1
Community Patrol Officer	4
Company Director	3
Compositor	1
Consultant Archaeologist	1
Control System Engineer	2

Job title	*Number*
Cook	1
Co-ordinator	2
Courier	1
Craft Operative	1
Credit Analyst	1
Creditor	1
Crew Manager	1
Crime Intelligence Analyst	1
Criminal Justice Worker	1
Customer Advisor	17
Customer Service Administrator/Rep	72
Dance Teacher	1
Data Entry Operator	4
Debt Advisor	1
Debt Recovery	2
Dental Nurse	6
Department Controller	1
Depot Operator	1
Design Assistant	1
Designer	1
Development Worker	1
Digger Operator	1
Director	2
Disc Jockey	1
Disclosure Officer	1
Draughtsman	1
Driver	14
Driving Instructor	5
Drum Tutor	1
Early Years Practitioner	2
Electrician	7
Electronics Technician	1
Electroplater	1
Employment Officer	2
Engineer	31
Engineering Support Assistant	1
Estate Caretaker	1
Events Support Team Leader	2
Factory Worker	2
Financial Consultant	5
Finisher	1

Job title	*Number*
Fire fighter	3
Fiscal Officer	5
Fishmonger	1
Fitness Instructor	23
Fitter	1
Football Coach	8
Footballer	2
Fraud Investigator	2
Funeral Director	1
Furnisher Repairer	1
Gamekeeper	1
Gardener	2
General Assistant	2
Go-kart Supervisor	1
Golf Pro	2
Graphic Designer	2
Green keeper	5
Hairdresser	4
Health & Safety Officer	1
Health Support Workers	2
Heating Engineer	1
Help Desk Operator	2
HGV Driver	8
HM Forces	1
Home Shopping Driver	1
Hospitality Rep	4
Hotel Manager	1
Housewife/husband	1
HR Assistant	2
Income Administrator	1
Information Assistant	3
Insolvency Administrator	1
Instrument Technician	1
Insurance Agent/Broker	6
Insurance Underwriter	3
Investigator	2
IT Consultant	2
IT Technician	7
Joiner	15
Karaoke Presenter	1
Kennel Assistant	1

Job title	*Number*
Key Worker	1
Kitchen Assistant	1
Labourer	4
Landscape Gardener	2
Lead Advisor	1
Leisure Attendant	5
Liaison Officer	1
Lifeguard	4
Loans Advisor	1
Logistics Technician	2
Loss Adjuster	2
Loss Preventions Investigator	1
Loss Protections Supervisor	1
Machinist	2
Mailroom Assistant	1
Maintenance Planner	2
Manager	117
Marine	1
Marine Ecologist	1
Marketing Assistant	1
Marketing Executive	2
Medical Lab Scientist	1
Merchandising Co-ordinator	1
Mobile Crane Operator	1
Mortgage Consultant	3
Motor Mechanic	4
Multi Disciplined Instructor	1
Navy	1
Nurse	13
Nursery Worker	2
Nursing Assistant	2
Office Fitter	1
Operational Manager	4
Operations Assistant	3
Overhead Linesman	1
Overland Operator	1
PA	4
Packer	1
Panel Beater	2
Paralegal	3
Paramedic	1

Job title	*Number*
Parts Advisor	1
Parts man	2
Passenger Service Assistant	1
Payroll Administrator	1
PCSO	10
Personal Banker	1
Personnel Trainer	4
Pharmacy Assistant	1
Pharmacy Technician	1
Phlebotomist	1
Photo Processor	1
Planning Co-ordinator	1
Plasterer	1
Play Activity Motivator	2
Plumber	2
Police Cadet	63
Police Controller	2
Police Officer Transfer	17
Police Staff	15
Port assistant	1
Porter	1
Post Person	9
PPC Exec	1
Presentation Officer	1
Press Setter	2
Printer	3
Prison Officer	4
Process Assistant	3
Procurement Administrator	1
Procurement Buyer	1
Productions Operator	5
Project Controller	4
Project Mgr	1
Projects Assistant	1
Property Management Assistant	1
Property Valuer	2
Quality Officer	2
Quantity Inspector	1
Quantity Surveyor	2
Radio Operator	1
RAF Officer	1

Job title	*Number*
Railway Track Assistant	1
Receptionist	6
Recreation Assistant	2
Recruitment Consultant	4
Research Scientist	2
Researcher	3
Reservation Consultant	1
Resource Worker	1
Revenue & Customs Officer	4
Roofer	1
Route Representative	1
Rugby Coach	1
Sales Assistant	126
Sales Executive	8
Sales Rep	3
Scaffolder	1
Schools Supervisor	3
Secretary	3
Security Consultant	2
Security Guard	14
Self Employed	1
Service Advisor	15
Service Engineer	1
Service Leader	2
Service Manager	1
Sheriff Officer	1
Shop fitter	1
Sign maker	1
Site Co-ordinator	1
Skincare Specialist	3
Social Care Worker	2
Soldier	5
Solicitor	1
Solutions Consultant	1
Sorter/Loader	1
Special Constable	1
Sport Assistant	1
Sports Coach	2
Staff Sergeant	1
Station Assistant	4
Steelworker	1

Job title	*Number*
Steward	2
Stock Controller	4
Stonemason	2
Store Manager	4
Stores Person	5
Student	44
Student/Sales Assistant	2
Student/Bar Supervisor	2
Student/Greenkeeper	1
Studio Co-ordinator	1
Supervisor	24
Support Learning Assistant	1
Support Worker	20
Surveyor	1
Switchboard Assistant/Operator	1
Tax Analyst	2
Taxi Driver	7
Teacher	4
Team Leader	9
Technical Analyst	8
Technician	11
Telecom Fraud Specialist	1
Telesales	15
Ten print ID Officer	1
Tiler	1
Topographic Surveyor	1
Trace Officer	1
Track Marshall	1
Traffic Scheduler	1
Train Driver	1
Trainee Coachbuilder	1
Trainee Dispenser	1
Trainee Optician	1
Trainee Paralegal	1
Trainee Parts Advisor	1
Trainer	3
Training Sergeant - Army	1
Transport Manager	1
Travel Agent	5
TV Productions Co-ordinator	1
Typist	1

Job title	*Number*
Underwriter	1
Unemployed	62
Veterinary Nurse	1
Visualisation Assistant	1
Waiter/Waitress	15
Warden	3
Warehouse Asst	3
Warehouse Operative	4
Warehouse Supervisor	2
Web Developer	5
Wedding Co-ordinator	1
Window Applicator	1
Wine Retailer	1
Work Allocation Officer	1
Workshop Operator	1
WPO	1
Yacht Repairer	1
Youth Worker	1
TOTALS	1539

Source: Police Recruit Profile Information (Strathclyde Police Force 2010).

REFERENCES

Abrams, L. and Brown, C.G. (eds) (2010) *A History of Everyday Life in Twentieth-Century Scotland*, Edinburgh: Edinburgh University Press.

ACPOS (Association of Chief Police Officers) (2008) *Diversity Booklet*, Glasgow: ACPOS.

ACPOS (Association of Chief Police Officers) (2011) *A Flexible Approach to Offending Behaviour by Children and Young People*, Glasgow: ACPOS.

Anderson, S. (1999) 'Crime and social change in rural Scotland', in G. Dingwall and S.R. Moody (eds) *Crime and Conflict in the Countryside*, Cardiff: University of Wales Press, pp. 45–59.

Archibald, T.W. (1990) *A History of the Lothian and Borders Police*, Edinburgh: The Author in association with The Edinburgh and East of Scotland Military Collectors' Society.

Atkinson, C. (2011) 'From Life on Mars to Life on Venus: gender, civilianisation and cultural change in the Scottish Police', paper delivered to the Sociology, Anthropology and Applied Social Science Postgraduate Conference, 8–9 December 2011, Glasgow University.

Audit Scotland (2012) *Managing Performance: Are You Getting it Right?* Edinburgh: Audit Scotland.

Barrie, D.G. (2008a) *Police in the Age of Improvement: Police Development and the Civic Tradition in Scotland*, Devon: Willan.

Barrie, D.G. (2008b) 'Patrick Colquhoun, the Scottish Enlightenment and police reform in Glasgow in the late eighteenth century', *Crime, History & Societies*, 12(2): 59–79.

Barrie, D.G. (2010a) 'A typology of British police: locating the Scottish municipal police model in its British context, 1800–35', *British Journal of Criminology*, 50(2): 259–77.

Barrie, D.G. (2010b) 'Police in civil society: police, Enlightenment and civic virtue in urban Scotland, c. 1780–1833', *Urban History*, 37(1): 46–65.

Barrow, J. (2011) 'Foreword', in I. Green, *Fuzz to Folk: Trax of My Life*, Edinburgh: Luath Press Ltd, pp. 11–12.

BBC (2013) 'WPC 56', forthcoming TV series in 2013.

Blair, I. (2009) *Policing Controversy*, London: Profile Books Ltd.

Blair, I. (2010) Interview on *A Life in Question*, BBC Radio Scotland, 22 August.

Bradley, D., Walker, N. and Wilkie, R. (1986) *Managing the Police: Law, Organisation and Democracy*, Sussex: Wheatsheaf Books Ltd.

Brettle, J. (2007) *A Contemporary Portrait of Scotland's Police*, Edinburgh: National Galleries of Scotland.

Bridgeman Report (1924) *The Report of the Committee on the Employment of Policemen*. Cmd 2224, London: HMSO.

British Council (1945) 'The man on the beat: the training and duties of a British police officer', British Council Film Collection, available at http//film.britishcouncil.org/the-man-on-the-beat (accessed 3 May 2012).

Brown, L. and Jeffrey, R. (2007) *Glasgow Crime Fighter: The Les Brown Story*, Edinburgh: Black and White Publishing.

Burnett, A. and Harrigan, T. (2010) 'The police and ethnic minorities in Scotland', in D. Donnelly and K. Scott (eds) *Policing Scotland*, 2nd edn, Devon: Willan, pp. 259–90.

Cachet, L., De Kimpe, S., Ponsaers, P. and Ringeling, A. (eds) (2008) *Governance of Security in the Netherlands and Belgium*, Amsterdam: Boom Juridische Uitgevers.

Campbell, D.J. and Campbell, K.M. (2010) 'Soldiers as police officers/police officers as soldiers: role evolution and revolution in the United States', *Armed Forces & Society*, 36(2): 327–50.

Carnohan, J. and McCluskey, K. (2010) 'Violence, culture and policing in Scotland', in D. Donnelly and K. Scott (eds) *Policing Scotland*, 2nd edn, Devon: Willan, pp. 401–26.

Carrier, J. (1988) *The Campaign for the Employment of Women as Police Officers*, Aldershot: Avebury.

Carson, W.G. (1984) 'Policing the periphery: the development of Scottish policing, 1795–1900 (1)', *Australian and New Zealand Journal of Criminology*, 17(4): 207–32.

Carson, W.G. (1985) 'Policing the periphery: the development of Scottish policing, 1795–1900 (2)', *Australian and New Zealand Journal of Criminology*, 18(1): 3–16.

Carson, W. and Idzikowska, H. (1989) 'The social production of Scottish policing, 1795–1900', in D. Hay and F. Snyder (eds) *Policing and Prosecution in Britain, 1750–1850*, Oxford: Oxford University Press.

Clabby, K. (2004) *Careers and Jobs in the Police Service*, London: Kogan Page.

Clark, A. (1873) *Reminiscences of a Police Officer in the Granite City*, Aberdeen: Lewis Smith.

Clark, H. and Carnegie, E. (2003) *She Was Aye Workin': Memories of Tenement Women in Edinburgh and Glasgow*, Dorchester: White Cockade Publishing.

Conley, C.A. (2007) *Certain Other Countries: Homicide, Gender and National Identity in Late Nineteenth-Century England, Ireland, Scotland and Wales*, Columbus, OH: Ohio State University Press.

Crown Office and Procurator Fiscal Service (COPFS) (2013) *Knife Crime Scotland*, Edinburgh: COPFS.

Cumming, M.T. (2010) *Police Practice Papers: Information Handling Tests Based upon the Scottish Police Forces Standard Entrance Test*, Glasgow: Recruitment Practice Papers.

Daily Mail (2012) 'Police in schools', 24 September, p. 12.

Daily Record (2012a) 'Revealed – 333 serving police officers in Scotland have criminal convictions', available at: http://www.dailyrecord.co.uk/news/scottish-news/2012/07/05/revealed-333-serving-police-officers-in-scotland-have-criminal-convictions-86908-23904396/ (accessed 5 July 2012).

Daily Record (2012b) 'Scottish police tackle big rise in complaints about crime on Twitter and Facebook', available at: www.dailyrecord.co.uk/news/uk-world-news/police-forces-swamped-with-rising-number-1508159 (accessed 28 December 2012).

Day, J.P. (1918) *Public Administration in the Highlands and Islands of Scotland*, London: University of London.

Devine, T.M. (2011) *To the Ends of the Earth: Scotland's Global Diaspora, 1750–2010*, London: Penguin Books.

Dinsmor, A. and Goldsmith, A. (2010) 'Scottish policing: a historical perspective', in D. Donnelly and K. Scott (eds) *Policing Scotland*, 2nd edn, Devon: Willan, pp. 47–71.

Dinsmor, A. and Urquhart, H.J. (2001) 'The origins of modern policing in Scotland', *Scottish Archives*, 7: 36–44.

Donnelly, D. (2008) *Municipal Policing in Scotland*, Dundee: DUP.

Donnelly, D. (2013) *Municipal Policing in the European Union: Comparative Perspectives*, Basingstoke: Palgrave Macmillan.

Donnelly, D. and Scott, K. (eds) (2005) *Policing Scotland*, Devon: Willan.

Donnelly, D. and Scott, K. (eds) (2010) *Policing Scotland*, 2nd edn, Devon: Willan.

The Economist (2010) 'Voting blue: elected commissioners are on the way', 31 July, 24.

Emsley, C. (2010) 'Was the British police officer ever different?', lecture delivered at the SIPR Conference on Crime and Policing: Past and Present, 19 May, West Park Conference Centre, Dundee.

Equality and Human Rights Commission (Scotland) (2011) *Inquiry into Human Trafficking in Scotland: Executive Summary*, available at: http://www.equalityhumanrights.com/uploaded_files/Scotland/Human_Trafficking_in_Scotland_/inquiry_into_human_trafficking_in_scotland-exec-sum_pdf_.pdf (accessed 5 June 2012).

Etherson, P. (2010) *A Comparative Study of Scottish Police Boards: A Profile of the Composition of the Police Boards in Scotland* (ERSC and Scottish Government-funded PhD study), Scottish Institute for Police Research, Summary No. 4, available at: www.sipr.ac.uk/downloads/Research_Summaries/Research_Summary_4.pdf (accessed 1 February 2010).

Evening Telegraph (2008) 'We're losing drugs war says top cop', 12 May, available at: www.eveningtelegraph.co.uk/output/2008/05/12/story11348986t0.shtm (accessed 1 August 2010).

Fraser, J. and Ludwig, A. (2010) 'Forensic science and policing in Scotland', in D. Donnelly and K. Scott (eds) *Policing Scotland*, 2nd edn, Devon: Willan, pp. 375–98.

Fry, M. (2001) *The Scottish Empire*, East Lothian: Tuckwell Press.

Fry, M. (2005) *Wild Scots: Four Hundred Years of Highland History*, London: John Murray.

Gallacher, G. (2011) *Gangsters, Killers and Me: A Detective's Story*, Edinburgh: Black and White Publishing Ltd.

Garda Siochana (2009) *Annual Report 2008*, Dublin: Garda Siochana.

Glasgow Herald (1983) 'More police on the beat in problem areas', 25 November.

Glasgow Housing Association (GHA) (2012) 'Justice Secretary launches new safety partnership', 20 August, available at: http://www.gha.org.uk/content/default.asp?page=s25_1&newsid=3991&back=s25 (accessed 30 September 2012).

Golden, M.C. (2003) 'Criminality and the development of policing in Dundee, 1816–1833', unpublished thesis, University of Dundee.

Goldsmith, A. (2002)' The development of the City of Glasgow Police, 1800–1939', unpublished thesis, University of Strathclyde, Glasgow.

Gordon, P. (1980) *Policing Scotland*, Glasgow: Scottish Council for Civil Liberties.

Gowri, A. (2003) 'Community policing is an epicycle', *Policing: An International Journal of Police Strategies and Management*, 26(4): 591–611.

Grabosky, P. (2009) 'Community policing, east and west, north and south', *Police Practice and Research*, 10(2): 95–8.

Grant, D. (1973) *The Thin Blue Line: The Story of the City of Glasgow Police*, London: John Long.

Grant, J. (2010) 'Police unionism in Scotland', in D. Donnelly and K. Scott (eds) *Policing Scotland*, 2nd edn, Devon: Willan, pp. 144–72.

Green, I. (2011) *Fuzz to Folk: Trax of My Life*. Edinburgh: Luath Press Ltd.

Heidensohn, F. and Brown, J. (2011) 'From Juliet to Jane: women police in TV cop shows, reality, rank and careers', in T. Newburn and J. Peay (eds) *Policing: Politics, Culture and Control*, Oxford: Hart Publishing Ltd, pp. 111–34.

Hellawell, K. (2002) *The Outsider*, London: HarperCollins.

The Herald (2012) 'Police lose 3000 working days due to assaults on officers', 30 December, available at: www.heraldscotland.com/news/crime-courts/police-lose-3000-days-due-to-assaults-on-officers-.19792893 (accessed 30 December 2012).

HM Government (2012) *First Annual Report of the Inter-Departmental Ministerial Group on Human Trafficking*, Cmnd 8421, Norwich: TSO.

HM Inspector of Constabulary for Scotland (2006) *Annual Report 2005/2006*, Edinburgh: Stationery Office Bookshop.

HM Inspectorate of Constabulary for Scotland (2000) *Without Prejudice? A Thematic Inspection of Police Race Relations in Scotland*, Edinburgh: HMSO.

HM Inspector of Constabulary for Scotland (2006) *Annual Report 2005/2006*, available at: www.scottish.gov.uk/Publications/2006/11/29160835/3 (accessed 1 December 2012).

HM Chief Inspector of Constabulary for Scotland (2007) *Thematic Inspection: Selection for Promotion in the Scottish Police Service*, www.scottish.gov.uk/Publications/2007/12/13115024/1 (accessed 5 September 2011).

HM Inspectorate of Constabulary for Scotland (2008) *Natural Justice: Joint Thematic Inspection of the Arrangements in Scotland for Preventing, Investigating and Prosecuting Wildlife Crime*, report jointly compiled by HMICS and the Inspectorate of Prosecution Scotland. Edinburgh: Scottish Government.

HM Inspectorate of Constabulary for Scotland (2012a) *Annual Report 2011–2012*, Edinburgh: Scottish Government.

HM Inspectorate of Constabulary for England and Wales (2012b) *Taking Time for Crime*, available at: http://www.hmic.gov.uk/media/taking-time-for-crime.pdf (accessed 1 December 2012).

Hogg, I. (2009) 'Scenes of crime', in W.D.S. McLay (ed.) *Clinical Forensic Medicine*, 3rd edn, Cambridge: Cambridge University Press, pp. 171–6.

Home Office (1929) *Royal Commission on Police Powers and Procedures*, Cmnd 3297, London: HMSO.

Home Office (1962) *Royal Commission on the Police: Final Report*, Cmnd 1728, London: HMSO.

Home Office (1978) *Committee of Enquiry on Police (Lord Edmund Davis): Report on Negotiating Machinery and Pay*, Cmnd 7283, London: HMSO.

Home Office (1981) *The Brixton Disorders, 10–12 April 1981 (The Scarman Report)*, Cmnd 8427. London: HMSO.

Home Office (2008) *Workforce Modernisation*, available at: www.police.home.office.gov.uk/human-resources/efficiency-and-productivity/workforce-modernisation-programme (accessed on 30 January 2009).

Home Office (2010) 'Radical reform for police announced', available at http://www.homeoffice.gov.uk/media-centre/press-releases/radical-reforms-police (accessed 10 August 2010).

Hoogenboom, B. (2010) *The Governance of Policing and Security: Ironies, Myths and Paradoxes*, Basingstoke: Palgrave Macmillan.

House, S. (2012) 'Chief Constable's address to members of the Strathclyde Police Authority', 13 December, Glasgow City Chambers.

Hunter, J. (2007) *Scottish Exodus*, Edinburgh: Mainstream Publishing Company.

Hyde, R. (2008) 'Rethinking the response of part-time professionals: the case of the part-time police officer', *International Journal of Public Administration*, 31: 1095–9.

IPPR (2010) *Capable Communities: Towards Citizen-Powered Public Services*, Joint Report by IPPR and PwC, available at: www.ippr.org/publicationsandreports/publication.asp?id= (accessed 26 November 2010).

IPSOS (2010) *Evaluation of Campus Police Officers in Scottish Schools*, Edinburgh: IPSOS/MORI Scotland, available at: http://www.scotland.gov.uk/Resources/Doc/305489/0095816.pdf (accessed 2 June 2012).

Irvine, H. (1972) *Diced Cap: The Story of Aberdeen City Police*, Aberdeen: Corporation of the City of Aberdeen.

Jackson, J. (2008) *Chasing Killers: Three Decades of Cracking Crime in the UK's Murder Capital*, London: Mainstream Publishing.

Jackson, L.A. (2006) *Women Police: Gender, Welfare and Surveillance in the Twentieth Century*, Manchester: Manchester University Press.

Jones, T., Newburn, T. and Smith, D.J. (2011) 'Democracy, police and crime commissioners', in T. Newburn and J. Peay (eds) *Policing: Politics, Culture and Control*, Oxford: Hart Publishing Ltd, pp. 219–44.

Juniper, B., White, N. and Bellamy, P. (2010) 'A new approach to evaluating the well-being of police', *Occupational Medicine*, 60: 560–5.

Kelly, P. (2011) *Scotland's Radical Exports: The Scots Abroad and How They Shaped Politics and Trade Unions*, Glasgow: The Grimsay Press.

Kerr, J.A. (2010) *Scotland and the Impact of the Great War, 1914–1928*, Paisley: Hodder Gibson.

Laybourn, K. and Taylor, D. (2011) *Policing in England and Wales, 1918–1939: The Fed, Flying Squad and Forensics*, Basingstoke: Palgrave Macmillan.

Livesey, A.H. (1927) *The Women Police Question*, Westminster: Social Services Ltd.

Lycett, A. (2007) *Conan Doyle: The Man Who Created Sherlock Homes*, London: Weidenfeld and Nicolson.

Lynch, T. (1991) *The Bill*, London: Boxtree Ltd.

MacAskill, K. (2012) Speech delivered at the International Policing Conference, 22 November, Edinburgh.

MacGregor, W. J. (2007) 'Policing and technology: A study of the impact of technology on the Police in Scotland 1920–1968', unpublished thesis, Open University.

Mack, J. A. (1963) *Police Juvenile Liaison Schemes*, London: Stevens and Sons.

MacKenzie, A. (1881) *The Highland Clearances*, Inverness: MacKenzie.

Malthouse, R. and Barentsen, J. R. (2010) *Verbal and Numerical Reasoning Exercises for the Police Recruitment Assessment Process*, Malthouse: Learning Matters.

Manson-Smith, D. (2008) *The Legal System of Scotland*, 4th edn, Norwich: TSO.

Mark, R. (1978) *In the Office of Constable*, Glasgow: William Collins & Sons.

Mawby, R.I. (2009) 'Perceptions of police and policing in a rural county of England', *International Journal of Police Science and Management*, 11(1): 39–53.

Mazeika, D., Bartholomew, B., Distler, M., Greenman, S. and Pratt, S. (2010) 'Trends in police research: a cross-sectional analysis of the 2000–2007 literature', *Police Practice and Research*, 11(6): 520–47.

Mazerolle, L. and Ransley, J. (2005) *Third Party Policing*, Cambridge: Cambridge University Press.

McGowan, J. (1996) *The Emergence of Modern Civil Police in Scotland: A case study of the Police and Systems of Police in Edinburghshire 1800–1833*, unpublished thesis, Open University.

McLaglan, G. (2003) *Bent Coppers: The Inside Story of Scotland Yard's Battle against Corruption*, London: Weidenfeld & Nicolson.

McLaughlin, B. and Smyth, B. (2012) *Crimestopper: Fighting Crime on Scotland's Streets*, Edinburgh: Black and White Publishing Ltd.

McLeish, H. (2012) *Scotland, the Growing Divide: Old Nation, New Ideas*. Edinburgh: Luath Press Ltd.

McMunn, R. (2011) *Police Tests; How to Pass the Police Initial Recruitment Test (PIRT)*. Kent: How2become.

McTaggart, J. (2010) *The Definitive Guide to Passing the Police Recruitment Process: A Handbook for Prospective Police Officers*, Oxford: How to Books.

Meade, R. (2010) *Building a Police Workforce for the Future: The Need to Scrutinise Changes to the Workforce*, London: Police Federation.

Metropolitan Police (2010) 'Metropolitan Police history timeline, 1850–1869', available at: http://www.met.police.uk/history/timeline1850-1869.htm (accessed 1 December 2010).

Moffat, A. (2012) 'Scotland's DNA: tracing the nation's ancestral history', available at: http://www.scotsman.com/lifestyle/heritage/scotland-s-dna-tracing-the-nation-s-ancestral-history-1-2465715 (accessed 15 August 2012).

Murray, W.H. (1973) *The Islands of Western Scotland: The Inner and Outer Hebrides*, London: Eyre Methuen.

Newburn, T. and Peay, J. (eds) (2011) *Policing: Politics, Culture and Control*, Oxford: Hart Publishing Ltd.

Nussbaum, B. (2007) 'Protecting global cities: New York, London and the internationalization of municipal policing for counter terrorism', *Global Crime*, 8(3): 214–32.

Office of National Statistics (ONS) (2012) *Job Classifications*, available at: www.ons.gov.uk/ons/index.html (accessed 2 June 2011).

Pearson, G. and O'Hare, K. (2008) *The Enforcer: A Life Fighting Crime*, Edinburgh: Black and White Publishing Ltd.

Police Complaints Commissioner for Scotland (PCCS) (2012) *Police Complaints: Statistics for Scotland 2011–2012*, available at: www.pcc-scotland.org (accessed 10 October 2012).

Police Federation (1924) *Report on the Question of Police Women*, London: Police Federation.

Police Mutual Assurance Society (PMAS) (2012) *Portrait of the Police 2012: A Police Mutual Study of Police Officers' and Staff's Financial Priorities, Lifestyle and Morale*, Lichfield: PMAS.

Police Oracle (2012) 'International dimension for new Scottish force', available at: www.policeoracle.com/news/International-Dimension-For-New-Scottish-Force-_59371.html (accessed 28 December 2012).

Police Review (2004) 'A quarter of officers fail to turn up for promotion exam', 30 July, 8.

Police Review (2005) 'No1 Detective Agency (Met Police Crime Agency in Hendon)', 11 November, 24.

Quick, R. (2009) 'Police in "uncharted territory" regarding extremism', *The Herald*, 13 February, 10.

Ricketts, K.D. (2008) *How to Pass the Police Recruitment Tests*, Oxford: How To Books Ltd.

Royal United Services Institute (RUSI) (2012) 'Emergency services must plan for lone terrorist attack', speech by the UK Security Minister James Brockenbridge, 18 October 2012, at the RUSI in London.

Savage, S. and Leishman, F. (1996) 'Managing the police: a force for change', in D. Farnham *et al.* (eds) *Managing the New Public Services*, 2nd edn, London: Macmillan, pp. 242–56.

Scheider, M. C., Chapman, R. and Schapiro, A. (2009) 'Towards the unification of policing innovations under community policing', *Policing: An International Journal of Police Strategies & Management*, 32(4): 694–718.

School of Forensic Mental Health (SoFMH) (2012) *Unusually Persistent Complainants against the Police in Scotland*, Lanark: SoFMH.

Scotland on Sunday (2012) 'Police Chief warns promise of more officers can't be kept', 30 December 2012, available at: www.scotsman.com/news/police-chief-warns-more-officers-promise-can-t-be-kept-1-2711830 (accessed 30 December 2012).

Scotland Today (1975) *The Making of a Policeman* – T2291, Scottish Screen Archive, National Library of Scotland, Ref No. Z00666, Glasgow: Scottish Television.

Scott, K. and Sproat, P. (2010) *An Evaluation of the Priority Crime Unit in Central Scotland Police*, SIPR Briefing Paper No. 9, Dundee: Scottish Institute for Policing Research.

Scott, M.I. (2003) *A Fair Cop*, Glasgow: Clydeside Press.

Scottish Crime and Justice Survey (SCJS) (2011) *Scottish Crime and Justice Survey 2010–2011*, available at: http://www.scotland.gov.uk/Topics/Statistics/Browse/Crime-Justice/crime-and-justice-survey (accessed 1 June 2012).

Scottish Executive (2007) *Evaluation of the Impact and Implementation of Community Wardens*, available at: www.scotland.gov.uk/publications/2007/03/22104147/0 (accessed 20 April 2008).

Scottish Government (2009) *The Effectiveness of Public Space CCTV: A Review of Recent Published Evidence Regarding the Impact of CCTV on Crime*, Justice Analytical Services and Police and Community Safety Directorate, Edinburgh: Scottish Government.

Scottish Government (2011a) *Commission on the Future Delivery of Public Services*, available at: www.scotland.gov.uk/About/Review/publicservicescommission (accessed August 2012).

Scottish Government (2011b) *The Carloway Review*, available at: www.scotland.gov.uk/Resource/Doc/925/0122808.pdf (accessed 20 April 2012).

Scottish Government (2011c) *Football Related Violence*, available at: www.scotland.gov.uk/Topics/Justice/law/sectarianism-action-1/football-violence/bill (accessed 1 February 2012).

Scottish Government (2012a) *Redesigning the Community Justice System: A Consultation on Proposals*, available at: www.scotland.gov.uk/Publications/2012/12/7292 (accessed 22 December 2012).

Scottish Government (2012b) *Police Officer Numbers in Scotland, 2006–2012*, available at: www.scotland.gov.uk/Topics/Statistics/Browse/Crime-Justice (accessed 10 December 2012).

Scottish Government (2012c) 'Criminals to pay for police assault', available at: www.scotland.gov.uk/News/Releases/2012/04/police12042012 (accessed 20 April 2012).

Scottish Government (2012d) *Police Officer and Police Support Staff Numbers (2008–2009 to 2011–2012)*, available at: www.scotland.gov.uk/Publications/2012/11/1397/7 (accessed 31 December 2012).

Scottish Government (2012e) *Breakdown of Full-Time and Part-Time Police Officers in Scottish Police (2010–2012)*, Justice Analytical Services. Edinburgh: Scottish Government.

Scottish Government (2012f) *The 2011 Census Results*, available at: www.scotlandcensus.gov.uk/en/censusresults/ (accessed 17 December 2012).

Scottish Government (2012g) *Scottish Index of Multiple Deprivation 2012*, available at: www.simd.Scotland.gov.uk/publication-2012/ (accessed 19 December 2012).

Scottish Government (2012h) *High Level Summary of Statistics Trend: Firearm Certificates*, available at: www.scotland.gov.uk/Topics/Statistics/Browse/Crime-Justice/TrendCert (accessed 10 December 2012).

Scottish Home Department (1947) *County Policeman*, Scottish Screen Archive, National Library of Scotland, Ref. No. 0494, Glasgow: Merlin Films.

Scottish Household Survey (2012) *Scotland's People: Annual Report Results from 2011*, Edinburgh: Scottish Government.

Scottish Police College (2012) *College Prospectus (2011–2012)*, Kincardine: SPC.

Scottish Police Federation (2012a) *Who We Are*, Briefing Paper, available at: www.spf.org.uk (accessed 20 December 2012).

Scottish Police Federation (2012b) *Police Assaults*, available at: www.spf.org.uk (accessed 31 December 2012).

Scottish Policing Performance Framework (SPPF) (2012) *Annual Report, 2011–2012*, Edinburgh: Scottish Government.

SIPR (2012) *The Scottish Institute for Policing Research*, available at: www.sipr.ac.uk (accessed 1 August 2012).

Smeets, S. (2008) 'New uniforms of local governance of security in Belgium – between shift of police function and activation of good citizenship', in L. Cachet, S. De. Kimpe, P. Ponsaers and A. Ringeling (eds) *Governance of Security in the Netherlands and Belgium*, Amsterdam: Boom Juridische Uitgevers, pp. 177–96.

Stenhouse, D. (2005) *How the Scots Took Over London*, Edinburgh: Mainstream Publishing.

Stenning, P. (2009) 'Governance and accountability in a plural policing environment: the story so far', *Policing*, 3(1): 22–33.

Stewart Research (2009) *Civilianisation of Policing in Scotland: Final Report*, Glasgow: UNISON Scotland.

Strathclyde Police Force (2010) *Profile Information of Police Recruits, October 2008–October 2010*, Glasgow: Strathclyde Police Force.

Strathclyde Police Force (2012) *Questions to Be Considered by Potential Police Recruits*, Glasgow: Police Recruitment Department, Strathclyde Police Force.

The Spectator (1962) 'Public and police – comment on the Royal Commission on the Police', 8 June, p. 740.

Sunday Herald (2009) 'Roma to quit Belfast for good, in wake of race attacks', 21 June, p. 25.

The Telegraph (2010) 'German policeman wins extra week of holiday for time spent getting dressed', 14 July, available at http://www.telegraph.co.uk/news/worldnews/europe/germany/7889572/German-police-wins-extra-week-of-holiday-for-time-spent-getting-dressed-htm (accessed August 2010).

The Times (2008) 'Metropolitan Police's proud boast sets off police alarm in Glasgow', 4 July, p. 9.

Tolley, H., Hodge, B. and Tolley, C. (2010) *How to Pass the New Police Selection System*, 3rd edn, London: Kogan Page.

Tozer, C.M. (1996) *The Guide to Police Recruitment and Promotion: The Assessment Centre Process*, Hockley: Career Management Techniques.

UNISON Scotland (2012) *Police Support Staff*, available at: http://www.unison-scotland.org.uk/police/index.html (accessed 10 December 2012).

Vaughan, B. (2006) 'Reforms of policing North and South', *Irish Criminal Law Journal*, 16(2): 17–20.

Vejnovic, D., Lalic, V. and Sikman, M. (2010) 'Private security in Bosnia and Herzegovina', in G. Cordner, A. Cordner and D. K. Das (eds) *Urbanization, Policing and Security – Global Perspectives*, Boca Raton, FL: CRC Press, pp. 389–402.

Violence Reduction Unit (2012) Violence Reduction Unit, available at: www.actiononviolence.org.uk (accessed 1 September 2012).

Waddington, P.A.J. and Wright, M. (2010) *What Is Policing?*, Exeter: Learning Matters Ltd.

Wakefield, A. (2005) 'The public surveillance functions of private security', *Surveillance and Society*, 2(4): 529–45.

Walker, N. (2000) *Policing in a Changing Constitutional Order*, London: Sweet and Maxwell.

Walmsey, B. (2007) *Succeed at Psychometric Testing: Practice Tests for the National Police Selection Process*, London: Hodder Arnold.

Wells, H.G. (1904) *The Country of the Blind*, London: Strand Magazine.

Whatley, C.A. (1997) *The Industrial Revolution in Scotland*, Cambridge: Cambridge University Press.

Whatley, C.A. (2000) *Scottish Society 1707–1830: Beyond Jacobitism, towards Industrialisation*, Manchester: Manchester University Press.

Wilson, J.M. (2012) 'Articulating the dynamic police staffing challenge: an examination of supply and demand', *Policing: An International Journal of Police Strategies & Management*, 35(2), 327–55.

Wilson, J.Q. and Kelling, G. (1982) 'The police and neighborhood safety: broken windows', *The Atlantic Monthly*, March, 29–38.

Winsor Review (2012) *The Independent Review of Police Officer and Staff Remuneration and Conditions*, available at: www.review.police.uk/ (accessed 20 December 2012).

Wood, J. and Shearing, C. (2007) *Imagining Security*, Devon: Willan Publishing.

INDEX

Locators shown in *italics* refer to tables, figures and boxes.